RENÉ GIRARD AND
SECULAR MODERNITY

RENÉ GIRARD AND
SECULAR MODERNITY

Christ, Culture, and Crisis

SCOTT COWDELL

University of Notre Dame Press

Notre Dame, Indiana

Library of Congress Cataloging-in-Publication Data

Cowdell, Scott.
    René Girard and secular modernity : Christ, culture, and crisis / Scott
Cowdell.
        pages   cm
    Includes bibliographical references and index.
    ISBN 978-0-268-02374-4 (pbk. : alk. paper) — ISBN 0-268-02374-3
(pbk. : alk. paper)
    1. Girard, René, 1923– 2. Secularization. 3. Violence. 4. Civilization,
Modern—20th century. 5. Philosophical theology. 6. Philosophy,
French—20th century. 7. Philosophy, Modern—20th century. I. Title.
    B2430.G494C69   2013
    194—dc23
    2013000465

In Memoriam

JOAN MEYERS

1923–2009

Many waters cannot quench love . . .
Song of Songs 8:7

CONTENTS

I came late to René Girard, and after three false starts. In the early 1990s, when I was completing my PhD dissertation on the uniqueness and finality of Jesus, I discovered and was much influenced by Walter Wink on the New Testament "powers and principalities," though without appreciating Girard's influence on Wink's trilogy. In the late 1990s I was asked to review *Why Must There Be Scapegoats?* by the Girardian Jesuit theologian Raymund Schwager, but I could make neither head nor tail of it. I attended a gathering of Australian Anglican theologians where Girard's work was introduced, and again things failed to spark. What finally awakened me from my dogmatic slumbers was an invitation in 2004 to review James Alison's book *On Being Liked*. The time was right, and I was hooked.

Here was an intellectual vision of great simplicity and power, combined with a level of spiritual and psychological insight that has helped me greatly both personally and professionally. Reading Alison and Girard followed, then other Girardians. I advanced some way toward my own Girardian synthesis in a 2009 book, *Abiding Faith: Christianity Beyond Certainty, Anxiety, and Violence,* but it became clear to me that I needed to learn a lot more about Girard before proceeding with my longer-term theological project. Hence this volume, which undertakes a Girardian account of secular modernity.

I am grateful for a relatively new and (in Australia) rare opportunity to be doing this type of work more or less uninterrupted, so I thank Charles Sturt University for a Research Fellowship in Public and Contextual Theology. Within the life of our Research Center, based in Australia's national capital, I thank Rev. Prof. James Haire, AC, our director, for his support and encouragement, along with my colleague Wayne Hudson for valuable conversations. My thanks also to the always helpful Kaye Malins, at St. Mark's National Memorial Library.

In early 2010 I spent four months in the reading phase of this project on sabbatical leave in Collegeville, Minnesota, which Andrew M. Greeley described as the last magical place in American Catholicism. Life together with fellow resident scholars at the Collegeville Institute for Ecumenical and Cultural Research was delightful, as was worship with the St. John's Abbey monastic community in their iconic Marcel Bruer Abbey church. At the Institute I thank Donald Ottenhoff, Carla Durand, and Elisa Schneider, as well as Kilian McDonnell, OSB, and Wilfred Thiesen, OSB, who made me welcome at St. John's University.

In Australia undergraduate and research degrees do not normally have a compulsory language requirement, so I had managed to get this far without learning French. Galvanized by this project, however, and in the company of my adventurous wife, I started from scratch during 2009, two nights a week at the Canberra Institute of Technology. To Jen Bateman, Christine Moore, and Jacqueline de Montmollin go my thanks for beginning my induction into this most beautiful and wonderful language and opening for me a deeper engagement with Girard. During the aforementioned sabbatical we also braved a one-month intensive course in French at the Université Catholique de Lyon, enjoying (patient) hospitality with the Communauté de Chemin Neuf. We have fond memories of our French teachers, Stéphanie Rabin and Christine Nodin, and our Chemin Neuf hosts at Rue Henri IV, Tim and Kate Watson.

I now want to mention those who helped me with preparation and publication. Special thanks to Charles Van Hof at the University of Notre Dame Press for commissioning this volume and seeing it on its way. Canberra is a long way from South Bend, but I hope to enjoy another boutique Indiana beer with Chuck at the Morris Inn on the UND campus before too long. I also thank Wendy McMillen and Sheila Berg, who have done me a great service with the editing and design of this book. I am especially grateful to the leading Australian painter, Jeffrey Smart, for once again allowing me to use his work on a cover, and to his archivist Stephen Rogers for invaluable assistance. Wolfgang Palaver of the University of Innsbruck, Jeremiah Alberg of the International Christian University, Tokyo, and Kevin Mongrain of the National Institute for Newman Studies, Pittsburgh, very kindly read the manuscript and made a number of helpful suggestions. Fr. James Alison graciously added his endorsement when I first proposed this project for publication. My friend and mentor Bishop Bruce Wilson offered his Girardian expertise and editorial eye in detailed comments on draft chapters one by one, then on the whole manuscript. Bruce's "Girardian therapy" saved my bacon during a difficult parish appointment several years back. I hope this Girard book will serve as a tangible "thank you."

Two last words of thanks, the first posthumous. Joan Meyers was my (adoptive) mother's sister and our next-door neighbor during my boyhood in suburban Brisbane. Joan was a spinster who cared for her aged mother. She was well traveled, independent, and something of an exotic figure. She made me her project, and it wasn't always smooth sailing. But, man and priest, my debt to her is deep, though I was not clear enough in expressing my gratitude before it was too late. Hence the dedication of this book to Joan's memory. Finally, I thank Lisa Carley—my partner in faith, hope, and love—for sharing this Girardian journey with me, along with much wifely support and encouragement.

Canberra, Australia
Feast of Saint Francis of Assisi
4 October 2012

Introduction

In 2009 humanity marked the sesquicentenary of its arguably greatest intellectual achievement: the theory of evolution by natural selection. Darwinian molecular biology is now foundational for everything we know about life's development, illuminating so much complexity by an essentially simple mechanism. Similar attempts to unify the human sciences have met with less success, from grand positivistic aspirations in nineteenth-century cultural anthropology— fictionalized by George Eliot in the character of her scholar-parson Edward Casaubon, who collapsed under the weight of his search for "the key to all mythologies"—through to today's skeptical postmoderns, who question not only the likelihood but also the morality of encompassing cultural diversity within a single theory. And of course the possibility of a Christian intellectual synthesis holding faith and reason together has scarcely been conceivable since the late Middle Ages, when faith and reason went their separate ways in the West and the modern *saeculum* began to emerge.

But, wonder of wonders, an audacious claim to do just this has been in place for thirty-five years and is winning both intellectual and spiritual converts. In 2005 the French American thinker René Girard, in his ninth decade, was formally welcomed by Michel Serres on his election as an Immortel of l'Académie française as the "new Darwin

of the human sciences."[1] The postmodern intelligentsia, deeply wedded to the dogma of cultural relativism, remains largely unimpressed.
They also despise any attempt to rehabilitate the Queen of the Sciences. Girard, with a dash of Gallic insouciance, shrugs off these
detractors, referring to their small intellectual ambitions as "the comprehensive unionization of failure";[2] and of course his mimetic theory
gives a good account of such academic rivalry, along with the arrogant
individualist's refusal of personal conversion that appreciation of his
theory demands. Besides, his agenda is bigger than the intellectual
or indeed the theological: Girard believes that having uncovered the
origin of culture and explicated the emergence of secular modernity,
he has revealed the apocalyptic acceleration of history toward a tragic
denouement. Hence, from his study at Stanford, this scholar's scholar
has become a planetary prophet.

I have decided to focus on the issues of secularization and modernity in this project because they provide both a privileged perspective for surveying the whole Girardian vision and an opportunity for
commending that vision by demonstrating its explanatory power in
conditions familiar to us. In this introduction, then, it will be helpful to concentrate on three questions: Who is René Girard? What is
secular modernity, and what is distinctive about Girard's take on it?

WHO IS RENÉ GIRARD?

René Girard (1923–) was born under the shadow of history in
Avignon, France, where his father was curator of the Castle of the
Popes. In Nazi-occupied Paris, he trained in his father's discipline,
medieval history.[3] The young Girard then left behind the French
avant-garde (he knew Picasso, along with many other artists as well as
writers) for postwar America. In his new country Girard was initially
unable to find his feet academically, struggling in his intellectual life
with the personal demons he later unmasked with the mimetic theory.
His PhD in history at Indiana University, on American perceptions of
wartime France, led to the teaching of French literature and a necessary move to Duke University (he also taught at Bryn Mawr College).

Meanwhile, the need to read all the novels that he had to teach opened Girard's eyes to significant insights into the human condition, though the avant-garde had taught him that no universal truths were available in such texts.

It was at Johns Hopkins University in Baltimore that Girard published his first book, introducing the first of three major intellectual breakthroughs: the mimetic theory of desire. *Deceit, Desire, and the Novel* traced his discovery of a new psychology in Cervantes, Dostoyevsky, and the great nineteenth-century French novelists: Stendhal, Flaubert, and Proust. These writers had broken through to a deeper perspective on human motivation, having shed the self-deceiving superiority of black-and-white moralism and the self-serving fictions of romantic individualism. They laid bare the dynamics of groupthink and the craven hunger for being that existentialism had named, with Proust and Dostoyevsky in particular learning to live more modestly, wisely, and ironically.

It is no accident that Girard's conversion back to the Roman Catholicism of his boyhood took place at this time, for he was on a path to understanding what religion most truly is and is not. His second book followed in 1963, focusing on the psychology of Dostoyevsky's "underground man"—a book appearing thirty-five years later in English as *Resurrection from the Underground.*

Subsequently, Girard grasped the primal role of scapegoating in the fostering of human peace and solidarity through reading classical literature, from which he advanced to mastering sociology, anthropology, and ethnography during the 1960s. Girard knew that he was onto something big. He moved from the chair he had held at Johns Hopkins since 1961 to Upstate New York and a Distinguished Professor position at the State University of New York in Buffalo, then returned to a named chair at Johns Hopkins in 1976. Girard published the French original of *Violence and the Sacred* in 1972 (the English translation in 1977) to great interest and acclaim. Here he revealed through its traces remaining in prohibitions, rituals, and myths the scapegoat mechanism that is hidden at the root of culture and religion. This uncovering of the bloody hands that humanity has used to build its venerable institutions and sacred narratives has not always been well received. Girard waited until his next book, *Things Hidden Since the Foundation of the World* (1978), to drop his great intellectual bombshell. This originally French volume, written in the form of an extended conversation with the psychiatrists, and his collaborators, Guy Lefort and Jean-Michel Oughourlian, reworked the mimetic and scapegoat theories. But, most notably, it explicated Girard's new conviction that a remarkable anthropological breakthrough has taken place at the level of history, which is explicable purely in terms of scientifically objective evidence. The Judeo-Christian Scriptures in general and the texts of Jesus' passion in particular are expounded by Girard as revealing and hence disempowering the scapegoat mechanism. This insight was of course cultural dynamite. Girard attributes its modern discovery to Nietzsche, who hated what he had found and was ultimately driven mad by it. Girard develops this insight in subsequent volumes, in particular, *The Scapegoat* (1982) and *I See Satan Fall Like Lightning* (1999). Girard moved to his final academic post in 1981, as Andrew M. Hammond Professor of French Language and Literature at Stanford University.

In *A Theater of Envy* (1991), Girard went on to provide a detailed reading of Shakespeare as a sophisticated analyst of mimetic desire who also understood the scapegoat mechanism and its disempowering by the gospel. From the mimetic lovers of *A Midsummer Night's Dream* to the failed sacrifice of *Julius Caesar* to the resurrection of Hermione at the end of *The Winter's Tale*, Girard presents Shakespeare as a psychological genius and Christian prophet.

Girard extended his reflections on mimeticism as revealed in great literature, and on the nature of scapegoating culture and its scriptural undoing, in *Job: The Victim of His People* (1985) and *Oedipus Unbound* (2004), with both figures presented as the victims of Soviet-style show trials. Girard has also engaged with the Indian Vedic literature, in which he finds only a very limited awareness of the scapegoat mechanism. His 2003 French lecture series on the Vedas has been published in English with the title *Sacrifice* (2011). In 1990 the Colloquium on Violence and Religion was initiated, with annual conferences alternating between the United States and Europe, to explore, critique, and develop Girard's work. An international community of

Christians, Jews, atheists, and others have found in one, two, or all three aspects of Girard's vision the intellectual and, in many cases, the personal and spiritual inspiration for their work and their lives.[4]

More recently Girard has offered something of a retrospective volume, *Evolution and Conversion* (2007), drawn from extended conversations in the late 1990s. His interlocutors there, in a book which updates *Things Hidden Since the Foundation of the World*, were Pierpaolo Antonello (Cambridge) and João Cezar de Castro Rocha (Manchester). A particular theme is the scientific nature of Girard's conclusions, on the model of Darwin's big, all-encompassing idea. Those who are disinclined to accept the truth of Christianity are shown how Girard makes visible a diagnosis of human ills that can commend itself apart from Christian belief, though it is clear that he sees no way beyond those ills apart from the healing of mimetic distortion and the abandonment of sacrificial violence that comes with repentance and conversion.

This issue became urgent for Girard in his eighties, in the decade after 9/11, when he turned his mind to the nature of warfare and fully crystallized his long-standing apocalyptic instincts about the direction and likely outcome of modern history. The escalation of violence has nothing reliably to restrain it once the scapegoat mechanism has been revealed, so unification at the expense of a common enemy or culprit becomes increasingly desperate, strident, one-eyed, and bloodthirsty—precisely because it is unreliable and ineffective. Through reflecting on Napoleon's campaigns, such an escalation to extremes was discovered by Carl von Clausewitz, the early-nineteenth-century Prussian general and military theorist, who quickly resiled from his insight into a comforting but erroneous conviction that war could continue to be rule-bound and containable. Hence Girard's 2007 book titled *Achever Clausewitz* (completing Clausewitz), which again took the form of an extended conversation—in this case with the French philosopher Benoît Chantre. It was later published in English as *Battling to the End*. In today's era of globalization, rampant militarism, environmental crisis, and the resurgence of archaic violence since 9/11, Girard is convinced that we are on an apocalyptic roller coaster that mocks Hegel's intellectual vision of peaceful resolution within history.

René Girard and his wife, Martha, have raised three children in America. The French Immortel now lives quietly in the seclusion of advanced age at Stanford.

WHAT IS SECULAR MODERNITY?

The meanings of *secular* and *modernity* are increasingly contested.[5] Modernity, that once clean-cut specimen, now appears in scruffier postmodern dress, and it proves harder to recognize in a variety of non-Western guises.[6] Its pedigree is less clear than we once thought,[7] with Bruno Latour showing how modernity's anxious myth of rational purity conceals a menagerie of strange hybrids.[8] Secularization, too, is in trouble. This sociological theory, which attempts to explain the inexorable desacralizing drive toward functionally atheistic modernity, must now account for major international variations, postcolonial hybridity, and a number of frank reversals.[9] Today's rise of militant Islam is one such reversal *and* a distinctively modern phenomenon.[10]

Secular modernity is a narrative available in various versions. One popular account—from the likes of Richard Dawkins—is that scientific advances have rendered belief in God obsolete as nature's laws were brought to light, creating a go-ahead society of human self-betterment through technological spin-offs and by liberating our creativity from the oppressions of church and tradition.[11]

The stubborn religiousness of Africa, the Middle East, and much of the rest of the world outside Western Europe, the United States, and a few satellites is surely exasperating for those proposing this view.[12] Equally stubborn, and irritating to the skeptic, is the wonder and sense of deep obligation that still draws many Westerners to consider Wordsworth's "sense sublime of something far more deeply interfused," even if it is true that they are less and less likely to seek it in Western churches. So this view of secularization seems to put the cart before the horse. If modern people claim scientific reasons for abandoning "their faith," it is likely that a lively faith has eluded them already, with science perhaps providing the catalyst for their unbelief, though not its cause.

A more believable account of secular modernity might go like this.[13] Until the late Middle Ages in the West, human societies were more integral and holistic than has proved either sustainable or desirable in modern times. "Religion" and "society" were significantly interwoven. Likewise, a transcendent God underpinned a rationally ordered cosmos and human world. Church and state, pope and emperor, archbishop and king, were structurally interdependent in the sociopolitical manifestation of a deeper metaphysical belonging. A Durkheimian account of religion underwriting social cohesion is entirely appropriate here.[14] Of course, explicit Christian belief, personal holiness, and devoted Christian discipleship were widespread in presecular times, but such focus and personal intensity by no means exhausted the meaning of belonging to a Christian society. Typically, these were *tribal* Christians who *belonged*, compared to the characteristic posture of *individual* choice usually associated with modern Western Christians who *believe*.

The breakdown of this unified synthesis had a number of elements. The shift in Western thinking about God that took place under the influence of late medieval nominalist philosophy (Duns Scotus, William of Ockham) made God *sovereign over* rather than transcendently present everywhere within the order of things. The nominalist metaphysic proved conducive to the emergence of the *saeculum*—an independent natural order standing apart from the newly sovereign God, which could be left to scientific investigation and theorizing. The recovery of Greek learning and the shift of Europe's intellectual center from the monasteries to the new universities furthered this bifurcation of the sacred and the secular. Shifts from feudal hierarchy to the naked sovereignty of monarchs, with a recognizably modern notion of the individual emerging for the first time in medieval romances and a newly prosperous middle class, extended the picture. Lay devotion, with its emphasis on individual belief and practice, developed under the influence of manuals, lay spiritual communities, and the new orders of preaching friars.

Next came the Reformation, inheriting this nominalist vision of God and the world. Doctrinally distinctive denominations jostled for position with "the universal Church," while the newfound emphasis on lay devotion was quickly diverted into the cultivation of markets and commerce, as Max Weber famously proposed.[15] A public world increasingly understood as the work of voluntary human association, preserved by human know-how, for the pursuit of human well-being, left less room for God and less need for religion.

Key aspects of modernity are reform and diversification, with the one world of Christendom splitting its functions between agencies, economic classes, professions, and churches, as humanity for the first time began to take its own future in hand. Religion became a separate undertaking, with its values remaining in the public square while its doctrine and practice retreated behind a veil of privacy. Only thus could nation-states and markets begin their annexation of the modern world.

Into this account of an emerging *saeculum* fits Dawkins's very partial picture, whereby science makes enormous strides in understanding and control. The machine age, the medical revolution accompanying the germ theory of disease, the revolutionary creation of our first great modern democracies, the prosperity growing with colonial markets and expansion on the North American continent, all contributed to a truly brave new world where divine providence—surely the deepest vein of popular religious sensibility—was outsourced to human agents. The unplanned evolutionary etiology of human being (Darwin) and its irrational inwardness (Freud) furthered the isolation of religion from a suitably triumphant, publicly shared view of reality. While both simple and sophisticated theological imaginations never lost Hopkins's celebrated sense that "the world is charged with the glory of God," nevertheless individualized faith became increasingly fragile as an essentially isolated matter of personal preference within a larger worldview that was secular.

The result is a degree of spiritual homelessness in the secular modern West, with few finding their way to churches and even fewer deeming those churches authoritative. Those who do are often retreating from the uncertainty and exposure that existentialism identified in Western modernity. Human inwardness tends to follow more romantic directions today, with consumer culture ensuring that it remains on a tight leash.[16]

Tribal faith survives in particular localized forms—among ethnic groups, for instance, seeking cohesion in immigrant contexts as a stage on the way to fully inhabiting their new home in a secular modern manner. It also survives in particular national contexts, such as Ireland and Poland where church and Christianity served to maintain identity and resistance in the face of an invasive "political religion" (Ireland) or political ideology (Poland).[17] Likewise, militant Islam provides a rallying point for the disaffected in today's Middle East.

The impact of all this on church attendance throughout the West is a major issue in secularization theory, as is accounting for differences within a general pattern of decline. In Europe, for instance, where church attendance is plummeting but church taxes are still widely paid, the church is typically conceived of as a public utility to which one might occasionally need to have recourse. In America, however, where the actual extent of church attendance can be disputed, the church model is closer to that of a business competing for customers in the open market. My own country, like Canada and New Zealand, seems to lie somewhere in between,[18] so that in the Anglican Church of Australia our current trials in the ministry remind me of doughy public utilities struggling to reinvent themselves as sexier and more relevant once privatization and the need to become competitive is forced on them.

The narrative of secularization that I have been sketching seems right enough, as far as it goes. However, the resurgence of religion in step with feral manifestations of modernity lends an air of tentativeness to these conclusions. Aspects of Western culture today make sense in the light of this narrative, but not all of them. Remember Durkheim and his key insight that religion ultimately has a social function, literally binding together communal life.

An obvious question is, therefore, what binds together the life of secular modern communities now that the old premodern synthesis is gone and "formal" religions are increasingly sidelined? An adequate answer must include nation-states and global markets, programmatic national enmities and grand ideologies, all seen to fulfill formerly religious functions (i.e., when religion and society were two sides of the same coin). Some sociologists of secularization, like Steve Bruce, confine themselves to measuring religion as private belief and ecclesial affiliation, drawing predictable conclusions in accordance with the narrative of religious isolation and decline.[19] But what if religion needs to be understood more broadly, more socially, less privately, less obviously—less *religiously*? This possibility indicates the direction of Girard's approach.

WHAT IS DISTINCTIVE ABOUT GIRARD'S TAKE ON SECULAR MODERNITY?

First, Girard's account of secular modernity is not about loss of faith eventually ushering us into a brave new world once we have grown up and abandoned the consolations of religion. Religion for Girard is not about finding or making personal meaning. It is less of a private search and more of a specific public function, having to do with managing violence for the preservation of society. If there is a felt sacred aura, then it is likely to be a powerful effect of human togetherness. And if that felt sense has dwindled in secular modern times, it is because a particular social function is no longer working as it once did.

Second, Girard distinguishes between religion as an evolved concomitant of human culture and religion (typically, Judaism and Christianity) as a form of countercultural witness. Girard sees the Christian gospel outing and undoing the violent false sacred that undergirds human religiousness. Thereafter, the transformed "religion" typically colonizes the structures and legacies of the old, which generates a perennial unease for Christianity. New wine in old wineskins is Jesus' image for this awkwardness (Mt 9:14–17; Mk 2:18–22; Lk 5:33–39). "A religion is revealed that is entirely other and yet inseparable from the old," as Girard puts it.[20] The archaic human religious impulse identified by Girard will always attempt to reconstitute this protective sacred, too, which while mortally wounded by the gospel was not killed outright. Consequently the gospel finds itself socially marginalized, within the church as well as outside it, for its countercultural unwillingness to maintain anybody's status quo. This leads to some of history's lowest points in terms of gospel values deserting the church—as when a pope blesses crusaders, for instance, or righteous Protestant clergy hold out for the death penalty. But there remains a Christian alternative to typical human religiousness, even if regularly compromised throughout history.

Third, for Girard the rise of a sovereign individual God, and of the sovereign human individual, finds inspiration much earlier than the rise of nominalism—certainly much earlier than the modern individual whom we first glimpse in medieval romance and the emerging middle class. This separation of God from the social matrix, and the indiscriminate honoring of all human persons, was first of all a biblical development, as the victim mechanism began its undoing by the real God. So Girard provides a deeper, more anthropologically savvy account of imaginative and social transformation than standard versions of how secular modernity emerged.

Fourth, while Girard's take on secularization accords with the influential account of Charles Taylor in *A Secular Age*, as the Girardian theologian Wolfgang Palaver also points out,[21] nevertheless I have one important reservation. Girard's understanding of the human person varies in emphasis from Taylor's description of secular modern selves as less "porous," and more "buffered."[22] These terms refer to a secularizing, modernizing shift in how people typically experience their world: from premodern, traditional societies in which attitudes and options were culturally given and constrained, with lives more scripted and limited—more porous, that is—to today's experience of independent, freer, self-determining individuals, who are thus more buffered. This is true, but with a caveat. Girard's mimetic theory shows that in an important sense we all remain porous. The independent buffered self is in reality a fragile metaphysical poseur, and the modern romantic individual is an illusion. Today it remains a question of what models of desire we follow, and what metanarrative we inhabit, just as in premodernity—though we have the illusion of greater and freer choice. With Taylor, Girard certainly recognizes the social disembedding of modern Western people by comparison to their forebears in traditional societies. He does not see modern people as any less mimetic, however, but likely more so.

Fifth, Girard seeks to identify a new "religious" face of society in modernity, denying that the measurable behavior of a "religious minority" in secular modern societies exhausts how "religion" might be functioning. There is a *resacralizing* going on within secular modernity, which Girard tries to name. In his analysis of the violent false sacred returning under the championship of Nietzsche, he offers an alternative to viewing the secular modern West as a realm of declining religious engagement. Belief in the Christian God is definitely in decline, admits Girard, but this is chiefly because the preferred deity of secular modernity is Dionysus, who is worshiped in various (often unacknowledged) guises. So Girard sees secular modernity in the West as functionally religious. However, its "religious" dimension does not work as well in restraining violence as did archaic religious forms, because the gospel has begun their undoing. Hence Girard's essentially apocalyptic account of modern history, based on there being greater risks with less protection.

Sixth, Girard concurs with Hans Blumenberg, Max Weber, and Marcel Gauchet—to name three proponents of this thesis—in finding the ultimate source of secular modernity in Christianity. This is certainly closer to the truth than Dawkins's naive proposal, which sees Christianity expelled kicking and screaming from the modern world once noble-minded scientists had outsmarted it. Charles Taylor, by the way, scores a tidy point against this Dawkins-style view by identifying its religious roots in the spurned evangelicalism of Victorian-era skepticism.[23] But Girard differs from all three in the details. Rather than Blumenberg's late medieval nominalist account[24]—which Taylor welcomes as "the intellectual deviation story" and which is championed today by the Radical Orthodoxy movement in theology[25]—or Weber's economic path to modernity focused on the Protestant ethic secularizing monastic discipline,[26] or Gauchet's structural theory whereby belief in a transcendent God who remains incarnationally and ecclesially invested in the world provides a perfect seedbed from which secular modernity might emerge,[27] Girard goes deeper, darker, and further back. He declares the defeat of a violent cultural *habitus* that had evolved among mimetic creatures. The fact of such mimeticism, the scapegoat mechanism with its various religious echoes, and the way things are unraveling since that religio-cultural bubble was burst by the gospel, together account for the rise of secular modernity. Girard's version is highly explanatory and predictive—for instance, the return of religion and pseudoreligion.

Seventh, Girard does not wring his hands with the existentialists and the New Age movement over secular modernity's spiritual homelessness. The disenchantment of which Weber wrote (as a necessary consequence of our grasping the levers of history to make our own future) is closer to Girard's view, and is not a thing to be lamented. However, Girard accounts for this disenchantment differently from Weber. The unified religio-cultural world, extending from human origins to premodern societies, provided a sense of metaphysical belonging, a unified cosmos, and a place for us in the scheme of things, all of which has departed to the sound of lament from modernity's various critics. Yet Girard reminds us that togetherness and personal security are typically rooted in a violent compact and its mythico-ritual reinforcement, so that the price of liberation for a future of genuine human dignity and self-determination is the risk of isolation, exposure, and emotional flatness. This is because the false sacred has been punctured. Disenchantment is thus the price of Christian maturity and closeness to God, according to a Girardian reading, as Saint John of the Cross intuited at the onset of modernity with his "dark night of the soul." Of course, Girard is also aware that a form of enchantment returns in secular modern times as we struggle to get by without the former social protection that religion provided. For instance, historical enmities, nation-states, political ideologies, and market forces are invested with transcendent meaning. In light of all this, and of resurgent Islam, Gauchet's declaration of an end to enchantment appears premature.

Eighth, Girard seems torn about how to respond politically. He is a conservative in his pragmatic sense of society's need for law, order, and religiously motivated disciplines, as well as in his robust dismissal of romanticism, sentimentality, political correctness, and pacifism.[28] Yet he is a progressive in the hermeneutic of suspicion with which he confronts today's several sacred cows: the state, the global market, ideology, and militarism. Hence Girard calls himself a moderate, disavowing whichever political or ideological program of human perfectibility.[29] This position may also have something to do with his genuine perplexity on being faced by the apocalyptic future that he predicts. He dismisses the modern myth of progress, expressing as it does Hegel's confidence that the back-and-forth of history will eventually achieve resolution. It is a fragile modernity, an incomplete secularization, and a dark future that Girard offers us. Unless we learn the Gospels' lesson and draw back from the brink.

OUTLINE OF THE BOOK

Girard's conclusions about secular modernity need to be set out in terms of his overall project in order to make proper sense. So chapter 1 explains the mimetic theory and demonstrates some of its explanatory power, showing how modernity and secularization look in light of Girard's early work on Proust, Dostoyevsky, and Freud. Chapter 2 sets out systematically the second element in his vision, archaic violence and its sacrificial containment. I try to make clear the detail, which includes piecing together elements of the argument from various sources as is sometimes necessary with Girard. Chapter 3 discusses the revealing and unraveling of this violent cultural-religious matrix. We advance from the Hebrew Scriptures to the New Testament to various stages of the false sacred returning in later Christian societies, most notably with Nietzsche and his legacy.

The final two chapters involve something of a shift in gear. They refer essentially to Girard's late thought, in many cases to the reflections of his ninth decade on contemporary events. His work in this period is more episodic than was the case during his most productive decades when the theory was being hammered out in forensic detail, then refined and broadened across a series of books. Also, the bulk of Girard's earlier work was concerned with the past—from prehistoric civilization to antiquity to early modernity to nineteenth-century fiction—so it is understandable that his focus on contemporary events is less extensive and comprehensive. The student of Girard's formidable earlier work is struck by an element of tentativeness in his more recent comments on Islamist terrorism, for instance. However, a body of wider Girardian reflection is emerging in commentary on modern culture in general and contemporary events in particular, on which I also draw in the two final chapters.

Chapter 4 looks at modern institutions, chiefly the nation-state and the market, considering how they hold violence in check. Some forms of contemporary violence are identified that reintroduce aspects of Girard's archaic sacred under secular modern conditions. Chapter 5 turns to modern warfare and terrorism, and what they can tell us about the course of history, culminating in a reading of Girard's late, troubled work, *Battling to the End*. In the conclusion, I take up and extend Girard's own hints concerning an alternative to apocalypse. What sort of conversion must humans undergo before it is too late?

CHAPTER 1

Mimesis, Modernity, and Madness

Our journey toward understanding secular modernity begins with the first plank of Girard's controversial threefold program, the mimetic theory. *Mimesis* is typically defined in terms of human imitation. It is about the representation of external reality and other people.[1] But mimesis goes deeper and further for Girard. It is a particular kind of representation, involving imitation not so much of others' actions but of the desires that find expression in them. Mimesis according to Girard reveals the key thing about our desire, which he sees as awakened by and following the desires of another—of a "model" or "mediator" of desire. This individual or group shapes our desiring, which is less about this or that "object" of desire than it is about the model who awakens that desire.

Quite at variance with how modern Westerners typically understand themselves and their motivations, Girard's mimetic theory replaces the sovereign, autonomous individual with a nonromantic, rather more prosaic figure. The active desiring agent becomes a passive product in the reflection of others' desire; the self's private inner sanctum turns inside out, becoming a potentially disorienting hall of mirrors. Girard uses this account, which he originally discovered in great literature, to theoretically outperform Freud and depth psychology, with their speculative complement of unconscious interior states. Shakespeare, Dostoyevsky, and Proust prove the better psychologists, according to Girard, illuminating even the most puzzling aspects of human motivation and group interaction, and their pathological dynamics "which become *interdividual* . . . rather than *interindividual*—that is, which progress beyond the point at which ego and other can still be meaningfully distinguished."[2] I begin in this chapter with an overview, then sketch an interdividual account of normal and abnormal psychology, especially as these illuminate the secular modern condition. Because skepticism dogs Girard's program, I want to also present some hard scientific evidence for mimetic theory that has emerged in the past two decades.

AN OVERVIEW OF MIMETIC THEORY

The rational, choosing individual reigns supreme in today's popular Western imagination. Yet simple observation and honest introspection, aided by a perceptive guide, reveal a different reality. From children mimetically mastering language and basic life skills to the emerging sexual personae of mimetically fascinated teenagers to the supposedly highly personal styles, habits, and occupations of adults, the desires of others fascinate, awaken, and direct our own.

Some examples. Inspired and apprenticed, our particular skills and commitments are evoked and formed by others. How many of us can testify to the formative effect on our desires of fine teachers, exemplary craftspersons or musicians, inspiring colleagues—indeed, any kind of influential role models? Less positively, perhaps, advertising mimetically draws our desire into one or another of the proliferating niche markets that our growth economies demand. Through television, popular novels, films, magazines, and social networking websites, celebrities, fictional characters, and wannabes possess our imaginations, shaping our sensibilities and even our bodies. Internet porn, along with mainstream cinema, is transforming the sexual desires of a generation in line with what Girard sees as the onanistic voyeurism of modern literary eroticism—a mimetic entanglement marked by "a double inaptitude to communion and to solitude."[3] Likewise, violent computer games awaken violent desires, with Girard arguing that "violence exerts a mimetic fascination without equal."[4] He can explain all this and more by approaching human desire *and human consciousness* mimetically.[5]

"Love by another's eyes"

La système Girard is there in Shakespeare—all three elements[6]—but as far as mimetic desire goes, Shakespeare's first mature statement is found in *A Midsummer Night's Dream.* The young protagonists fall in and out of love all night long, their attraction directed toward the one whom another first desires, with knowing Puck and his love juice standing in for the mimetic principle of "love by another's eyes."[7] Dostoyevsky in *The Eternal Husband* paints a later version of his underground man,[8] who provokes another's ardor for his fiancée in order to mimetically awaken his own desire for her—as Shakespeare's Troilus also did, "recklessly inviting cuckoldry in order to strengthen an uncertain passion."[9] From Shakespeare and Dostoyevsky to Woody Allen's knowing (and underrated) 2008 film, *Vicky Cristina Barcelona,* the unstable and unflattering mimeticism of romantic desire accounts for why "the course of true love never did run smooth." Here the longer shadows of mimetic theory stretch toward us—how envy and rivalry annex desire, risking masochistic self-destruction (more on this shortly).

Girard finds the origins of human mimeticism in the evolutionary modification of our animal appetites, which "with the help of this imitation, turn into what we call desire."[10] A simple formula might go like this: *instinct* or *appetite* + *mimesis* = *desire*. And the basic mimetic dynamic of what Shakespeare called "borrowed desire" is triangular. The *subject* desires the *object* (e.g., the blonde, the Mercedes, or the accolade) not for the object primarily but because the desire of a model (or mediator) awakens this desire. Someone we admire desires and lays hold of an object, so we start desiring it too. Indeed, we do not know what to desire, according to Girard, so that authority in the matter of desiring lies with its mediator.[11] What is more, as he puts it in his first book, *Deceit, Desire, and the Novel*—in which the mimetic theory is already extraordinarily fully formed—"The impulse toward the object is ultimately an impulse toward the mediator."[12] The object develops a kind of aura but only thanks to the mediator whose desire illuminates it. Indeed, we will see how "acquisitive mimesis"—directing desire toward an object—can lose sight of that object altogether, becoming entirely caught up with the mediator in what Girard calls metaphysical desire.

Desire's model or mediator can of course be fictional. Hermione and Lysander in *A Midsummer Night's Dream* desire according to their reading habits,[13] as do Paolo and Francesca in Dante's *Inferno,* whose illicit passion began after reading the romances of Lancelot and Guinevere.[14] Flaubert's flighty protagonist Emma Bovary yearned predictably with all the other readers of romantic fiction (in a story nicely updated by Tom Perrotta in his 2004 novel, *Little Children*).[15] First among Girard's mimetically attuned authors was Cervantes, whose crazed Don Quixote desired according to a model from chivalric literature, Amadis of Gaul.[16]

Girard's interpreter Paisley Livingstone seeks more clarity on the attraction and influence of mediators, wishing to explicate in mimetic terms the sociological distinction between primary and secondary socialization of the young. He distinguishes between "proximal" examples such as "an imitative relation to a particular actor who appears in television advertisements" and "the more distal and more longstanding type of mediation that we may associate with developmental processes and social learning."[17] Girard does not explore themes of childhood at length. But he does explore at great length the primary means by which a particular subject will be caught up in the desire of a particular mediator. This happens when subject and model become entwined in mutual envy and rivalry[18]—a state of mimetic interference, by the way, to which children are especially prone.

Rivalry and Mimetic Desire

Playpen squabbles provide a standard illustration in the explication of mimetic theory, wherein intense infant desire is suddenly and irresistibly drawn to whichever toy another infant first desires, so that envy arises—because of course the toy itself is never the cause of desire. One of the skills grownups learn if they are to get along in the world is how to conceal such desires, so that envy and hence rivalry in others is not stirred up. The ability to keep a poker face is one aspect of such skill, but ordinary "common sense" involves a number of others.[19] Once awakened, envy readily detaches from its object to fixate on the model of desire, who can in turn take on the envious desire of the one whose desire he or she had formerly stimulated.

Shakespeare's plays are full of this (as Girard lays out in *A Theater of Envy*). And so is the real world. We can come to feel ambivalent about employers, leaders, and "heroes," for instance, when their role as models of our desire becomes one of obstacle to the fulfillment of the desire that they have awakened in us. Medieval chivalry manifested such bad faith, according to Girard, with competing knights both admiring and despising each other.[20] Frantz Fanon was explicit about a similar dynamic in colonial environments: respect and hatred for the master coinhere in the frustrated bosom of colonized peoples.[21] A likely escalation sees rivals becoming indistinguishable as mimeticism spirals toward crisis, bringing about the all-out frenzy into which crowd violence readily descends. Meanwhile, police can become indistinguishable from the violent criminals they pursue, just as opposing regimes successively in charge at Baghdad's Abu Ghraib prison treated their respective prisoners in similar ways. I testify to my own mimetic entanglements with control-minded lay opponents in my last appointment as a parish priest. I demonized them as they did me, to the point that our mutually reinforcing rivalrous desires annexed the original object, which was control of our parish. Unlearning this mind-set came with my developing grasp of Girardian theory.

All such escalation to extremes begins with the shift from what Girard calls "external mediation"—which is relatively stable and uncontroversial, when the model or mediator is unlikely to become a rival of the subject—to "internal mediation," where the model of desire is close to us, on our level or in our space, becoming an obstacle to the fulfillment of desires that they have awakened in us.[22] Here, as Girard explains, "envy is merely the reciprocal borrowing of desires, under conditions of sufficient equality to ensure the development of mimetic rivalries."[23]

Girard identifies external mediation as the kind you might find between child and adult and internal mediation as that between children.[24] Children are rivals with each other in their peer group, though less typically with adults—unless adults harass and seek excessively to control children, as intrusive parents with inadequate boundaries are prone to do, whereupon generational rivalry does emerge. I note, for instance, that adults never appeared in the comic strip *Peanuts* because, as external mediators, they were clearly off the mimetic radar. Instead, mimetic dynamics were confined to the children—and to that quixotically mimetic dog, Snoopy, who lived in their world.

The shift from external to internal mediation is observed whenever two mimetically prone individuals who were previously perhaps only mildly competitive friends suddenly have to work together at close quarters, or one becomes senior to the other, whereupon mimetic rivalry emerges as the old friendship recedes. An edgy 2010 British comedy, *The Trip*, in which the comedians Steve Coogan and Rob Brydon play themselves on a weeklong fine dining tour of England's North, provides an excellent illustration of internal mediation. Rivalry surfaces immediately between two entertainment professionals who obviously crave aspects of the other's "being," chiefly the lonely and insecure Coogan who is secretly jealous of Brydon. Their constant competitive mimicry of Sean Connery, Michael Caine, and Woody Allen highlights the mimetic nature of their formerly externally mediated acquaintance, which had become internally mediated and envious thanks to their physical proximity on the trip. Similarly, Coogan's rivalry with his absent girlfriend, Misha, with whom he appears to be breaking up, is evident as he counters her imagined infidelity by his own one-night stands with a hotel receptionist and a magazine photographer during the trip.

From internal mediation arises what Girard called "double mediation" or, as it builds, "reciprocal mediation," where the desire to thwart rivals replaces desire for whatever constituted the original object of rivalry (as I discovered in that former parish).[25] In a variation of this, such rivalry can return attention to an object, which suddenly becomes desirable because to have it would foil the rival. Each "becomes the other's rival for acquisition of increasingly symbolic objects."[26] So obsessions with "forbidden fruit" are more typically the result rather than the cause of rivalry.[27]

Soon we arrive at what Girard calls the "scandal," or the *Skandalon* to give it its New Testament name. He is referring to anything addictive and obsessive that both attracts and repels, such as "drugs, sex, power, and above all morbid competitiveness, professional, sexual, political, intellectual, and spiritual, especially spiritual."[28] Such stumbling blocks come to exert a chronic fascination in the escalating reaches of mimeticism.[29] For Girard, "*Skandalon* is the aching tooth that we cannot stop testing with our tongue, even though it hurts more."[30] The speck in our rival's eye is readily identified while we fail entirely to notice (let alone evaluate soberly and realistically) our own heightened suspicion and vitriol. Hence our behavior and the behavior we deplore in our rival become progressively indistinguishable. We do not see the log in our own eye (Mt 7:1–5).[31] For Girard:

> Mimeticism is indeed the contagion which spreads throughout human relationships, and in principal it spares no one. If the model himself becomes more interested in the object that he designates to his imitator as a result of the latter's imitations, then he himself falls victim to his contagion. In fact, he imitates his own desire, through the intermediary of the disciple. The disciple thus becomes model to his own model, and the model, reciprocally, becomes disciple to his own disciple. In the last resort, there are no genuine differences left between the two, or, to put it more precisely, between their desires. . . . In rivalry, everyone occupies all the positions, one after another and then simultaneously, and there are no longer any distinct positions.[32]

Thus emerge what Girard calls "mirror doubles," at worst "monstrous doubles," when subject and model have become interchangeable.

This escalation toward mimeticism's terminal phase begins when status, prestige, or honor becomes the sole desired object. "These notions are in fact created by rivalry; they have no tangible reality whatsoever," explains Girard. "Yet the very fact that there is a rivalry involving them makes them appear to be more real than any real object."[33] And they are sought *in the being itself* of our model, or in a plurality of models. Thus through internal mediation our rivals potentially multiply without end. The *vaniteux* of Stendhal's novels and the *snobbisme* of Proust's salons point to this "ontological sickness" of modernity, where hunger for being propels a world of addicts and compulsives—from failed gamblers and junkies to high-functioning sports heroes, public figures, and celebrities—in pursuit of diminishing returns, desiring the mojo of their models, yet never able to attain it. Indeed, were they to succeed they would soon awaken to a sense of their model's limitations, their lack of the "being" that they were expected to deliver. Whereupon such subjects relaunch themselves on the ever riskier pursuit of a more unattainable model, one whose very unattainability surely guarantees the presence of the "being" that is desired.

Here we arrive at the very heart of Girard's mimetic theory. "Metaphysical desire" represents Girard's take on existentialism, though without its individualistic preoccupations. It yields an *interdividual* psychology revealing much that is considered normal in our world to be pathological while declaring much that seemed pathological to be far more normal: "The 'metaphysical' threshold or . . . the point at which we reach desire properly speaking, is the threshold of the unreal. It can also be seen as the threshold of psychopathology. Yet we should insist upon the continuity, even the identity, between such a level of desire and everything that passes as completely normal because it is defined in terms sanctioned by society, such as the love of risk, thirst for the infinite, stirrings of the poetic soul, *amour fou*, and so on."[34]

So internal mediation and reciprocal mediation move us from acquisitive mimesis, with the original object still in view, perhaps via metaphysical desire and prestige rivalry,[35] to ontological sickness (of which more later in the chapter) to the cusp of what Girard calls "conflictual mimesis."[36] There the focus shifts to one individual among a conflicted group of increasingly indistinguishable rivals who is made a scapegoat and dispatched for the restoration of order. Chapter 2 begins with Girard's account of this age-old means for resolving such mimetic crises.

Internal Mediation as the Key to Modernity

It is timely to begin considering how modernity heightens these mimetic dynamics. In what we might call a traditional society, with a clear social hierarchy, there is certainly external mediation. Girard points out that Sancho Panza desires and covets according to his station as a valet, and only desires the imaginary island because Don Quixote promises it to him, so that any desire shared between master and man remains externally mediated and nonrivalrous.[37] Nowadays, however, anyone can observe lifestyles of the rich and famous on television and desire mimetically to emulate them. Such aspirations to share in the good fortunes of one's "betters" have grown apace in modern times. For instance, Josiah Wedgwood began making white porcelain tea sets for the middle class, advertised as identical in style and quality to those he made for royal clients, apart from the lavish decoration.

Girard points to a moment in history when the social shift to internal mediation took place. In the intensely mimetic goldfish bowl of Versailles, while rivalry no doubt flourished among Louis XIV's courtiers, such internal mediation was inconceivable vis-à-vis their universal mediator, the Sun King, whose divine right placed him at an unbridgeable remove from his subjects. Girard points out that Louis's royal infidelities were tolerated at court for this reason; cuckolded husbands accepted what would have awakened rivalry had any ordinary mortal taken such liberties.[38] All this changed with the revolution, ending the divine right of kings. Idolatry of the tyrant as mediator "is replaced by hatred of a hundred thousand rivals," who crowded into the Latin quarter to seek their fortune once it was no longer available at Versailles. Girard concludes that "democracy is one vast middle-class court where the courtiers are everywhere and the king is nowhere"—hence *"men will become Gods for each other."*[39] Here hangs Girard's account of secular modernity.

Hobbes's analysis "of the Naturall Condition of Mankind, as concerning their Felicity, and Misery," in *Leviathan*, centers on the development of tension between equals as the mimetic heart of emerging modernity, so that "from this equality of ability, ariseth equality of hope in the attaining of our Ends. And therefore if any two men desire the same thing, which nevertheless they cannot both enjoy, they become enemies."[40] From there it is a very short step to Hobbes's "warre . . . of every man, against every man,"[41] indicating a world of internal mediation out of control. In chapter 4, the way Western modernity has hitherto been dodging Hobbes's bullet is considered.

Girard is particularly interested in Alexis de Tocqueville—France's aristocratic envoy to the young United States—and his classic, closely observed analysis of the new republic. *Democracy in America* sees an association between modern equality, what Girard calls internal mediation, and a newfound competitive, never-quite-satisfied, stubbornly unquiet mood that seemed likely to succeed the ancien régime.[42] Of course, attachment to the group, the family, the place, typically looms larger in French culture than in American, so that a different, less isolated flavor of modern individualism emerges there. Nevertheless, Tocqueville and his near-contemporaries Stendhal and Flaubert sensed the escalation of petty rivalry, and ambition to distinguish oneself from the crowd, as "the truly schismatic tendency of romantic and modern society."[43]

This modern mood was analyzed philosophically early in the twentieth century by Max Scheler, sharpening Nietzsche's identification of an embittered, spoiling attitude that he thought typical of powerless, jealous Christianity. When I first read Scheler's *Ressentiment,* I was struck by his old-fashioned aristocratic sensibility in conservative opposition to modern trends. Scheler's lost world, like that of Tocqueville, Flaubert, and Stendhal, is essentially the premodern world where sufficient differentiation remained to keep internal mediation in check. "They perceived the grotesque element of the era that was about to begin," Girard concludes, "but they did not suspect its tragedy."[44]

From this reading of modernity as mimetically volatile, Girard extrapolates his bleak account of deteriorating human social relations, personal instability, and madness, all underpinning his emerging apocalyptic assessment of modernity as the final stage in history. I propose to say more about this apocalypticism in chapter 5. For now, it will be helpful in setting the scene to see how Girard deploys his mimetic theory in a new and comprehensive psychology fit to illuminate the troubled modern Western mind.

THE HELL OF THE HYPERMIMETIC

In a characteristically provocative statement, Girard claims that "the mimetic is . . . the real 'unconscious.'"[45] He proposes a straightforward interdividual explanation for our various experiences of being driven by an irrational otherness, which the West has long reckoned to be taking place entirely within the subject. In antiquity the womb coming adrift in women or the intracorporeal movement of withheld semen in men constituted an "intraphysical other" understood to cause "hysteria," while in medieval times it was an "external other" that then moved to a position inside us to take us over, in the form of demonic possession. The "intrapsychic other" of Freud's unconscious brings this tradition up to date—of seeking a chimerical "other" within, in place of actual human models remaining *outside us* who influence us mimetically.[46]

But none of these "others" working within are real, as the psychiatrist and Girardian thinker Jean-Michel Oughourlian explains: "The Id, the Superego, Eros, Thanatos, and the rest have neither more nor less actual existence than Asmodeus, Beelzebub, Leviathan, and the various other demons." The devil is best understood in Girardian terms as a way of talking about extremes of the concrete and potentially dangerous mimetic principle rather than the theatrical supernatural figure of popular imagination.[47]

Oughourlian traces "discovery" of the unconscious to nineteenth-century psychological investigations of hysteria and the hypnosis used to treat it.[48] Yet both Girard and Oughourlian strike out boldly for an alternative, interdividual account of these phenomena. Indeed, they are confident that hypnosis provides an empirical confirmation of Girard's mimetic theory,[49] sufficient to unseat the Cartesian rational individual at the center of modern Western philosophical anthropology.[50] Of course we remain wedded to that self-defining myth of rationality, so that modernity copes uneasily in its encounters with madness. Girard offers a mimetic account of this discomfort too: "The madman makes us feel uneasy not because his game is different from ours but because it is ... the same old mimetic game in which we all engage, but a little too emphatic for our taste, as if played with excessive application by a man who lacks a sense of proportion.... We prefer to leave the matter alone and not to look at ourselves in the mirror that is offered to us."[51]

Mimesis and the Mirror of Mental Illness

I begin here with the example of hysterical neurosis, which represents the attempted camouflage of interdividual influence. The subject seeks to gain control of an actual rival by internalizing the rival in the form of a paralyzed limb, for instance; or else an actual obstacle blocking the subject is manifested in the form of anxiety, phobias, inhibitions, or neurasthenia.[52] Hypnosis effects the temporary cessation of hysterical symptoms by overcoming the unacknowledged influence of the model rival or obstacle so that a new unified self is constituted by the hypnotist/model's desire. It directs the subject to new desires and away from unacknowledged influence by his or her former model.[53]

Hysteria is the pathological condition to which demonic possession used to refer, according to Oughourlian. He contrasts it with cathartic forms of possession such as Tarantism, which in certain premodern cultures constitutes a publicly licensed admission and ritual exploration of unhelpful mimetic influence. The subject identifies the right tune from a succession offered by musicians present for the ritual and then begins imitating the tarantula. From this came a popular dance form, the tarantella. The choice of a particular tune to dance to dramatizes the subject's acknowledgment that a particular mimetic model is causing the ailment.

This cathartic type of possession observed ethnographically is different from today's hysterical type, in which interdividual influence is denied.[54] Oughourlian finds an example of this more modern version in the infamous mid-seventeenth-century possession of nuns at Loudun, France, which he thinks was a case of obsession with the mimetically fascinating local curé rather than possession by the devil.[55] Girard himself identifies a mimetic reading of possession in Dostoyevsky, whose underground psychology explicitly becomes a demonology in *The Possessed* and *The Brothers Karamazov* in terms of just this fascination with the obstacle/rival.[56] Because the devil has vanished from modern Western psychology, the alien influence experienced in hysteria has become a piece of the individual self that has broken loose. Hence an "unconscious" is invented.[57] But the mimetic fascination and control exercised by others' desires, as distasteful as it is for modern Westerners (with their authentically personal desires and their autonomous selves) to admit, provides a simpler explanation. Think of unruly crowds and the prompt unraveling of individual rationality that they bring about, described by Oughourlian in terms of "plural somnambulism, fusion of desires, mimetic gigantism, dissolution of the self."[58]

Oughourlian goes on to argue that psychotic as well as neurotic conditions are based on the interdividual dynamic of models, rivals, and obstacles, with delirious subjects no longer able to distinguish themselves from the models of their desire. So, for instance, the subject might *take himself to be the model*—Napoleon, say—hence experiencing cosmic deliria, delusions of grandeur, or paranoid symptoms.[59] Girard's account of paranoia is simply the aforementioned rivalry persisting after the initial object of rivalry has dropped from awareness.[60] As the type of identification between subject and model shifts, according to Oughourlian, the model as *obstacle* is expelled in what we know as schizophrenia, or else the model as *rival* engenders a merciless battle for the subject manifest in a range of chronic, nonschizophrenic psychoses.[61]

For Girard, psychosis persists while we remain wedded to non-interdividual thinking, exhibiting our "metaphysical hubris" in trying to find a stabilizing element within the self.[62] Hence the ratcheting up of desire by feedback between subject and rival until Girard's "doubles" emerge—which neither romantic individuals nor their therapists can countenance, insisting instead on confining this interdividual dynamic to the "within." Madness follows directly for Girard, understood as our modern Western inability to integrate these doubles into a differential scheme.[63] The resultant psychotic delirium is "nothing but the obligatory entrance of a desire that imbeds itself in the impasse of the obstacle-model," which Girard identifies with the double bind theory of Gregory Bateson.[64]

The physical playing out of these conditions in the three major systems of the human brain is not overlooked by Oughourlian. Our *limbic system* registers the emotional concomitants of interdividual experience, from depression to euphoria, also stimulating concrete bodily symptoms of basic rivalrous desires. Our *cortical system* clothes the mimetic with moral judgments, religious sentiments, and dualistic assessments of our interdividual situation. Significantly, our *mirror neuron system* has been shown to escalate the impact of rivalry through the other two cerebral systems.[65]

Girard and Freud

I now want to turn to Freud, who loomed large for Girard from the beginning (1) for his notable clinical and theoretical ability; (2) for his intriguingly close approach to the mimetic theory in *Group Psychology and the Analysis of the Ego,* from which he resiled, refusing to let his dawning insights about mimeticism revolutionize his program;[66] and (3) as an example of a stubborn wrongheadedness present more widely in modern Western understandings of human motivation.

Girard as good as admits that Freud was the great rival against whom he worked out the mimetic theory, while Freud saved the role of great rival for the father.[67] Having come in time to feel less defensive of his mimetic theory, Girard admitted in a 2000 interview that he would like to be more positive about Freud than had been possible for him in earlier years. "Mimetic desire was invented in such a Freudian atmosphere," he explains, "that I felt if you gave an inch to Freud, you would be completely swallowed by him."[68] Girard's earlier decision not to give an inch is clear in what follows.

The obvious difference between Girard and Freud is that between an individual and an interdividual account. As the Girard expert Chris Fleming writes, "Where the Freudian unconscious defines an individual repository of repressed trauma, the Girardian subject is constitutionally imbricated in a *public field* of misrecognized beliefs and behaviours that inheres between individuals and which, in turn, shapes them."[69] In light of my earlier observations linking modernity, equality of individuals, and internal mediation, it is interesting to note with Fleming that psychoanalytic theory fares particularly well in the United States, where equality officially reigns and the most distinctive thing about each of us is our desire.[70] Psychoanalysis denies a necessary link to the mimetic model of our desire, so that like existentialism it deepens bourgeois individualism. Girard's alternative position was awakened not by psychology but by literature. He discovered great authors who saw beyond the individualistic illusion "that endeavours to place a god-like self beyond the influence of others."[71]

Going deeper still, Girard denies the originally Platonic reification of mimetic relations into intrapsychic states or entities—into making something inner, private, and static out of something essentially relational, shifting, and public. Freud standardizes positions that exist only as functions of each other,[72] whereas Girard insists on a smooth continuum of mimetic phenomena across the standard psychological range of neurotic and psychotic "conditions."[73] So Freud is a typically Platonic Western researcher in positing his Oedipus complex, for instance, because "there must be an archetypal triangle somewhere of which all the other triangles are reproductions."[74] This is a trap into which all psychoanalysis falls. Girard:

> Because Freud is a Platonist, all the psychoanalytic heresies are platonic heresies. In Jung, the element of rivalry is totally expelled, and nothing is left except a Platonian mystic contemplation of the archetypes. In Melanie Klein, by contrast, there is nothing but conflict, but fundamentally this conflict has no real existence because it is fixed and given an almost otherworldly status by a notion of the first relationships with the mother. In Deleuze and Guattari, not the Oedipus complex itself but the text of psychoanalytic theory—Freud's Oedipus text—multiplies rival triangles, as a result of the universal tendency to simulate that it incites.
>
> All the problems of Platonism return in psychoanalysis. As it is impossible to contain dynamic processes within a system of archetypes, Freud finds it necessary to create more and more essences, rather like structuralism, which takes more and more synchronic

"cuts" because of its own incapacity to conceive of any genuinely diachronic mechanism.[75]

This is why the three great modern intellectual movements of structuralism, Marxism, and psychoanalysis got on so well: they all looked for hidden differentiations—for example, Lacan's unconscious, which is structured like a language.[76] Indeed, because structuralism can only see difference, it reifies difference, turning the undifferentiated into a real category of thing: a monster.[77]

One of the many pre-Copernican "epicycles" to Freud's account is the death instinct, which he creates to account for the fact that suffering-inducing behavior is so common in non-neurotic patients, who are supposed to be governed by his "pleasure principle." For Girard, however, a non-neurotic person who habitually courts disaster is more readily understood in mimetic terms.[78] The great writers, from whose insights Girard first developed mimetic theory in *Deceit, Desire, and the Novel*, are fully aware of such self-destructive behavior—most notably sadism, masochism, and so on—on the part of ordinary people.[79] These along with the other important Freudian themes of narcissism and the Oedipus complex are all present in Girard's attempt to "complete Freud," as we might call it, much as he has more recently sought to "complete Clausewitz." Hence the abnormal end of the normal according to Girard's version of Freud's analysis—"Freud by another's eye."

Achever Freud

The Oedipus Complex

As set out in *The Ego and the Id*, the Oedipus complex involves sexual attachment—"object cathexis"—by the son to his maternal object and, in light of that primary desire for that particular object, identification with his father. This identification progressively deteriorates, becoming one of jealousy and opposition toward the father as obstacle to the fulfillment of the son's desires for the mother. Girard notes that Freud had seen identification with the father as primary and the sexual rivalry as secondary in his earlier book, *Group Psychology and the Analysis of the Ego*, whereupon he turned away from this nascent mimetic insight into the primacy of "identification": toward a sex-based, wholly interior account of the object itself being desirable, hence shaping identification.[80]

For Girard, however, sexual appetite does not account for desire, nor is desire object oriented. Neither is it a duality, with Oedipal and narcissistic poles, but single and mimetic.[81] From Dostoyevsky, Proust, and Nietzsche, Girard learned that desire only lights upon an object thanks to a mediator, so that if there is desire on the son's part toward the mother, it is not her intrinsic desirability but the desire of the father as model of desire that guides it.[82] Likewise, if there is to be any incest and parricide, as in the original Oedipus myth, these will arise only as mimesis manifests itself in the family triangle.[83] In Girard's assessment, "The Oedipus complex is what Freud invented to explain triangular rivalries, when he failed to discover the remarkable possibilities of the principle of imitation, precisely in connecting with issues of desire and rivalry."[84]

Girard adds that sons will normally follow their fathers' desires in an apprenticeship manner but not in terms of sexual desire or rivalry.[85] This is because, ideally, their relationship is sufficiently differentiated to remain externally rather than internally mediated. Fathers can of course exert a malign influence on their sons but only as an example of the wider mimetic reality rather than because there is some special Oedipal hardwiring. Dostoyevsky is certainly alert to this possibility. Fathers who become rivals to their sons tend to be less like fathers and more like brothers, whereas if they maintain their fatherly distance, whether as an ideal model or as a tyrant, they will avoid becoming rivals to their sons.[86] So, for instance, "Father Karamazov is certainly a mimetic rival for two of his sons, but this is precisely because he no longer has anything of the father in him."[87] It is a matter adequately accounted for in the shift from external to internal mediation.

I now want to mention two related issues: first, some interesting Girardian implications in wider Western culture of our having abandoned repressive parenting; and second, a possible place for family-of-origin issues in Girard's account.

At the level of contemporary Western culture, many younger "dads" dress like "dudes" and "hang out" with their sons, while attractive thirty-something mothers swap jeans and cosmetics with their teenage daughters. Traditional parental socialization of children based on hierarchy and discipline has become a thing of the past, with the resulting generation of young adults entering universities and workplaces having scarcely if ever known sustained constraint or parental disapproval. It is interesting, therefore, to consider why that generation shows a marked resistance to external control and objective standards of accountability when they are unlikely ever to have experienced them. Why is it that focus groups tell us (and the advertisers) that choice and self-determination are everything for this generation when they has never been denied them?

I was struck in this connection by footage on a French news website of a civil union—a *pacte civil de solidarité*—involving gathered friends singing the song "Freedom Is Coming" by Sarafina, presumably to celebrate the long-denied possibility of a legally sanctioned life together in France *sans mariage*. Yet the decidedly average-looking young couple *avec bébé* celebrating this union seemed for all the world to be unexceptionally, conventionally bourgeois. The nonmarital status of their "PACS" was obviously crucial to these *jeunes françaises* for maintaining sufficient "differentiation" from the values of their parents' generation, which must presumably have burdened them with many constricting rules.

Girard's explanation involves an example from Shakespeare's *A Midsummer Night's Dream.*

> Hermia rejects the tyranny of external mediation in favour of what she regards as no tyranny at all, her own autonomous and spontaneous choice. On the road to self-sufficient bliss, she sees no obstacle except for fathers and father figures. In reality she is dominated by what most people nowadays would call "peer pressure"; she has exchanged one modality of alienation for another. The single and normally placid external mediation has turned into a multitude of nasty little demons.[88]

So mimeticism requires that the possibility if not the fact of repression calls forth an eternal vigilance. As every barrier to the constraint of individualism is removed—as "I" and "my" appear in the names of more and more software applications and IT products—nevertheless today's rampant mimeticism ensures that "I" and "my" become less and less differentiated from "you" and "yours." All this is to be expected, says Girard, in "a society that believes itself to be enlightened but in actuality simply projects upon institutions that are in the process of breaking down . . . the mimetic difficulties provoked by that very breakdown. Who believes in the repressive father any more?"[89] We crave differentiation, and deprived of it we blame the failing institutions that once might have delivered it.

Perhaps Girard's eagerness to mark out a case against Freud accounts for his rarely mentioning the extent of mimetic influence from the family of origin.[90] Yet these are persistently important considerations. Today we are aware of so-called attachment issues, for instance, and how they might influence our emotional development. I suggest that early conditioning determines our greater or lesser mimetic vulnerability, as we might put it in Girardian terms, establishing what we would once have thought of in terms of "ego strength," or else "weakness." Occasionally Girard does admit the importance of such considerations. He notes that Dostoyevsky, when his child characters are treated like serfs, "shows us how individuals, traumatized in their early infancy, imprint the most diverse situations with irrational imaginings, transforming each one of them into a repetition of the initial trauma."[91] Likewise: "The adult who scandalizes a child runs the risk of imprisoning him forever within the increasingly narrow circle of the model and the mimetic obstacle."[92] These acknowledgments go some way to answering Paisley Livingston's concern, noted earlier, that there must be a role for especially formative relationships in setting the longer-term mimetic patterns of our lives: "Parents, friends, lovers, and educators serve as long-term personal mediators whose desires, real or imagined, inspire longings patterned after them."[93] Negatively, too, of course, though always mimetically.

Attachment theory teaches that traces of our secure or insecure patterns of early connectedness are wired into our brains. Understood in Girardian terms, this would mean that the mimetic dynamics of our early formation become the default setting of our future relating, for good or ill. So the family of origin *is* important, though not as Freud saw it. Non-Girardian literature on shame and its implications for relationships can be read accordingly. The familiar observation that strong, positive role models in early childhood foster a firm, confident self is readily explicable in terms of positive models of desire, whereas the early reinforcement of shame (which involves a more global assessment of our whole self than guilt does) and subsequent lack of self-acceptance for life—of "a predisposition to shame"—is regularly found to be rooted in incompetent, preoccupied, or narcissistic parents and in active shaming by parents (or by others acting under the influence of social norms such as racism).[94] And, as Girard knows, "shame is a mimetic sentiment, in fact the most mimetic of sentiments."[95]

Shamed children can grow up ideal-hungry, prone to creating an ideal whether artistically, by fabulation, or by seeking acceptance in groups.[96] In intimate relationships, one partner with a background of inadequate attachment places heavy burdens of emotional insecurity on the other, whereas a more adequately attached, more secure partner can assist the insecure one—we would say mimetically—helping undo insecurities which poor family-of-origin modeling has established. But two insecure partners in the same marriage swerve with seeming inevitability into the rut of constant acrimony because they have become rivals for attention, which we would understand in terms of internal mediation.[97]

If the family scene is an especially favored site for shaping us, as Girard on balance seems willing to acknowledge, it is as a notable example of the same mimetic dynamics that pertain everywhere else rather than as a Freudian wellspring of object-generated desire and sexual foundationalism. For Girard, when families go bad "relationships within the family . . . become similar to what they are outside the family; they become characterised either by total indifference or by the type of morbid attention that accompanies mimetic desire wherever it flourishes, within the family or outside it."[98]

Narcissism—or Coquetry

We have seen that one pole of Freud's foundational desire is located in the mother, hence the Oedipus complex. The other object in Freud's duopoly of fundamental desire is the self, hence the "condition" he calls "narcissism." This whole approach is rejected as inadequate by Girard in favor of a single mimetic mechanism. Likewise, whereas Freudian narcissism entails a weakening of desire for objects outside the self, Girard allows that narcissism can actually imbue objects with mimetic intensity while even fostering an unlikely altruism in the narcissist.[99] Think of those high-minded charity galas attended by the rich and otherwise frivolously narcissistic for showing off their superior being when the usual display of luxury trappings will not suffice. For Girard, what Freud calls narcissism is but one more symptom of metaphysical desire rather than something independently real. Narcissism is a strategy, not an essence, based on acquiring "the metaphysical mirage of self sufficiency."[100] So Girard prefers to call it "pseudo narcissism," or by the more literary term *coquetry.* Here we find perhaps the most intriguing and persuasive application of mimetic theory, but one that involves some chicken-and-egg subtlety.

Freud's account of narcissism is hardly what you would call pro-women. Narcissism for Freud is the natural condition of children, with boys typically growing up to invest their desire in external objects (first the mother) while women can remain turned inward in a state of intact self-love. This referred especially to the beautiful, eternal feminine types to which Freud was especially partial among his young admirers, having given up sex with Frau Freud at a young age, and whose adulation Freud craved during the period he was actually writing about narcissism.[101] Their coolness and indifference were more significant than their beauty, however, in terms of awakening desire.[102] Freud saw this deployment of indifference at work in the appeal to us of cats and other large predators, as well as in literary portrayals of great criminals and humorists who seem to maintain an unassailable libidinal position. Here Freud draws close to Girard's insight, which views all this in terms of metaphysical desire.[103] "Tout désir est désir d'être [All desire is desire for being, or desire to be],"[104] as Girard once put it. And the desire expressed by a fascinating model or mediator whose being we crave lies at the root of our further desires for this or that object—a Tag Heuer wristwatch like the one Brad Pitt wore in the advertisements or perhaps a seersucker suit like the one Gregory Peck wore in *To Kill a Mockingbird.* But it is the being of Pitt or Peck (or of Atticus Finch), rather than the watch or the costume, where mimesis most truly focuses.

So coquetry adds a further iteration—a strategic one—to metaphysical desire. Coquettes first exhibit a desire for themselves, whether by feminine adornment and allurement—for example, Vivien Leigh playing Scarlett O'Hara in *Gone With the Wind*—or in a more suavely aloof masculine form. This pseudonarcissistic strategy of desire on the part of a mediator awakens longing in an opposite-sex subject (or same-sex—more on this shortly), whose resultant desire for the coquette is in turn copied by the coquette, whose self-love escalates (perhaps indefinitely). Thus coquettes manage to bootstrap themselves into a situation of being coveted and held in a kind of metaphysical awe, though "the illusion of self-containment is produced by precisely that which it itself produces, i.e. the fascinated stare of men."[105] Or women! The inherent contemptuousness of coquettish desire, and its nonsubstantial nature—including that of its male versions, such as the dandy with his studied affectation of indifference[106]—is nicely set out by Girard's leading theological interpreter, James Alison.

> That maximally cool person is in fact entirely dependent on the others imitating him to keep up his apparent poise and self-possession, and will quickly come to have a contempt for those who imitate him, since he is half aware that there is nothing 'there' beyond a negotiating ruse. The contempt itself will betray the dependence on the other. Or, should a bigger star swim into the galaxy, one capable of exercising a stronger gravitational pull, so that the regard of the others becomes redirected, watch Mr Cool's self-possession and poise disintegrate.[107]

I once witnessed such a meltdown when a textbook Girardian coquette in my former parish discovered that I had rostered someone else for her accustomed highly visible spot in the sanctuary team for Christmas midnight mass, with its big crowd of potential admirers. As Girard puts it, "The flame of coquetry can only burn on the combustible material provided by the desire of others."[108]

Here we arrive at "the fundamental paradox of human desire," according to Girard, which is "that the more morbidly self-centred an individual becomes the more morbidly other centred he also becomes."[109] This reference comes from an article on how Proust discerns the mimetic truth behind what Freud calls narcissism. Such "fascination for an alien 'self-sufficiency'" is entirely wrongheaded, however. This "blissful autonomy" is never actually experienced by anyone in Proust because it is only a mirage of desire, despite everyone wanting and believing in that kind of self.[110] Let's face it: we may want to be James Bond, but we live in an Inspector Clouseau world.[111]

This mirage of desire is eventually revealed to whichever unlucky individual finally wins the coquette. His success soon turns to ashes, as Rhett Butler discovered having at last married Scarlett. His hope of acquiring the enhanced being of his coquettish model dies as surely as their child had died, with Rhett discovering that he can no longer "give a damn." As for the indefatigable Scarlett, however, the voices of new mimetic models immediately fill her head, as fresh desires take the place of old ones, her advanced mimeticism most reliably ensuring that "tomorrow is another day."

Freud himself did not see the strategic nature of coquetry, and was taken in by it, whereas once again a great literary intelligence proved itself more psychologically astute—as Girard sets out in the following, going on to reveal the affinity to coquetry of some quite diverse modern attitudes.

> In Molière's *Le Misanthrope*, Célimène acknowledges the strategic character of coquetry; she cynically tells Arsinöe that she might well turn into a prude on the day she is no longer beautiful. Prudishness is also a strategy. Indeed, misanthropy—which is very like it—is akin to an intellectual prudishness, which Nietzsche would call ressentiment: that is to say, the *defensive* strategy of the losers, of those who speak against desire because they are unsuccessful in their attempts to attract it and capitalize on it.[112]

Homosexuality

A brief word now on homosexuality, in light of some comments made in the previous discussion of coquetry, and as a step toward the highly significant Freudian themes of sadism and masochism, which Girard both demythologizes and normalizes.

Girard's approach to the whole gay question is less clear than we might wish. His characteristic insistence that desire is chiefly mimetic, extending beyond natural appetites, along with his refusal to countenance Freud's vaporous interior states, leaves him with little room to accommodate homosexuality as a nonpathological state. Girard does not condemn it, however. He singled out "le père Alison" among his significant Christian teachers, for instance,[113] while Alison was prosecuting a strong Girardian case for the acceptance of homosexual orientation. But Girard does not go as far as Alison. As recently as 2008, for example, he noted with approval that the toleration of homosexuality was never in the past offered legal parity with marriage and family.[114]

His reservations arise from his identification of a mimetically driven version of same-sex attraction that Freud misunderstands but which Shakespeare and Cervantes, Proust and Dostoyevsky, acknowledge and explore. "I do not say it is bad," explains Girard, "but I say there certainly is one type of homosexuality which was interpreted this way by Shakespeare," referring to the conflictual element in *Two Gentlemen of Verona,* as well as the military struggle between the hero and Aufidius in *Coriolanus.*[115] Girard opines that Proust may have understood the erotic modern so well because of his own homosexuality (presumably understood by Girard as a mimetic product of these modern forces).[116]

Freud on the other hand views homosexuality as one more essence, having to do with a boy's failure to mature sexually. Or he tries to account for the fascination the Oedipal boy can have with his father as rival by claiming a latent passive homosexual desire on the boy's part, which is supposed to coincide with his more primal desire for the mother. To accommodate this multiplying confusion, Freud posits bisexuality as yet one more distinct state of being.[117] Girard of course resists all such Platonic multiplication of entities, looking instead to mimetic dynamics. He suggests that at an advanced stage of mimetic desire, morbid obsession with the rival occluding the object can result in the transfer of sexual desire to the rival. Girard points to literary examples of such eroticizing of rivalry while recognizing how this can also assume a heterosexual form. Thus he acknowledges that all sexual desire is highly mutable under the sway of mimetic forces. Girard explicitly refuses to pass judgment on the possibility of a nonmimetic homosexual orientation, however.[118] What happens at the level of appetite and instinct is of far less importance to Girard than what happens at the level of actual desire, which exhibits the added dimension of mimetic influence.

It is left to Oughourlian and especially Alison to carry the Girard-ian conversation in a more explicitly gay-friendly direction. In *The Genesis of Desire* Oughourlian never treats homosexuality as a special case. Nor does Alison, who reads Girard on the basic mimetic fact of our being run by the desires of others as applying equally to gay and straight people. Perhaps Alison thinks that the "mimetic gayness" to which Girard refers is simply how advanced mimetic phenomena might play out among people of same-sex orientation.[119]

Masochism and Sadism

These exotic and theatrical sexual deviations are two more dis-crete psychological entities in Freud's sex-based account of desirable objects, whereas for Girard they are entirely normal and widespread examples of advanced mimetic desire, and only derivatively sexual *if at all*. The key for Girard is mimetic fascination with the being of the mediator through metaphysical desire, as rival and obstacle, who becomes a repository of deviated transcendence: an idol worshiped by the masochist, and aspired to by the sadist.[120] Comparing them-selves unfavorably with their mediator, masochistic subjects desire the brutalities that they believe the mediator ought to be inflicting on subjects as unworthy as they are. Sadism is the obverse of this; a sub-ject achieves the illusion of attaining the being of his or her violently contemptuous mediator by transferring the unworthy status he or she claims onto some other unlucky victim.[121]

Masochism reveals for Girard the whole process of mimetic desire, the escalation of which leads ultimately to shame and futility. The masochist, as it were, embraces this inevitability of defeat and disappointment.[122] It is not about Freud's death instinct or any sexual appetite for pain but simply the mimetic tendency to seek out increas-ingly resistant models/obstacles that heighten the sense of value invested by the subject in its model.[123] The more resistant the ob-stacle, the more being it appears to possess. Hence the model may be chosen for the amount of disgust demonstrated toward the subject, with the model's contempt and obstruction redoubling the subject's desire because such treatment confirms the model's superiority. No kindness can be allowed to intrude, nor can any criticism be rejected, with salvation in terms of accessing superior being only available from a sufficiently contemptuous deity.[124] Indeed, these unpleasant effects once experienced shape the future playing out of masochistic desire, ensuring a passionate embrace of the most discouraging obstacles to the exclusion of anything pleasant or positive in life.[125]

So who are these people? In intimate relationships, according to Girard, "mimetic addicts cannot possibly desire someone who responds positively to their own desire, and they cannot remain permanently indifferent to someone who is really indifferent to them."[126] These are today's proliferating tragic romantics for whom to say that they are "unlucky in love" is to sentimentalize what is in actuality a deliberate (if not self-aware) program of relationship mayhem and self-destruction. Their addiction is effectively to indifference and rejection. Girard likens this to the search for treasure hidden under a stone, in which the obsessed seeker finds no satisfaction turning over stone after stone: "So he begins to look for *a stone which is too heavy to lift*—he places all his hopes on that stone and he will waste all his remaining strength on it."[127]

Heroes and great figures engaged in grand romantic pursuits are also deeply mired in this pathology, as are the ordinarily ambitious. Nothing relieves the hero of mimeticism's dialectic of pride and shame even at the height of their glory—for instance, Napoleon (serving here for the first time as a Girardian example) resolutely seeking and finally finding his Waterloo, his ultimate obstacle.[128] As Girard puts it, "Behind every closed door, every insurmountable barrier, the hero senses the presence of the absolute mastery that eludes him, the divine serenity of which he feels deprived. To desire is to believe in the transcendence of the world suggested by the other."[129]

Ordinary ambition is also regularly dissatisfied with its attainments, exhibiting "the permanent restlessness inherent in the mimetic principle"[130] and forever looking to "new challenges"—as we like to label a series of increasingly insurmountable and potentially dangerous obstacles behind which we hope at last to find the cure for our perennial dissatisfaction. Hence the poor judgment regularly afflicting the ambitious, for which I can vouch personally (again, from my pre-Girardian phase), having taken not one but two leadership jobs in theological education that wiser heads in both cases left well alone. I demonstrated the mistaking of walls for doors of which Girard speaks in his assessment of mimetic desire in its typical downward spiral.[131] In all such cases he discerns no clear boundary between risk-taking ambition and masochism. The mimetic slave remains glued to the obstacle like a limpet.[132]

Girard mentions subtle variants of this self-destructive profile. *Snobbisme* is the obvious one, into which Proust and Dostoyevsky prove to be expert guides. It belongs to modern conditions of equality, where the mimetic subject hungry for the being of another must pursue distinctiveness to an escalating extent. "When individuals are inferior or superior to each other," Girard explains, "we find servility and tyranny, flattery and arrogance, but never snobbism in the proper sense of the word. The snob will fawn and cringe in order to be accepted by people whom he has endowed with an arbitrary prestige.... The snob bows before a noble title which has lost all real value, before a social prestige so esoteric that it is really appreciated by only a few elderly ladies."[133]

He identifies this as a major theme of Proust's *In Search of Lost Time* and also in Dostoyevsky's *Notes from the Underground*, where snobbery flourishes among a bureaucracy of equals in the mimetic microcosm of St. Petersburg civil service life.

Another variant is what Girard calls "counter-imitation," which typifies the proud among life's perennial losers: those who demonstrate their independence (that they possess, after all, the *being* of a worthy model) by systematically pursuing courses opposite to those that the winners have chosen.[134] There is also today's dominant myth of contemptuous intellectuals, with whom Girard is fully acquainted among his many detractors, and which he identifies with the coquettish modern figure of the antihero who feels empty before the obstacle and divinizes his impotence as critical lucidity.[135] Antiheroes despise the stability of traditional forms, preferring to export the misery of their own lack of being, all of which Girard links to the spirit of modern revolutionary movements that end up uniformly oppressive.[136] Closely related to this is the protest profile of the romantic hero in late-twentieth-century youth culture, whereby "an entire youth personalizes its anonymous anguish at small expense by identifying with the *same* hero *against* all other men."[137]

Tabloid culture also comes to mind as an example here with its love of scandal, feverish in exposing, denouncing, and hence differentiating. Thus our own distinctiveness is assured but at the expense of vastly extending the scandal that was supposedly being combated.[138] Vendettas in public life seem similar. Remember Ken Starr going after Bill Clinton, mimetically drawing all of America into the scandal of their president and "that woman, Miss Lewinsky." Such a mimetic brouhaha tells us more about the tabloid editors and crusading morals campaigners than about their targets, however. "The victim of ontological sickness is always excited to fury at the sight of others less sick than himself and he always chooses his mediator from among them," muses Girard, so that "he tries constantly to bring his idol down to his own level."[139] The Internet is surely today's new frontier for this legion of the chronically dissatisfied whose mimetic obstacle fascination drives their life's work of aggrieved posturing by blog and tweet. Another example is the increasingly popular hate campaign against this or that public figure carried out anonymously by email.

"Scandal gratifies our craving for a sense of our own worth," concludes the Girardian thinker Andrew McKenna, providing us with "a moral rectitude that is fashioned over against its transgressors rather than requiring any foundation of its own."[140] McKenna identifies this "intense, prurient disgust"[141] in the radical Islamist thinker Sayyid Qutb, and we can speculate about the same "underground psychology" among the 9/11 terrorists (more on this in chapter 5).

Tired of being the martyr, according to Girard, the *sadist* chooses to become tormentor.[142] "In order to desire to persecute," he explains, "we must believe that the being who persecutes us thereby attains a sphere of existence infinitely superior to our own. One cannot be a sadist unless the key to the enchanted garden appears to be in the hands of a tormentor."[143] Thus shame, weakness, and a history of being or feeling abused coalesce in the mimetic addiction of those who relinquish the entrenched victim status of masochism—whether as an "existential masochist,"[144] as Girard calls them, or the more overtly sexual type—for a sadistic profile.

One cannot help thinking of certain violent criminals here—superficially hard men plainly doomed to die violently, perhaps in prison—but also of today's fast-proliferating class of workplace bullies. The crisis of clergy sexual abuse may find its simplest explanation here, too, as those abused by a clerical culture of outward conformity cloaking inner emptiness—with a violent god image thrown in—reject the standard clerical masochistic responses of obsequious compliance, or of self-oblation driven by careerist ambition and perhaps by a desire for approval, in favor of the sadistic option, taking out the pain of their own unhealed mimetic wound on the church's "little ones."[145] All such masochistic and sadistic dynamics are particularly well represented in secular Western modernity, as Girard amply illustrates in his reading of the great modern novelists, and especially in a secular culture as deviated transcendence waits eagerly to usurp the real thing.

Modernity, Secularization, and "Ontological Sickness"

Our myth is one of cool individualism, and of a pride in our metaphysical autonomy that Girard traces from the Renaissance[146] to become the underlying principle of every new Western doctrine since the Enlightenment.[147] Before modern individualism the role of models was more readily admitted, and success meant being able to imitate them, but individualism led to the denial of models and a brave new world in which mimeticism went into the underground, where Dostoyevsky found it. Alternatively it went into the unconscious, where Freud unwittingly but effectively maintained its concealment. The mimetic truth behind individualism, however, is its attachment to every desire promising difference, distinctiveness, and enhanced being, all taken from models whom we can never fully acknowledge if the myth is to remain alive.

In its modern romantic form, the myth tries to pretty up the reality of Western societies that are characterized by the envy and jockeying for position that internal mediation produces. Romantic individualists believe that they can do and be who and what they want in today's world of deregulated desire, though in reality they are simply devoting themselves unawares to mimetic captivity and rivalry. So, ironically, while pursuing desires that create the illusion of individual differentiation at a superficial level, people are drawn by internal mediation into an ever greater similarity. "Far from acknowledging the reciprocity besetting it," Girard concludes, "desire always flees into more imitation in the insane quest for difference."[148]

Now that our manner of dress no longer provides sufficient scope for showing how different and special we are, we see in America and Australia a mainstream mimetic epidemic of body piercing and tattooing. A more widespread example of exactly the same phenomenon is the way we seek the being of mimetic models by acquiring what they have through the purchase of a mass-produced replica. We mark out our specialness by choosing it in a different color or finish, however—the blue Gaggeneau espresso maker rather than the red one, perhaps, or going one up on our model of desire by opting for leather rather than cloth seats in the new Audi (more on this in chapter 4).

Secularization and the Early Girard

In this context it is timely to make some preliminary comments about secularization because of its strong connection with modernity in Girard's account. But we need to be careful. At the level of explicating these first, mimetic aspects of Girard's three-part program, secularization features negatively as part of our modern Western eagerness to remove perceived constraint—in effect, as the by-product of increasingly deregulated mimetic desire. Hence Girard sees nothing good about secularization in his earlier work, remaining concerned in his later writings, too, about the loss of social protection that it entails. Secularization becomes a worthwhile breakthrough for Girard, as we shall see, though at this stage in the discussion, with reference to his mimetic theory alone, secularization shows only its darker side.

Girard identifies this negative aspect of secularization with the impossibility of our tolerating God any more thanks to the spirit of rivalry that underpins self-understanding today. It is a matter of *Lebensraum*, with God as one-competing-individual-too-many in the modern Western project of self-creation. *Rivalry secularizes*, as constraining prohibitions and the God underwriting them are set aside. Hence modernity and secularization can be understood as two dimensions of disembedding the Western individual from constraint, which is in reality our submission to even greater constraint from the unacknowledged play of mimetic forces.[149] Demystifying the claims of religion, with the accompanying commitment to debunking reputations of the great and disdaining time-honored customs of personal behavior in traditional societies, strikes Girard as all of a piece. That signature modern figure of the debunker labors to preserve "the greatest myth of all, that of his own detachment."[150]

Clearly God could not compete, as individualism took over God's priorities. "What is this God who is in the process of dying?" asks Girard. "It is the Jehovah of the Bible, the jealous God of the Hebrews, the one who tolerates no rivals."[151] We moderns might be able to tolerate a less distinctive god, but not this one. Because with the rejection of this God the promethean self can come into its own—though of course it is really internal mediation that reigns, driving history by its own simple logic toward "the great fury of the Revolution and the triumph of unbridled rivalry."[152] Here the roots of Girard's apocalyptic vision are revealed, which Dostoyevsky also perceived. And Proust, who came to understand the nature of desire better than Freud, discerning the course of mimeticism's unrestrained engine of undifferentiation from the belle époque to World War I and beyond. All this reveals to Girard a new, final stage of history.[153]

"It is desire which puts into the mouths of the romantics exclamations of revenge and curses against God and men," as Girard explains. "The misanthrope and the coquette, the underground man and his beloved persecutor are always the two sides of the same metaphysical desire."[154] Here we see the great simplicity of Girard's account, with so many elements lining up as dimensions of the one, secular modern escalation of mimesis. Dostoyevsky and Nietzsche help us to see how this looks from the inside.

In Hell with Dostoyevsky and Nietzsche

Dostoyevsky was Girard's chief deconstructor of the romantic myth and its dream of a pure soul,[155] revealing the combination of rivalry, undifferentiation, and masochism that Girard collectively labels "underground psychology." For Girard, Dostoyevsky's "underground man" as "the victim of romanticism always becomes more and more unfit for life, while demanding of it things more and more excessive."[156] It is a mind-set that readily disproves today's widespread fiction of economists and libertarians that rational utilitarianism proves a reliable guide, when in reality a life of haunted mimetic entrapment in lonely and hateful obsession with rivals and obstacles is closer to the truth.[157] Eroticism and gambling are two chief ordeals for underground pride,[158] which is obsessed with unattainable being and spends itself in self-destructive futility. Girard points to this hellish quality into which the romantic period descends, as promethean idealism readily takes the place of a gracious God,[159] concluding that "Masochism and sadism constitute the sacraments of the underground mystique."[160]

A key text is Girard's early essay "Proust and Dostoyevsky," in which the trajectory of this "ontological sickness" is traced. There are three stages in Proust, from the conventional hypocrisy of Cambray to the contrary posture of the Verdurin salon to the final emptiness of Baron Charlus. Girard unearths the same insight in "the Dostoyevskian *summa* which is *The Possessed*."[161] Girard:

> Each generation embodies one stage of ontological sickness. The truth about the parents remains hidden for a long time but it breaks out with incredible force in the feverish agitation, the violence, and the debauchery of the children. The parents are amazed to discover that they have brought forth monsters; in their children they see the opposite of themselves. They do not see the connection between the tree and its fruit. The children, on the contrary, are fully aware of the histrionics in their parents' indignation.... They fully understand that middle-class dignity is a form of "bad faith."... Dostoyevsky places great emphasis on the generations and on the parents' responsibility.... Beneath middle-class "loyalty to principles" is the furious agitation of the possessed, and beneath this furious agitation is immobility and nothingness, the frigid acedia of Stavrogin[,] ... the pure nothingness of absolute pride.[162]

This is prophetic of "ontological sickness" in its twentieth-century generational form. Here I think of a 2008 German film, *Der Baader Meinhoff Komplex* (based on a 1985 book of the same name by Stefan Aust), about the young of Germany's postwar generation who founded the terrorist Red Army Factions. Theirs was a conscious protest against the bourgeois complacency of an older generation with unacknowledged blood on its hands, yet they were at one with their elders in doing violence despite their resolute pursuit of "differentiation." The film's self-righteous youth, distressed parents, and uncomprehending judicial officials all confirm Girard's reading of Dostoyevsky. I also think of the mainstream 1960s youth movement and a high-minded ideology of individual self-determination made manifest via the sexual revolution but which quickly spawned the Stavrogin-like figure of Charles Manson. Subsequently we have reaped a mainstream pornographic culture of programmatic sexual addiction and exploitation. Every element confirms Girard's identification of a "bestial sensuality always underlying discarnate idealism."[163]

With Nietzsche, who developed the term *ressentiment* and found its epitome in Dostoyevsky's *Notes from the Underground*,[164] we see the logical extension of hypermimeticism toward madness. The object of Nietzsche's own desire, according to Girard, was intellectual and artistic omnipotence—the curse of the modern intellectual world since the French Revolution, when patrons as models were replaced by fellow intellectuals.[165] The mediator of this desire for Nietzsche was Wagner, who became his obstacle and the focus for Nietzsche's *ressentiment*. Girard sees *Ecce Homo* as Nietzsche's attempt to establish his own cult, based on what Wagner tried to do at Bayreuth,[166] and in which any Greek would have discerned signs of madness accompanying Nietzsche's unprotected courting of the Dionysian[167] (more on ritual protection from dangerous mimetic escalation and its foundational role for human culture in chapter 2).

Nietzsche's mimetic striving with Wagner's unsurmountable model-obstacle pointed beyond the solipsism and egotism of earlier romanticism toward the hypercompetitiveness of the world we now live in, so that Nietzsche's "will-to-power mystique might be called the *ideology* of mimetic desire."[168] But it brought him undone. "The will to power is a Wagnerian giant, a colossus with feet of clay that collapses pitifully," as Girard observes, so that "the movement toward madness in Nietzsche is identical with a perpetual metamorphosis of the will to power into ressentiment, and this metamorphosis is identical to the schizophrenic oscillation of 'extremes,' the terrible alternation of exaltation and depression."[169]

Here is the hypermimetic Western "individual" whose illusory independence and greatness grow proportionally with their mimetic compulsion and self-engineered adversity in the grip of an insurmountable obstacle. This is what Cervantes meant by calling Don Quixote mad, as Girard observes.[170] The path away from madness, not surprisingly, is the path away from mimetic compulsions, back to the more real world of uneventful everyday life and its concrete responsibilities. "Being rational—functioning properly—is a matter of having objects and being busy with them," as Girard points out, while "being mad is a matter of letting oneself be taken over completely by the mimetic models."[171]

Yet this sanity is harder to ensure without God, both for mad individuals and for the modern West as a whole—which Girard believes is afflicted by a systemic madness. He is clear that "the development of the psychopathological symptom and the place it holds in psychiatry have kept pace closely with the stages of desacralization that govern our culture as a whole." This downward path of ontological sickness, once God is out of the way, involves divinizing the obstacle, hence begetting idols and monsters as inevitable by-products of mimeticism's infernal engine.[172] Such illusory divinity proves a perennial reproach to masochistic subjects, ensuring that everything that threatens and diminishes them develops a sacred aura.[173] Here Girard finds the most worrying aspects of secular modernity—in a love for the negative, the ugly, the rough and coarse, the demeaning, the dangerous, the indifferent, all of which are cherished under the banner of individual freedom. This is true for Girard in art, in architecture, in sexuality, and in the intrepid explorer's death-dealing obsession with the unforgiving void (the sea—think *Moby Dick*; the ice—think Scott of the Antarctic; or outer space—think of the comforting early *Star Trek* myth of progress challenged by the antipromethean *Alien* film franchise).[174] He concludes that all Dostoyevsky's possessed are "in quest of a wrong way redemption whose theological name is damnation."[175] Hence in modernity, at least since Hegel, the supposed affirmation of the self and of life has tended toward self-negation, mimetic slavery, and death.[176]

Shakespeare was aware of this apocalyptic slide toward self-destruction inherent in the hypermimetic, as in the wholly unnecessary death of a beloved Desdemona in *Othello,* and in the lamentable ending of *Romeo and Juliet,* where mimetic forces out of control ensure that "All are punish'd."[177] Dostoyevsky variously addresses the same point, most notably in *Crime and Punishment* with the figure of that posturing nonentity Raskolnikov, whose ontological sickness at its paroxysmal stage led to an orgy of destruction.[178] As one last example of this, I predict that the narcissistic among Generations X and Y, with their guiding values of freedom and self-expression, will eventually reveal the logic of their mimetic condition in an equally mimetic holocaust of euthanasia, once age and the indifference of others make their myth of networked desirability unsustainable.

Girard returns to these earlier apocalyptic insights in his most recent work, to which I give significant attention in chapter 5. For now, I devote the final section of this chapter to some hard scientific evidence for Girard's mimetic theory, lest this all seem too speculative.

HARD EVIDENCE: INTERSUBJECTIVITY AND MIRROR NEURONS

The evidence for Girard's account of mimesis lies in the capacity of these great literary figures to explain human behavior with insight and economy, and in the straightforwardness and power of interdividual psychology in comparison with Freudian psychology. Freud's theory, based on the individual unconscious, object desire, and sexual motivation, is surpassed—effectively, made redundant—by Girard's account of mimesis, of desire according to the the desire of another, and of sexuality under mimetic control. This is a paradigm-style argument for the truth of a scientific hypothesis based on its simplicity, comprehensiveness, and predictive power. Girard believes, however, that there is further, concrete evidence on offer. He points to Darwin's elegant work on evolution as a youthful inspiration, believing that

science now strengthens his case for mimetic theory as an evolutionary account of human nature.[179]

Up to the mid-1990s, partial descriptions of what Girard would
call mimetic behavior were found here and there among the scientifically minded: from Adam Smith on the taking up of others' emotions
in *The Theory of Moral Sentiments* to Darwin himself on imitation
in children and his contemporary Anton Mesmer on "animal mag-
netism" to Gustave Le Bon and Elias Canetti on the influence of
crowds on individuals caught up in them to Desmond Morris in *The
Naked Ape*. There was also the recognition that feeling regularly follows action, which William James saw as the most valuable precept
in moral education. Emotion proved bodily detectable in demeanor,
in voice patterns, and via electrodes placed on the skin. Likewise,
mimicry and synchronous posture in interpersonal encounters were
recognized as establishing the bodily sharing of emotions at a largely
preconscious level.

One group of psychologists providing a handy compendium of
this research initially found themselves taking on the emotions of
therapy patients, including nodding off while listening to the de-
pressed (through being caught up mimetically in their emotional ex-
haustion). Another example concerns the way in which actors can
be deeply affected by the characters they portray—for instance, Kirk
Douglas, brought very low while playing Vincent van Gogh. They also
mention the Stanislavski or method-acting school, whereby the real-
istic portrayal of emotions is achieved through imaginatively entering
into the emotions of another.[180] Conversely a lack of such connection
is reported among the autistic, psychopaths, and blind babies. "If one
has worked very largely with blind babies for many years," as Selma
Fraiberg testifies, "the encounter with a sighted baby is absurdly like
the experience of meeting a compatriot abroad after a long stay in a
country where the language and customs are alien."[181]

Developmental Psychology

The connections to Girard's program in such research are suggestive but not conclusive. Up to the mid-1990s, studies of infant intersubjectivity by Andrew Meltzoff provided the strongest scientific

evidence for the mimetic nature of desire. Piaget thought that babies learned to imitate facial expressions as part of a developing sense of self, at about a year old,[182] but the reality is that babies are native imitators. Meltzoff demonstrated this with an infant born only forty-two minutes previously, who was yet to see a human face. Meltzoff looked the baby in the eyes and stuck out his tongue, in a gesture that the newborn repeated immediately.[183] But this imitation, which has been confirmed by cross-cultural experiments to be innate, is more than a simple reflex. Make this face when the baby has a pacifier in its mouth, and it will not be diverted from its sucking, but remove the pacifier, keeping an impassive face, and the baby will soon produce the withheld action in imitation of your earlier one.[184] Likewise, infants will have a stab at imitating and try to improve in subsequent attempts.[185] They will also complete actions which the adult has left incomplete, for instance, trying to get the end off a dumbbell which an adult has only ineffectually pulled at.[186] In other words, and this is highly significant for our purposes, the infant intuits the goal of the action rather than just copying it. *It is oriented to knowing and responding to the desire of another.* Contrary to a behaviorist reading, which separates rigorously the fact of perceived action from the supposition of internal mental states associated with that action, "such imitative behaviours reveal a capacity to map internal states on to externally perceived behaviour, a kind of aboriginal mentalism."[187] Such imitation is understood as part of cognitive development, with the likely value of helping infants identify particular adults ("Are you the one who made this face at me last time, or not?") and, through the imitation games that infants love, of forming their emerging minds by learning to experience the mental state of another through bodily synchrony.

Meltzoff and Moore have called their scientific hypothesis AIM—Active Intermodal Mapping—making concrete and immediate the presence of intentions read through bodily processes. Hence we learn imitatively that we are alike.[188] Autistic infants are unable to do this.[189] This finding is confirmed by the new science of mirror neurons, which explains why all these things are so. Meltzoff was very excited when he first heard about mirror neurons, convinced that they accounted for his findings.[190]

Cognitive Neuroscience

Mirror neurons were discovered in the early 1990s in area F5 of the macaque monkey brain, which while smaller than the human brain is anatomically similar to it. Using brain implants, investigators at Italy's University of Parma found *motor* neurons that also performed *perceptual* functions, but only regarding actions. Other so-called canonical neurons fire as part of perceiving and distinguishing objects,[191] but these newfound mirror neurons only fire when action is involved—when the monkey does something, usually grasping food and bringing it to its mouth. But the big news is that these mirror neurons also fire, though to a slightly lesser extent, when another monkey or a human experimenter is observed performing the same action, and even when the observing monkey only hears the action.[192]

As with observed infant simulation, this is not a matter of reflex copying. The monkey captures the investigator's intention with the aid of context and memory. If the monkey knows that an orange is concealed behind a screen, for instance, and the experimenter reaches behind the screen for it, the observing monkey's mirror neurons will fire as if the orange were visible.[193] When the experimenter grasps food and puts it in her mouth, while occasionally introducing a container to the scene into which the food is always diverted at the last instant, the monkey's mirror neurons for eating will not fire when the container is present.[194] Macaques can learn tool use from observing their human investigators, with mirror neurons then firing for use of pliers as once they did for hand use only.[195]

In all such cases, we discover a part of the monkey brain that catches on to intentions in a flash, reading the early stage of movements and their context in a way that is precognitive, preconceptual, and prelinguistic.[196] The macaques inhabit their world collectively; their perception and action are deeply intersubjective. They are not dispassionate, individual observers. Rather, the cognitive neuroscientist Vittorio Gallese regards their "shared mind" as built on an "intercorporeity" whereby "Self and Other are originally co-constituted."[197]

The placing of electrodes in human brains for such experiments is possible only in the rare cases of epileptic patients undergoing corrective surgery who agree to it, but newer brain imaging techniques achieve comparable results based on areas of the brain "lighting up" (i.e., receiving enhanced blood flow) in response to particular stimuli. Images sent to video goggles worn in the brain scanner and buttons pressed in response while physiological states are monitored allow experimenters to explore many different scenarios. It turns out that F5 in the *human* frontal cortex also contains mirror neurons but more sophisticated ones than monkeys have. As the brain mapper Marco Iacoboni puts it, they "fire when an individual kicks a soccer ball, sees a ball being kicked, hears a ball being kicked, and even just says or hears the word 'kick.'"[198] Also in humans, F5 and Broca's area, where language is generated, lie close together, which supports a theory of language developing from gestures, rather than from prelinguistic sounds, along with the predicted mimetic nature of language acquisition.[199]

Compared with monkeys, humans can read the influence of context more fully. Our mirror neurons will fire as a teacup is lifted from a table set for afternoon tea but not in a similar scenario with a disarrayed table showing that afternoon tea has been completed. We read the intention of identical hand gestures differently but automatically, depending on whether the context suggests grasping the cup for drinking or for clearing it away.[200] "Logically related" or "echo" mirror neurons allow these more lateral connections,[201] with a further level in humans that Iacoboni calls "super mirror neurons" providing a coordinating effect.[202]

Investigating these super mirror neurons involved a different, social psychological style of experimentation. So, for example, general knowledge tests were found to favor subjects who had been instructed to spend time before the test calling to mind university professors over others who called to mind soccer hooligans. It seems that the company we keep, even in mental imagery, affects our intelligence in measurable ways. The Dutch psychologist Ap Dijksterhuis concluded, "Relevant research has shown that imitation can make us slow, fast, smart, stupid, good at math, bad at math, helpful, rude, polite, longwinded, hostile, aggressive, cooperative, competitive, conforming, nonconforming, conservative, forgetful, careful, careless, neat, and sloppy."[203] That frontal lobe lesions can lead to echopraxia—a condition in which people uncontrollably mimic others—is suggestive of this oversight function being damaged.[204] These levels together comprise the mirror neuron system (MNS) in humans—also called the parieto-premotor cortical networks.

We now know that this MNS underpins human empathy, with a brain pathway connecting F5 via the insula to the amygdala and other parts of the limbic system, where emotions are experienced. Hence witnessing and simulating emotions in others lights up the brain as our own experience of the emotion would do.[205] There is also proven response to pain observed in others, measured by brain function and by muscle tension in the subject's finger while watching (through video goggles) someone else being pricked in the same finger. "This experiment demonstrates that our brain produces a full simulation—even the motor component—of the observed painful experiences of other people," Iacoboni concludes.[206] It turns out that the MNS is impaired in the autistic,[207] whose lack of cortical hardwiring for empathy and reading the intentions of others explains what emotion research and developmental psychology had previously recognized.

The MNS turns out to be involved in the communication of violence, the power of suggestion in advertising, and the reinforcement of prejudice.[208] At a 2007 conference on mirror neurons at Stanford University, Girard and his psychological collaborator, Jean-Michel Oughourlian, were excited to learn from Vittorio Gallese that the human MNS goes into overdrive in situations of rivalry.[209] So from "acquisitive mimesis" prefigured in monkeys reaching for food to sophisticated tests of human political preferences in the brain scanner, the discovery of mirror neurons is providing a biological basis for Girard's interdividual account of human being and acting. More work needs to be done on how the MNS undergirds key Girardian phenomena of violent unanimity, choice of victims, and ritual behavior,[210] which underpin his scapegoat account of human origins, culture, and religion. And to that scapegoat account I now turn.

CHAPTER 2

Violence, the Sacred Canopy

Our next step toward understanding Girard on secular modernity is to become acquainted with his singular approach to the archaic sacred, which he sees as the *fons et origo* of human life and culture. He argues that humanity emerged from the fires of mimetic crisis via a mechanism of "sacred violence," whereupon stability and civilization became possible. The sacred is thus a human agency, *though neither an invention nor a conscious discovery;* rather, it is the serendipitous chancing upon a viable form of life along the existing direction of evolution by natural selection. Reliable social order followed as the logic of this development played out, with emerging culture sustained by the universal phenomena of prohibitions, myths, and rituals that moderns customarily group together under the label of religion. Secularization, for good or ill, represents the collapse of this state of affairs that was coeval with human origins, while modernity is the type of society in which sacred protection is dwindling away and violence is less reliably held in check.

TERROR AND WONDER

We are dealing here with Girard's second major insight, and the second plank of *la système Girard*, following on from his literature-based discovery of desire's mimetic nature. I refer to the founding murder—a phrase borrowed from the Oedipal context of Freud's *Totem and Taboo*.[1] It is otherwise referred to by Girard as the scapegoat, or surrogate victim, mechanism. After writing his early masterpiece of mimetic theory, *Deceit, Desire, and the Novel*, Girard devoted the 1960s to studies in classical literature, anthropology, and ethnography, having discovered this scapegoat mechanism in *Oedipus* and *The Bacchae*,[2] culminating in his classic 1972 work, *Violence and the Sacred*.

The explanation is that mimetic conflict escalates dangerously, with each cast against all and no social mechanisms yet in place to apply any sort of brake on the escalation of violence. This burgeoning mimetic crisis will destroy the protohuman group unless some means for its control presents itself. "The rivalrous and conflictual mimesis is spontaneously and automatically transformed into reconciliatory mimesis"[3] as the group turns on a victim whose immolation creates unanimity and peace, and does so rather startlingly. The Dionysian mania, the Polynesian *amok*, the collective trance of Greek tragedy—all resolve into unexpected clarity and unanimity as a victim is singled out for having caused the crisis and is collectively set upon.[4] In the immediate transition from chaos to order that comes with the victim's lynching, the undifferentiation of frenzied mimetic doubles returns to the normal differentiation of group members at peace.

Hence the sacred emerges in its two classic elements of terror and wonder: Rudolf Otto's *mysterium tremendum et fascinans*,[5] a link that Girard properly explains for the first time.[6] What Otto described as metaphysical, Girard reveals as historical. "After a while," he explains, "the malevolence of the scapegoat is covered over by the benevolence of the god, which is retroactively extended to the preimmolation period."[7] "It is necessary that the victim first appear to 'merit' his punishment," however, "that he may later 'merit' his divinity."[8] This foundational breakthrough is mediated subsequently by religious practices, which reference the founding murder while concealing its shocking truth. So, in sum, to use an Australian bush fire–related metaphor: mimesis provides the fuel, mimetic conflict the spark, a founding murder the fire brigade, and the religious nexus of prohibition-myth-ritual the controlled burning that prevents a major conflagration from erupting.

Girard assembles extensive evidence to justify his claim from across a range of archaic practices, and from legacies of the scapegoat mechanism remaining in modern life. Significantly, it is among echoes and institutionalizations of the founding murder that Girard uncovers it, only later returning to reconstruct the story of how humanity must have emerged in prehistory for these outcomes to have followed. For the sake of clarity, however, I want to present this material in reverse order, beginning with Girard on human origins as pieced together mainly from earlier and later dialogues appearing in *Things Hidden Since the Foundation of the World* and *Evolution and Conversion*. I also want to consider briefly the counternarrative of human origins offered by the maverick Girardian Eric Gans. Then I set out the weightiest evidence for Girard's account, drawing on his comprehensive discussion of its ritual and mythical encoding in more developed religious and cultural forms. Girard's books *Violence and the Sacred* and *The Scapegoat* are of particular importance for the latter undertaking.

According to Girard, "Mimetic theory renders an account of sacrifice and archaic religion, to a purely natural force, human hypermimeticism."[9] Hence today's widespread and popular misunderstandings of religion are exposed by Girard. A more liberal take on religion, emphasizing the quest for meaning and the cultivation of personal spirituality, is revealed as a modern development—in richer or poorer forms, the latter in keeping with other aspects of consumer society—whereas religion originally served as a pragmatic cultural expedient primarily concerned with social cohesion and the restraint of violence.[10] Humanity's mimetic predisposition to violence, as emphasized by Girard, is also anathema to inheritors of the Enlightenment who champion a more rational and noble account of human motivations and capacities, contrary to all available evidence. All this is directly contradictory to the "atheist chic" agenda[11] of today's cultured despisers of religion, such as Richard Dawkins, who blame religion for violence while extolling humanity's natural capacity to sort itself out if left alone by the gods. Girard shows that, culturally and historically, the opposite is closer to the truth.

HUMAN ORIGINS

Girard admits that his version of human origins based on the surrogate victim mechanism involves imaginative reconstruction. He explains that "it bears upon a real victim, about whom we know nothing of course, but whose reality is attested by the frequency of the same accusations in mob phenomena today."[12] Girard's account also relies on traces still visible to the trained eye in prohibitions, rituals, and myths. Despite the speculative elements in his version of human origins, Girard claims "to have all the elements that make the mechanism possible and even statistically probable."[13]

Girard's approach emphasizes the continuity of animal and human along evolution's path, understanding surrogate victimage as "the primary adaptation of human beings to their own violent nature,"[14] conveying survival fitness to a threatened species. The necessity of deaths among nature's unfit individuals to foster the evolution of better-adapted life, according to Darwin's vision of "nature as a supersacrificial machine,"[15] suggests that Darwinian natural selection plays out at the level of protohuman groups by the same sacrificial means.[16] According to Girard, "Mammals mark their territorial borders with their excrement. Human beings have long done the same thing with that particular form of excrement that we call their scapepoats."[17]

Animal Legacies

The scapegoat mechanism for resolving conflict clearly represents an adaptation, and Girard looks for antecedents in animal behavior. He points to the rituals and prohibitions already present in some animal species,[18] in particular, to the imitation of dominant individuals as a way of providing survival-enhancing order and direction for a group. This is suggestive of human mimetic modeling,[19] pointing forward also to the more developed, follow-the-leader aspects of human ritual. It is an important consideration for Girard that instinctual dominance patterns typically prevent intraspecies violence from becoming lethal among animals, keeping their bickering and squabbling—born from something like acquisitive mimesis—from getting out of hand. The pack falls into a particular hierarchy that fixes and hence limits possibilities for the expression of desire and consequent violence (regarding food, potential mates, etc.).[20]

So-called animal rites provide a further example,[21] in which aggression from one animal toward another is at the last instant diverted onto an object or third party in an act of aversion that is mimetically reproduced by the opposing animal. Hence the two antagonists make common cause, which suggests a strong link from animal to human sociality (though compared with human tendencies such animal rites do not lead to immolation).[22] This instinctual pattern of behavior helps create the semipermanent bond between geese (notoriously cranky creatures), as Lorenz demonstrates in *On Aggression*. Girard sees this as "a kind of incipient scapegoat mechanism,"[23] which just needs extending to an entire pack.[24]

He speculates on what would happen if this deflection of hostility onto a third party caused its death.[25] Girard's main example here is the chimpanzee, our closest living relative (recently recovered Neanderthal DNA has been shown to mark the genetic halfway point between chimp DNA and our own). He reflects on studies of chimpanzee violence and the intensification of rivalry that they reveal.[26] He wonders what would happen if they surpassed their normal habit of throwing branches at each other—which is not restrained by instinctual inhibition because it represents no threat between disarmed adversaries—and learned to throw rocks instead.[27] More recently Girard has remarked on the collective killing and eating of monkey victims now known among chimpanzees, and the ritual aspects of their hunting, as a stage in the "long evolutionary process" leading to the scapegoat mechanism "in its final form and functionality."[28]

The Ur-Symbol

Chimpanzee brains, despite their adequacy for tool use, hunting, and protorituals, are not capable of using symbols, which demands more than brain size. It requires a center of signification, and that will be provided by the scapegoat victim. Here Girard mentions Stanley Kubrick's *2001: A Space Odyssey* and its Ur-symbol of the black monolith, which he reads as a metaphor for the slaughtered victim. In Kubrick's filmic vision its appearance catalyzes the emergence of a larger brain among the perplexed and unsettled protohumans, boosting their transition to a fully human state.[29]

The move to symbolic thinking, thence to desire proper, cultural development, and growth in brain size fit to cope with its complexities, on to language, writing, and cultural diversification, perhaps began with a single evolutionary innovation favoring a particular group of hominids. Here Girard agrees with Merlin Donald in his classic *Origins of the Modern Mind.*[30] But what sort of innovation? Following Terrence Deacon in *The Symbolic Species,* Girard identifies the breakdown of dominance patterns as the threshold of human emergence.[31] It arrives when the instinctually perceived inaccessibility of particular objects by creatures lower in the dominance hierarchy is overcome in a mimetic crisis. The strict presymbolic linking of signs to referents typical of this simple natural hierarchical mind-set is broken by a crisis of mimetic conflict in which formerly compliant creatures start fighting in earnest.

This dissolution of the prehuman group's instinctual inhabitation of their world is reset at a higher level as the first genuine symbol emerges, the slain victim. Girard imagines the state of the newly pacified group, as silence follows the mayhem of their mimetic crisis, with this "maximal contrast" between agitation and tranquillity providing favorable conditions for noninstinctual attention to emerge. "Consequently," Girard writes, "beyond the purely instinctual object, the alimentary or sexual object or the dominant individual, there is the cadaver of the collective victim[,] . . . the first object for this new type of attention."[32] This is not a complicated symbol system of binary oppositions such as we find developed in our languages but simply the opposition of a single trait standing out against an otherwise undifferentiated experiential field. Its newness, terror, wonder, and incomprehensibility at the level of instinct combine to make this first cultural symbol one of prohibition[33]—a warning and a reminder about the group's violent near-dissolution, now urging the group toward consolidating the miracle of its newfound accord. Thus the pattern of taboo, ritual, and symbolic exchange typical of human cultures emerges from an animal world of instinctual dominance patterns.[34] Girard's insight into human origins, then, is as remarkable as it is original: essentially, "the only thing an animal needs to become human is the surrogate victim."[35]

Girard also addresses questions of how the founding murder caught on and how many of them there might have been. The picture that emerges is of widespread parallel developments rather than a single moment of illumination that spread from only one point of origin. As Girard puts it, "We can conceive of hominization as a series of steps that allow for the domestication of progressively increasing and intense mimetic effects, separated from one another by crises that would be catastrophic but also generative in that they would trigger the founding mechanism and at each step provide for more rigorous prohibitions within the group, and for a more effective ritual canalization towards the outside."[36]

Rather than a one-off breakthrough, this is a new cultural pattern that gains traction and consolidates. Humanity's "discovery" of the scapegoat mechanism, according to Girard, is a process of incremental stabilization: "It is necessary to conceive of stages . . . , which were perhaps the longest in human history, in which the signifying effects have still not truly taken shape," and during which "next to nothing" may have been produced for periods "of dozens or even hundreds of thousands of years."[37] For Girard, this means that there must have been innumerable primal murders (because of the universality of this theme in myth and ritual, as we shall see),[38] which may have included "relatively original" repeat performances—"innumerable instances of unanimous violence that unified *or reunified* specific human groups"[39]—during which millions would have been killed.[40]

Beginning to Encode the Surrogate Victim

Consolidating the reconciliation of mimetic conflict achieved through the scapegoat mechanism calls "for substituting, in ritual, new victims for the original victim, in order to assure the maintenance of that miraculous peace," leading in turn to "the manipulation and differentiation of the sign constituted by victimage" in a variety of other forms that come to signify the victim while progressively masking and hiding it.[41] In the next section I set out some of the most suggestive echoes of the founding murder identified by Girard in prohibition, myth, and ritual, but for now it is helpful to note that many key early human practices and cultural developments involve just this "manipulation and differentiation" of the primal symbol of the slain victim.

I do not refer to figurines or cave art (from forty thousand years ago in France), burial customs,[42] or ritual spaces such as stone circles but to life's very basic necessities. The Neolithic practices of agriculture and animal domestication provide two obvious, though late, examples (under nine thousand years old). Girard notably ascribes animal domestication to a fortuitous outgrowth of the scapegoat mechanism, once it had transformed into early humanity's widespread practice of animal sacrifice. Animal species kept for sacrifice, when temperamentally suitable, became domesticated after generations of cohabitation with humans.[43] By way of comparison, pre-Columbian civilizations that continued human sacrifice into early modern times did not domesticate animals, as David Carrasco notes, which Girard sees as confirming his hypothesis.[44] Likewise, the otherwise odd-seeming practice of planting seeds in the ground recalls the burying of victims, whose immolation had proved the source of new life.[45] Here, a ritual practice provides the *seedbed* of concrete, beneficial human development.

Indeed, for Girard, it was the habit of performing rituals at certain fixed places that explains the emergence of sedentary life in the first place, which would not necessarily have occurred to hunter-gatherers as a pragmatic option—unless the nuts-and-bolts utility of ritual is acknowledged as the indispensable means for ensuring that humanity survives its own proneness to mimetically escalating violence.[46] Earlier still, the development of language had a ritual basis, according to Girard, also grounded in the founding murder. He notes the suggestive connection between pieces of the victim and languages all over the world. From the slain body of Hippolytus in Greece to Australian aboriginal society, body parts of sacred persons and animals became place-names, while in the Rg-Veda the primordial man Purusha is killed by holy men and his trisected body becomes the three castes in society.[47] The universal fact of sacred words at the basis of languages also extends to the likely influence of the repetitions, rhythms, and exchange patterns of ritual in the emergence, reinforcement, and learning of language.[48]

Then, taking the longest possible step backward in prehistory—certainly to the lower Paleolithic and to *Homo habilis* (two million years ago)—Girard posits an essential role for ritual protection at the remotest origins of the identifiably human.[49] His three examples are toolmaking, hunting, and human neoteny (here referring to the way humans are born relatively undeveloped, so that growth to viability and independence takes years of nurture outside the womb).[50]

First, Girard does not believe that the earliest humans could have made their potentially dangerous tools and weapons without violence first having been gotten under control and with some sort of religious fear-based taboos already in place. He finds an echo of this in widespread archaic customs concerning the class of persons who forged dangerous objects. These blacksmiths were kept in a kind of quasi-sacred, permanently scapegoated outsider position on the edge of human settlements; they were needed, yet regarded warily.

Second, Girard rejects the suggestion that killing animals for food was primary in establishing human bonds and that human sacrifice was derivative. Walter Burkert in *Homo Necans* (1972), like Girard, offers an account of religion based on the dissipation of violence. But for Burkert it is the direction of aggression toward a hunted animal that is primary and the unifying effect of subsequent feasting that sets the religious pattern.[51] Girard, to the contrary, views the hunt as a recollection of what first made human order possible rather than the means of establishing that order. Indeed, he regards the hunt as just the sort of complex, coordinated activity that would have first emerged out of prior ritual practice.[52] At a conference gathering, in response to Eric Gans also suggesting this formative role for hunting, Girard mocked the seamlessness of his own account by replying, "Well, if I accepted your theory I could no longer connect my theory of desire with my theory of victimage," but then added more seriously that he sees no evidence for the proposal.[53]

Third, the fact that babies are born significantly unprepared for autonomous living and require years of care from their mother in the context of relatively peaceful and stable community implies for Girard the prior presence of social protection, reflecting the coming together of biological and cultural factors in human evolution while creating a stable space for that evolution to advance.[54] Such a process of "self domestication" along the path from primates to humans can take place because "a sort of prohibition of a religious nature or some sort of fear of an immense invisible power at the most basic level triggered prohibitions against violence. These forms of prohibition protected the female, and made possible long-range care for infants."[55]

Eric Gans—A Kinder, Gentler Paleolithic?

Girard's first PhD student, Eric Gans, proposes an alternative, quasi-Girardian position without the primal scapegoating. For Gans, a Derrida-inspired literary theorist, the appearance of humanity's first sign dissipates potential mimetic violence by both differentiation and deferral—the two dimensions of Derrida's *différance*.[56] Gans's so-called generative anthropology begins, like Girard's theory, with an originary scene, though in Gans's case it is a gathering of protohumans all reaching for something, such as food, then drawing back in surprised acknowledgment of the thing that they have signified. The "fearful symmetry" (think of Blake, *The Tyger*) of this reaching-to-grasp has an awakening effect, and from this "aborted gesture of appropriation" emerges the sign.[57] Though the object has not been captured, it has been designated, and this new sign has the effect of giving pause to those who had reached out toward the object.

From this new, transcendent center in the object and the differentiated group members who have all been equalized with reference to it (hence establishing a sense of center and periphery) emerge the foundations of an incipient culture,[58] once the possibility of sharing has replaced the rivalrous exercise of desire and the threat of annihilation.[59] The sign becomes public and shareable, helping suppress resentment in the group by relativizing, introducing distance, and hence restraining those present.[60] "Diverting mimetic desire to the generation of new meanings is the most fundamental form of human interaction,"[61] as Gans proposes in his kinder, gentler account of human origins.

And language comes first, born in the cry of one present at the originary scene, a cry that does not signal action toward the object but that in *designating* the object succeeds in deferring action.[62] Gans accommodates those like Girard who claim a late origin for language, however, in his willingness to regard the first cry—the primary linguistic sign emerging in his originary scene—as separate from the later development of syntactical linguistic structures.[63]

Girardians respect and learn from Gans's wide oeuvre, but Girard is having none of this kinder, gentler version, countering, "The birth of language, or the very idea of substitution cannot come unaided."[64] He insists on an embryonic form of culture before language could develop; otherwise mimetic violence would have proven too intense and unstoppable for us to have lasted so long. Girard dismisses Gans's belief that violence has been averted essentially by talk, in what amounts to a prehistoric social contract. Gans denies this charge because you cannot have a social contract without equality arising first, whereas his scene is meant to be completely originary.[65] But there is force in Girard's assessment that this is all too gentlemanly, too tolerant-liberal, too modern-rational: "Gans presupposes a higher form of rationality that can only follow after a crucial event, like in my view, the victimary mechanism and the scapegoat resolution. It can never precede the event itself." And it is too *idealistic*, too *naive*. Girard again: "How can a simple gesture, regardless of how ostensible it may be, prevent the mimetic doubles from killing each other? As if violence did not exist! It is another way of denying violence. I think this is, again, a rhetorical manoeuvre to negate the primacy of religion in human culture."[66]

Girard embraces the claim of the primatologist Frans de Waal that modern notions of individual agency and choice are being imposed on the period of human origins by behaviorists, sociobiologists, and cultural materialists, whereas these notions actually have a history that must be unraveled. In Girard's view religion and ritual formed the human mind, from beginnings in the involuntary spasm of his scapegoat mechanism, so that the possibility of human individuality arises eventually as a product of the sacred and the differentiation it fosters.[67] I move on now to Girard's account of human culture and religion emerging from the archaic sacred as the ripe fruit and the full encoding of surrogate victimage.

REAPING THE WHIRLWIND: CULTURE AND RELIGION

Girard views the scapegoat mechanism, in Darwinian style, as human beings' primary adaptation to their own violent nature, enabling progress beyond the lethal infighting that would have destroyed many protohuman groups. It represents "a cultural degree-zero for survival's sake."[68] From this fortuitous discovery issued a sense of what we would now call religious transcendence, from a double transference onto the victim: first of the group's blame and aggression, then of its subsequent reconciliation.[69] Enter the sacred, which for Girard "is the sum of human assumptions resulting from collective transferences focused on a reconciliatory victim at the conclusion of a mimetic crisis."[70] Accordingly, says Girard, "the things you must not do are called *prohibitions,* and the things you must do are called *rituals.*"[71] Hence ritual is "the first specifically human technique, the origin of human culture."[72] Ritual gives way eventually to modern institutions,[73] such as the judicial system, which take from it their own version of power and transcendence.[74]

All this is nothing like our modern Western take-it-or-leave-it approach to religion. Girard mocks skeptical explanations of religion as if it were the invention of greedy priests, and as otherwise useless to a society of little Descartes. He asks how the universality of religion can be accounted for if not by its centrality in establishing human cohesion.[75] In a discussion of modern atheism, Girard insists that "l'humanité est la fille du religieux: elle n'existerait pas sans lui" (humanity is the offspring of the religious: it would not exist without it).[76] Here Girard follows Durkheim, to whom he ascribes the greatest anthropological insight of our time: the identity of society and religion.[77] This conjunction, which Saint Paul's letters refer to in terms of powers and principalities, and the sociologist Peter Berger as "the sacred canopy," points to "the juxtaposition of real immanence, a force arising with the social order itself, and a transcendental power."[78] Durkheim addressed this, though without the three pillars of Girard's theory.

This violent sacred is plainly not a good thing, according to Girard, although it is regretfully if temporarily necessary. "Archaic religions have little to do with Gods and a lot to do with two institutions: sacrifices and prohibitions," he reiterates, so that "their survival value justifies, *for a while*, their compromises with human violence."[79] I now want to offer a condensed overview of what happens during this period of "for a while"—that is, during the uninterrupted run of sacred violence-fueled religion that began to give way only under a pressure that first appeared on the human stage in the Hebrew Bible, then with Jesus Christ. Here I follow one possible path through Girard's classic *Violence and the Sacred*, supplemented occasionally from his other writings.

Sacred Technologies

The risks faced by primitive societies are likened by Girard to those faced by the hemophiliac, for whom peril is always near at hand.[80] "Religion, then, is far from 'useless,'" he insists. "It humanizes violence; it protects man from his own violence by taking it out of his hands, transforming it into a transcendent and ever-present danger to be kept in check by the appropriate rites appropriately observed and by a modest and prudent demeanour."[81] Hence the care taken in primitive societies to avoid giving offense, with lengthy palavers before nonritual actions and the cultivation of a reserved and noble bearing, because any careless action could have irreparable consequences. By comparison, our modern habits of informality and flexibility seem impossibly audacious and risky.[82]

Prohibitions

Likewise, signs of danger become the stuff of taboo. Hence the widespread sensitivities evoked by menstrual blood,[83] which like all blood recalls the specter of violence. Similarly, certain foods are declared off-limits, as are certain potential sexual partners (incest and moiety taboos)—in the latter case, not for reasons of prudery but to head off the possibility of dangerous mimetic rivalry erupting between indiscriminate would-be suitors.[84] A striking example is the way identical twins are treated in archaic cultures, including their exposure at birth, because, Girard says, "wherever differences are lacking, violence threatens."[85] Classical civilization was aware of twins as a "visible manifestation of the conflictual uniformity produced by mimetic rivalries," with the removal of one twin sufficient to end the mimetic crisis. Hence, in Rome's myth of origins, Romulus murders Remus and becomes the sacred king around whom nascent Rome can structure itself.[86] "Being the least differentiated relationship in most kinship systems, the status of a brother can become a mark of undifferentiation," Girard explains, "a symbol of violent desymbolization, the sign paradoxically that there are no more signs and that a warring confusion tends to prevail everywhere."[87]

The threat of a perceived loss of distinction that characterizes the mimetic crisis is also evident in the way victims are typically portrayed as gross boundary violators. Consider "that well-known delinquent Oedipus,"[88] cast as a monstrous exception to normal humanity and "framed" for bringing the plague to Thebes (once again, mimetic crisis).[89] Alain de Botton imagines the British tabloid headline "Royal in Incest Shocker."[90] But, as Girard insists, "Oedipus was innocent. The guilty party was the group."[91]

Rituals

The point of ritual is veiled reenactment of the primal murder in order to renew its pacifying effects,[92] using a surrogate from within the community to replace the original luckless outsider in "an inexact imitation of the generative act."[93] The ritual victim is both poison and antidote, as in the Greek *pharmakon*,[94] where slaves known as *pharmakoi* were actually kept for this ritual purpose.

Natural rhythms of death and rebirth are incorporated into this thinking, as the cosmic resonances of social practice manifest themselves in ritual.[95] This is because of a deep imaginative connection between the natural and the social that is not wholly gone even in modern times.[96] So, as Girard insists, the mimetic crisis is imagined in myths as a flood, a famine, a plague, or some other natural catastrophe because *actual* natural disasters like these are understood as manifestations of social disquiet, requiring the treatment of ritual and sacrifice.[97] Likewise, animal attackers standing in for human persecutors represent a mythic theme that Girard identifies from Sophocles to Racine.[98] This substitution conceals from the community its own role in the founding murder, emphasizing also the undifferentiation characteristic of social crisis—in this case, effacing the distinction between human and animal.

The conflation of nature and culture in all these examples points to the confusion of categories accompanying descent into violence, with ritual as the bulwark against social collapse. As Girard sums it up, "Rituals . . . repeat the initial sacrifice (the first victim leads to substitute victims: children, men, animals, various offerings), and repetition of rituals gives birth to institutions, which are the only means that humanity has found to postpone the apocalypse" (more on this in chapter 4).[99]

An example of one such institution, rooted in sacrificial ritual, is kingship. The king is a social figure whose person was typically understood to be rich in sacred resonances. So we are not entirely surprised to find that kings are treated as sacrificial-victims-in-waiting by a number of tribal societies[100]—as victims with suspended sentences.[101] For Girard, then, "the monarchy might be compared to the factories that convert household refuse into fertilizer."[102] Leaders have retained this function into modern times. For example, Girard thinks that the fate of France's ancien régime makes more sense in light of such "sacrificial kingship" than according to modern theories of monarchy.[103] Indeed, he proposes that political power first arose much like animal domestication—as the unimagined by-product of keeping a stock of sacrificial victims ready to hand, in this case prisoners who were "treated like kings" over long periods right up to the day of their sacrifice.[104]

Cosmic harmonization through sacrificial ritual is also achieved by Dionysian festivals in archaic and classical societies, where undifferentiated chaos is allowed to make its return and then vanquished in a veiled reenactment of the primal murder, all for the regular ritual reinforcement of society's status quo.[105] Girard identifies the presence of this dynamic even under erasure.

> The joyous, peaceful façade of the deritualized festival, stripped of any reference to a surrogate victim and its unifying powers, rests on the framework of a sacrificial crisis attended by reciprocal violence. That is why genuine artists can still see that tragedy lurks somewhere behind the bland festivals, the tawdry utopianism of the "leisure society." The more trivial, vulgar and banal holidays become, the more acutely one senses the approach of something uncanny and terrifying. The theme of holiday-gone-wrong dominates Fellini's films and has recently surfaced in various forms in the work of many other artists.[106]

The Greatness of Tragedy

Again, Girard is clear on how horrible all this is, praising the tragedians of classical antiquity for revealing the pathway from sacrificial immolation to communal catharsis[107] and for beginning its demystification, for example, Euripides in *The Bacchae* stripping any illusion from "a bacchanal that is pure frenzy, naked violence."[108] In a memorable image, Girard likens this myth-based world of violent catharsis to a beautiful, much-caressed fur coat that when turned inside out reveals the bloody skin of the victim from which its beauty derives.[109] He refers to the particular vulnerability of women in Dionysian festivals. Their relative weakness and lack of social power made women ready victims, yet also quasi-sacred, both "desired and disdained, alternately elevated and abused."[110] Elsewhere, Girard points to the suitability of orphans for sacrifice, because their lack of social belonging removed the risk that their immolation would upset anyone and fuel the violent mimeticism of revenge.[111]

The greatness of tragedy lies in its unveiling of this mimeticism, according to Girard. Tragedy refuses the Manichean distinctions that continue to manufacture the black-and-white heroes and villains preferred by romantically influenced moderns. For us, an unwavering blame, "an unyielding rancour that holds fast to its victims, has replaced the revolving oppositions of real tragedy."[112] Girard emphasizes the alternation and reversal of all the roles in tragedy, along with the mimetic attractiveness of violence that it exposes. In particular, he notes how divinity circulates in *The Bacchae*,[113] rather like the coveted yellow jersey in the Tour de France.

Ritual and Science

The pacifying and structuring effects of religion also underpin scientific advancement, though science is popularly regarded as antipathetic to religion in secular times. For Girard, however, "it is the surrogate victim who provides men with the will to conquer reality and the weapons for all victorious intellectual campaigns—having first secured society against violence. The myths of symbolic thought can be compared to a larva's cocoon: without this shelter, no development could take place."[114] Ritual provides the key in the way it helps us deal with impurity, undifferentiation, and mimetic jitters. It pushes the impure toward quicker resolution, not least the unsettling presence of the dead, hence helping to control disorder.[115] It gives the audacity to confront impurity and to broach the undifferentiated: "the rite overexcites the crisis and precipitates the mixtures in order to bring about a favourable resolution," as Girard explains, addressing the question of how humans must first have imagined the possibility of "experimentation on the rotten, the spoiled, the fermented."[116] All sorts of animal and vegetable secretions, milk, flour—the mixed states that are anathema in any number of purity codes—thus yield "the astonishing 'resurrections' that are called cheese, bread, wine, germination, and so forth."[117]

From Mythology to Modernity

Girard is the first to explain the founding role of religion in primitive societies together with the reason for our ignorance of that role. He reveals "the surrogate victim as that stone initially rejected by the builders, only to become the cornerstone of a whole mythic and ritualistic edifice. Or as the key that opens any religious text, revealing its innermost workings and rendering it forever accessible to the human intellect."[118]

Before considering (in chapter 3) how the Judeo-Christian vision definitively exposes and undermines this whole cultural and religious framework built on sacred violence, it will help to take an intermediate step by looking more closely with Girard at mythology, in particular, at the history of its transformation and decline. He analyzes myth in light of medieval and early modern persecution texts, showing first how actual victims of persecution were chosen and the way that fear of their "difference" manifested itself. He then identifies these same "stereotypes of persecution" in actual myths, outlining elaborate attempts in the developing mythological oeuvre to hide the actual victims whose murder stood at the origin of these narratives and suggesting why secular moderns fail to catch on. Finally, Girard shows how myth began to lose its capacity for concealing these victims. The first half of his book *The Scapegoat* will be our guide.

Persecution Texts

Guillaume de Machaut wrote that poisoning by Jews caused a mid-fourteenth-century plague outbreak in northern France. Jews also apparently brought lightning and a hail of stones. Such so-called persecution texts helped cause and sustain mob violence, backed by law, against a minority that everyone now knows to have been entirely innocent.[119] Women accused of witchcraft were similarly persecuted in the sixteenth century, essentially for crimes against a properly differentiated social order. They were symbolic victims, sacrificed for reasons of maintaining stability in uncertain times. This remains true even though many women accused of witchcraft confessed that they were guilty,[120] in typical show trial fashion.

One might have thought that the allegations in such persecution texts were so outlandish that even contemporary readers would have seen through them. Today, by comparison, such exaggeration in evidence given in court would typically be seen as a warning that deception is afoot. But not so with these obviously exaggerated texts of persecution, which remained persuasive in their day without any need for the denials and cover-ups that of necessity must accompany today's persecutions if they are to be effective.[121]

Whether the precipitating *crisis* was explicitly political or religious or linked to a real natural event like an epidemic or drought, the imagery used in such persecution texts typically has to do with the breakdown of stable order and its characteristic differentiations. This is the first of Girard's so-called stereotypes of persecution.[122] The second one is a moral transgression, because the victim always has to be guilty of something. Typically they are blamed for *crimes* involving the worst boundary violations: perpetrating the most unthinkable attacks, on the king or the father, perhaps more recently on children or the defenseless; also distinction-blurring sex crimes, like rape, incest, and bestiality; or religious crimes, such as profaning the eucharistic Host.[123]

Girard's third stereotype of persecution has to do with *criteria* for choosing the victim. It is a potentially random choice, though the unsettling presence of cultural or religious minorities in a community typically makes them fair game. However, explains Girard, "most myth-producing societies are too small and too homogenous to possess the religious or ethnic minorities that usually provide the large and heterogenous 'civilizations' with their reservoirs of scapegoat victims."[124] Hence physical criteria of sickness, madness, deformity, injury, and disability serve to attract attention, all of which cause unease of social exchange.[125] Indeed, Girard links this tendency of mobs to zero in on someone different to the way animal predators single out weak or abnormal prey from the undifferentiated herd.[126] Another mark of difference in potential victims is social divergence from the average, for instance, someone very poor or very wealthy, with mobs regularly turning on the powerful.[127] Girard finds an example of "the *crisis*, the *crime*, the *criteria* of choosing a victim, the first three stereotypes of persecution,"[128] in the singling out of Marie Antoinette by the mob, with the law court's connivance. France's prerevolutionary crisis, the allegation of incest with her son, and her foreignness as an Austrian tick all three boxes.[129]

It is insufficient to say that, according to Girard, human groups are wary of difference *tout simple*. Rather, Girard is just as insistent that it is the lack of difference that precipitates crises and ignites the search for a victim. Let me clarify what he means about the persecution of difference and the outsider.

Any culture is full of diversity. Humanity is plainly not the enemy of difference, because everything we do and are is structured by variations within our group that are endlessly noticed and evaluated. We are mimetic creatures after all. What any community does not want is for this order-preserving measure of internal differentiation to collapse, which is what happens when the group is confronted by the *really* different—by one who is so different that he or she makes everyone else look and seem the same. For instance, encountering someone so racially different or physically anomalous that he or she emphasizes the normality, *the relative sameness,* of everyone else puts the system of differences structuring a group's self-understanding into question. Consequently, immigrants with a different skin color and religion have been ill treated in racially and religiously monochrome societies, and the mentally and physically disabled have long struggled for acceptance and justice.

"Difference that exists outside the system is terrifying because it reveals the truth of the system," concludes Girard, exposing "its relativity, its fragility and its mortality."[130] It is not just a basic dichotomy of self and other, therefore, so that there is only one sort of difference that is deemed bad. Rather, Girard's insight is that there are "two ways of being different, two types of differences."[131] It is a subtle point, which he takes pains to clarify: "Even in the most closed cultures men believe that they are free and open to the universal; their differential character makes the narrowest cultural fields seem inexhaustible from within. Anything that compromises this illusion terrifies us and stirs up the immemorial tendency to persecution. . . . Despite what is said around us persecutors are never obsessed by difference but rather by its unutterable contrary, the lack of difference."[132]

Girard is also clear that his three stereotypes of persecution are deeply linked and in no way arbitrary. A common Greek root, *krino,* "to judge"—in the sense of to distinguish, to differentiate, but also to accuse and condemn a victim—underpins all three of his keywords here, *crisis, crime,* and *criteria.* "It implies an as yet concealed relationship between collective persecutions and the culture as a whole," concludes Girard, and "If such a relationship exists, it has never been explained by any linguist, philosopher, or politician."[133] He goes on to apply this understanding to mythology.[134] Here Girard lays bare *con brio* what George Eliot's scholar-parson in *Middlemarch,* Edward Casaubon, failed to discover: "the key to all mythologies."

Exhuming the Victim in Mythology

If a myth contains even two of his three stereotypes of persecution, Girard believes that behind it lies real crisis and real violence, with a real victim chosen not only for alleged crimes but also for a particular bearing, or signature, marking them out.[135] His comprehensive example is Sophocles' *Oedipus Rex*, which has all three stereotypes: a plague in Thebes, then the characteristic crimes of parricide and incest, and finally the singling out of a limping outsider as victim.[136] A further sign of Oedipus's outsider status is his exposure as an infant, which declares his nonbelonging (for Girard, the more signs of the stereotypical victim one bears, the more likely a target one becomes).[137] So why do we not read *Oedipus Rex* as a persecution text? It bears all the signs, and texts just like it from fourteenth-century France came to be read this way.[138] Girard certainly wants us to. He believes that the Oedipus myth is an undeciphered Dreyfus case,[139] confident that in fifty years people will read it that way: "There will be none of that attitude of our literary critics who say, 'All interpretations are good . . .' Either the Oedipus myth is a 'witch-hunt text' with an incredible surface that conceals a credible depth, like the accounts of the Salem trials, or it is not. There you have an either/or that you have to decide."[140]

It was only in the early modern period that eyes were opened to a correct reading of medieval persecution texts. The main reason that we have not made the same transition in reading myth, Girard thinks, is that we are confused by the presence of myth's other dimension, no longer found in persecution texts, and that is mythology's making sacred of the victim. "Medieval and modern persecutors do not worship their victims," he points out, "they only hate them."[141] It is harder to spot a real sacred victim when we are not used to them. As Girard explains, "Myths exude the sacred and do not seem compatible with texts that do not."[142] By the time the persecution texts appeared, however, the old mythic world of execration twinned with veneration was breaking down, although it was not entirely gone. An echo of this older dualism remained. Those persecuted Jews were not charged with total culpability, for instance; they had caused only a limited plague outbreak in northern France, unlike that in the Thebes of Oedipus. That is, they were not entirely demonized. Likewise, the supposed efficacy of Jewish medicine in medieval Europe represented a very limited survival of mythology's *pharmakon*. That is, the Jews remained at least a little bit divinized. But even such scant retentions of mythology's divinizing impulse would not last.[143]

Apart from this divinizing impulse, demonstrating myth's grounding in the archaic sacred, there is one other dimension in myth that hides the victim from modern eyes: mythology's active pursuit of concealment. It was necessary to keep hidden the violent human roots of culture and religion in order to preserve their "sacred" pacifying and ordering capacities. Early signs of this concealment are found in myths that take pains to disguise the founding murder. Girard might be accused of drawing a long bow with these interpretations, but he is resolute. "Myths that contain exactly what is needed to reflect a pattern of unconscious persecution I take at face value and regard as suggestive of the true nature of mythology," he responds, "and myths that contain something else and do not clearly support my case I regard as having been tampered with."[144] This tampering is evident to the Girardian eye in various categories of myth.

One such type of sanitized myth presents the victim as self-sacrificing, as if the death was not a collective act. The Aztec myth of Teotihuacan, in which one god offers himself to become the sun, then another the moon, and the remaining gods sacrifice their hearts to become the stars, gives a very public-spirited account of this pantheon. But Girard reveals the clear mood of intimidation in the text, along with his three stereotypes of persecution: the crisis of undifferentiation between night and day, along with the theme of burning bodies characteristically accompanying plague infestation; the hubristic crime of the god who becomes the moon, seeking mimetically to outdo the other gods; and the criteria marking out the little, pockmarked, outsider god who is the first to line up for immolation. There is also the mythic element of divinization in the victim becoming the shining light-giver.[145]

Another sort of myth showing signs of being cleaned up makes a caricature of the founding murder so that no one is really guilty, for example, the story of Baldr from Scandinavian mythology. Baldr is granted miraculous protection from harm in a game of mock attack, until Loki hands a harmless mistletoe to Baldr's blind brother, Hoehr, to use in the game, thanks to which Hoehr unwittingly kills Baldr. Girard sees a mythic evolution here in which the founding murder in an earlier version of the myth has been concealed by convoluted overlays.

Then there are myths reworked to hide the surrogate victim altogether. Girard's example is the birth of Zeus, whom the Curetes tried to conceal from the murderous Kronos by forming a circle and beating their weapons to drown the infant's cries. Girard identifies an earlier version of the same myth in the coaxing of infant Dionysus into a circle of Titans, who then kill and eat him (prior to his resurrection by Zeus, who kills the Titans). Moving from the Titans version, with its clear collective murder, to the Curetes- and Baldr-style of myth in which that murder is either concealed or else fudged demonstrates for Girard an evolution of mythology toward greater complexity for the sake of concealing its sacred violence. As Girard concludes, "Mythology eliminates collective murder but does not reinvent it, because all evidence indicates it was not invented in the first place."[146]

In yet other myths in which this spin-doctoring is evident, crimes by the gods are deemphasized so that we will not notice them. But surely Zeus having sex with Leda while she is in the form of a swan or the Minotaur marrying Pasiphae suggest a similarity with the more obviously boundary-blurring myths that involve sexual transgression. Or what of the subsequently "disappeared" Hittite god, Telipinu, whose rampage was excused—sort of—because it followed upon the other gods sending a bee to bite him?[147] Still, the crime of the god is never entirely hidden. "The elimination of the fault in one place generally means its reappearance somewhere else," Girard explains, "usually on the periphery and in an exacerbated form. Thus we see a god or a kind of demon appear who is even more guilty, a Loki or a Kronos who plays the role of a secondary scapegoat. Although this is a textual creation it nevertheless constitutes a trace of the real victim."[148]

Girard names two more variations in which blame is deflected away from the god. The divine trickster, impish and playful, is one way to go, and typical of many myths. The alternative of an angry god punishing in order to bless—a god who has to be cruel to be kind—is more familiar to us in the West. But, and here is a significant break-through according to Girard, this god at least shares blame with the wider community (whose wrongdoing is given as the cause of divine anger).[149] This shared sense of wrongdoing was evident to Girard in the Roman psyche, pervaded by collective guilt over Rome's violent origins. This remained despite the effective suppression of collective murder that Girard discerns in canonical and heretical versions of the Romulus and Remus myth.[150]

Beyond the Archaic Sacred

Girard views archaic myths and the more recent witchcraft stories as two different stages in the same fundamental process of mythic transfiguration while admitting that his interpretation "will remain controversial for a while."[151] It is a matter of continuity: "the text of persecution is not really a separate category," he concludes, "but a myth that failed."[152] That is, it failed to create the old sacred out of human sacrifice. Here we see the process of secularization at work, helping give birth to the modern world. Europeans on the cusp of modernity could still gang up on Jews or witches, though the scapegoating of these unjustly accused figures no longer delivered any lasting reconciliation among their persecutors. Indeed, these persecution texts represent a falling away from the peaceful unanimity of myth-based existence toward the sustained acrimony and the black-and-white blame game typical of today's increasingly irreconcilable world—a world of bitter civil wars, Middle Eastern stalemate, escalating conflict centered on terrorism, and environmental disaster spawned by modern mimetic rivalry manifested in unsustainable habits of consumption. Here is the apocalyptic theme in Girard noted in chapter 1 from his early writings on the hell of modern hypermimeticism and coming to full expression in *Battling to the End*.

We now know what is going on in medieval and early modern texts of persecution, and we are invited by Girard to cast our newly opened eyes back on archaic myth to uncover the same mechanism: "I think today the time has come to perform on mythology the operation that people in the seventeenth and eighteenth centuries were

able to perform on the witch-hunt. I think the greatest feat of interpretation in the Western world was what happened when the English
pastors decided that the witch-hunt laws had to go."[153]

But are we alert to even subtler *modern* versions of the same ac-
cusatory dynamic that we are now invited to recognize in myth?[154]
Having become attuned to the fact of scapegoating, we are now eager
to blame other people for doing it, and we deploy the term *scapegoat*
constantly. So when we do it ourselves there has to be adequate de-
niability. This is why scapegoating in the modern world can only be
carried out if we conceal the fact from ourselves (essentially by up-
dating earlier forms of its concealment). Girard wryly observes, "*We
have only legitimate enmities. And yet the entire universe swarms
with scapegoats.*"[155] He gives to all such misrecognition, perennially
necessary for a smoothly functioning scapegoat mechanism, the
French name *méconnaissance*. This breaks down progressively under
the impact of the gospel,[156] as we see for instance in the way persecution texts lost their power to convince. For Girard, "A society that
replaces myth by an awareness of persecution is a society in the process of desacralization."[157]

Where might we find the earliest signs of this revolutionary awareness? As late as 2003, in a series of lectures on the Hindu Vedic texts
given at the Bibliothèque Nationale de Paris, Girard suggested that
a conscious awareness of the scapegoat mechanism actually emerged
in the early Vedic tradition. He identifies the Hymn to Purusha as a
sacrificial myth, postulating an earlier, lost version in which Purusha
would have been culpable—because he ends up deified in typically
unreflective mythic fashion. In later texts of the Brahmanas, however,
a more obviously guilty victim is chosen, the incestuous Prajâpati,
who is not only deified after his killing, but becomes an actual god
of sacrifice. Thus the path from scapegoat mechanism to false sacred
becomes explicit.[158] As Girard concludes, "The Vedas go a long way in
their understanding of sacrifice, but without escaping . . . the source of
primordial error that characterises archaic religion: the sacralization
of reconciling violence."[159]

It is in the more developed Upanishadic tradition, from which
Buddhism took its departure, that Girard identifies the first appearance

of a critique. It comes in the story of Manu, a scathing satire on how the religious establishment exploits the piety of sacrificers. Girard concludes, however, that the critique extends no further than irony.[160] He also recounts one of the Buddha's birth stories, in which a would-be sacrificer falls victim to his own intrigues, though he does not rate this as an overcoming of the sacrificial imagination.[161]

For Girard, this overcoming is most fully revealed in the Bible—first in the Hebrew Scriptures, then more consistently in the Gospels and the wider New Testament. This is where we will find the earliest foreshadowing of modernity, as the Judeo-Christian vision begins to undo the false sacred and so to secularize the human experience. But this liberating secularization also brings an end to the false-sacred protection of our fragile human enterprise. Secular modernity is a potentially truer yet also a potentially more dangerous world.

CHAPTER 3

Scripture and Secularization

We come now to the third plank of Girard's vision, and the most controversial. In the Bible, from the innocence of victims first proclaimed in the Hebrew Scriptures to a full revealing and overturning of the scapegoat mechanism in the Gospels, Girard identifies humanity's greatest breakthrough.

On the other side of this Judeo-Christian watershed we find a draining away of the protection offered by what Girard calls "the false sacred" and "deviated transcendence" thanks to the real sacred and to genuine transcendence disrupting normal human cultural dynamics. The God we encounter in Jesus Christ unseats the ultimately false though useful and divinely tolerated gods assigned to the restraint of violence, and becomes the driver of secularization. And it is this God who underwrites Nietzsche's twilight of the gods. Thus, for Girard, secularization is reevaluated as a profound and liberating development. Yet he retains his earlier sense of its danger since, whatever else he now wants to say about it, secularization undermines humanity's naturally evolved protection against its own violence.

The breakthrough that Girard recognizes in the Bible is real but incomplete. Into the imaginative world of taboo, myth, and ritual, all founded on the dark secret of humanity's surrogate victim mechanism, comes a countervailing voice repudiating the persecution of innocents and the compulsive multiplication of saving divinities, both of which are churned up together from the mimetic maelstrom of human violence and self-deception. A new sacred—on the side of the victim, of a different order from the familiar archaic sacred—is on offer, yet humanity's wider imaginative transformation is still working itself out. So many echoes of the old false sacred remain in the Bible that a sacrificial reading can continue to find purchase there, for example, Christian fundamentalism whose angry God underpins a myth of redemptive violence in American culture. Yet Girard's alternative, nonsacrifical reading is plausibly based on biblical narratives, images, nuances, and hints that suggest something different, and exceptional.[1]

THE HEBREW BIBLE AND THE CRY OF THE VICTIM

The path chosen through Girard's various reflections on the Hebrew Scriptures starts with *Things Hidden Since the Foundation of the World* (1978) and his discovery of Judeo-Christian distinctiveness. I begin with a discussion of the mythologically freighted texts of Genesis and Exodus, looking more closely with Girard at the story of Cain and Abel, the Joseph novella, and the Ten Commandments (introduced for convenience at this point, from *I See Satan Fall Like Lightning*). I then mention the prophets, along with Girard's related discussions of the Psalms (chiefly from an article on their violent language) and Job (from *Job: The Victim of His People*).

Genesis and Exodus

Girard sees the Bible as beginning with an obviously mimetic story, when the borrowed desire of Eve and then of Adam and their rivalry with God (Gn 3) set humanity on a path to the primal murder of Abel by Cain at the foundation of humanity's first city (Gn 4). Genesis is marked by crisis moments like the Tower of Babel (Gn 11:1–9), the undifferentiated violence of Sodom and Gomorrah (Gn 19:1–26), and a mimetic meltdown undoing human civilization that is coded into the myth of a great flood (Gn 6–8).[2] Girard also identifies the all-against-one dynamic of collective violence, with the familiar mythological theme of conflicted doubles (one securing peace through the other's expulsion). This is the case between Jacob and Esau (Gn 27–33), though they finally renounce a lifetime of mimetic rivalry to achieve a real (if not entirely relaxed) reconciliation. Jacob wrestling with an angel at the Jabbok is another example. Jacob manages to limp away with his life, though he bears the distinguishing mark of a victim (Gn 32:24–30). At this stage of the discussion Girard is not yet announcing a breakthrough beyond normal mythological outcomes, but these unexpected survivals and reconciliations are surely suggestive of that.[3]

Noah and his family are also survivors of what Girard identifies as a mimetic catastrophe rather than the victims one might expect them to be in a mythical-sounding story like theirs—one beginning with a global crisis, complete with distinction-blurring divine human marriages, the monstrous birth of giants, and finally the flood (Gn 6–8).[4] It is notable, therefore, that it is violent humanity that perishes and not Noah's family. Likewise, Lot and his family survive the cataclysmic violence that destroys Sodom and Gomorrah (apart from Lot's wife, whose climactic death suggests to Girard the vestige of an earlier single-victim account) (Gn 19:1–26).[5] In both these cases, so redolent of myth, the standard mythological outcome is problematized.

Further evidence of a climb down from sacrificial religion begins with the substitution of ritual circumcision for human sacrifice.[6] Girard also discerns an arc leading away from human sacrifice to that of animals. His examples are the story of Abraham, in which a ram is sacrificed instead of Isaac (Gn 22:1–14); the use of animal skins on Jacob's body to fool his father, Isaac, and avoid a curse (Gn 27:14–23);[7] and the slaughter of Passover lambs in lieu of divine destruction, where the emphasis further shifts from sacrificial killing to the shared meal (Ex 12). Only one step remains along this arc in the Hebrew Bible, according to Girard, and that is the prophetic renunciation of sacrifice altogether.[8]

The Myth of Cain

Girard notes the typical mimetic elements in Genesis 4, of rival brothers one of whom kills the other, whereupon a community is founded. A law against murder is set in place, involving the restraint-inducing threat of sevenfold retribution. Cain's "mark" ensures differentiation, heading off descent into the undifferentiation of violent mimetic conflict. So far, so conventionally mythological.

Yet God's concern throughout sounds a new note. Unlike Romulus, Cain is never excused: "Where is your brother Abel? . . . What have you done? Listen; your brother's blood is crying out to me from the ground" (Gn 4:9–10). Also, although the typical mythical differentiating and founding are present, their effect here is short-lived; the violent crisis quickly reasserts itself clothed in undifferentiating imagery as the great flood.[9] The myth is not working. Moreover, there is a shift in perspective, away from the agenda of the persecutor to that of the victim, as Girard explains: "Certainly there must be, behind the biblical account, myths in conformity with the universal norms of mythology; so the initiative of the Jewish authors and their critical reappraisal must undoubtedly be credited with the affirmation that the victim is innocent and that the culture founded on murder retains a thoroughly murderous character that in the end becomes self-destructive, once the ordering and sacrificial benefits of the original violence have dissipated."[10] Girard concludes that "Abel is only the first in a long line of victims whom the Bible exhumes and exonerates."[11]

Joseph and His Brothers

The extended narrative of Genesis 37–50 begins with collective persecution fully visible. Young Joseph, Jacob's favorite son, has a dream establishing his superiority over his rivalrous brothers, who expel him into Egyptian slavery. They tell their father that Joseph has been killed by a wild animal. Yet Joseph flourishes in exile, eventually saving his family once his brothers repudiate their former scapegoating behavior. Girard is sure that in an earlier stage of this myth the sacrifice of a goat in order to bloody Joseph's coat and so to deceive his father would have been significant. We also note incestuous overtones typical of myth in the accusation against Joseph that he attempted to rape the wife of his Egyptian master (and father substitute), Potiphar. Girard expects that in an earlier version Joseph would have been blamed for causing disorder and his brothers exonerated, with Joseph subsequently providing benefits following his deification.

Hints of all these usual mythical themes are indeed present in the story, from Joseph's earlier hubris to his miraculous role in the family's survival.[12] And, not surprisingly, they feature in two later Egyptian versions of the Joseph story, dating from Hellenistic times, in which Joseph's dream-divining skills make him a magus and in which with Moses he is a leader of the Hebrews who are expelled by Pharaoh to pacify the Kingdom. "Joseph is thus an Egyptian gone awry, and although the Egyptian version does not divinize the entire group of Hebrews" (i.e., after first scapegoating them by expulsion), as James G. Williams points out, "Joseph is retained in the mythical tradition as a kind of divinity-victim."[13]

But things are very different in the way Genesis handles this material. The presence of separate adaptations edited together in the final text proves the presence of an earlier myth, which these later writers have altered. This transformation is evident, for instance, in the way Reuben (Elohist version, Gn 37:21–22) and Judah (Yahwist version, Gn 37:26–27) stand up for their victimized brother.[14] Girard makes a comparison with similar myths in order to highlight further differences. The parents of Oedipus and the brothers of Joseph rid themselves of their problem child in similar ways, with mothers and fathers or their substitutes serving as victims of the hero's alleged transgression in both stories. But that is where the similarity ends, as Girard points out: "Instead of being first demonized, then divinized— in the sense that Oedipus is—Joseph is admirably humanized."[15] In a French interview Girard highlights the fundamental discrepancy between these two stories as to their hero's innocence.

> Dans les deux textes le héros se trouve associé à un fléau social terrible, la sécheresse d'un côté, la peste de l'autre. Et la vraie question de deux textes est: est-il coupable? À cette question, le mythe païen répond toujours: « Oui Œdipe est coupable, oui il menace son père et sa mère, oui il a commis le parricide et l'inceste, oui c'est lui qui est responsable de la peste, il doit être châtié. » Tandis que le texte biblique répond: « Non, ce sont les douze [*sic*] frères hypocrites

et les Égyptiens qui colportent des mensonges au sujet de Joseph, faisant de lui un bouc émissaire. Joseph, en réalité, est innocent. »

(In the two texts the hero finds himself associated with a terrible social curse, drought in one case, plague in the other. And the real question of the two texts is, is he guilty? To that question, pagan myth always responds, "Yes Oedipus is guilty, yes he threatens his father and mother, yes he committed parricide and incest, yes it is him who is responsible for the plague, he has to be punished." While the biblical text responds, "No, it is the twelve [sic] hypocritical brothers and the Egyptians who are peddling lies about Joseph, making a scapegoat of him. Joseph, in reality, is innocent.)[16]

In another parallel Greek myth that Girard mentions, Hippolytus is understood to be justly punished for showing hubris, even though he was resisting Phaedra's improper advances, whereas Joseph's innocence in the episode with Potiphar's wife is emphasized.[17] Later in the Genesis story, when Joseph's brothers approach Egypt's grand vizier to buy food in a time of famine, they do not recognize him as Joseph, and he decides to see if they have changed. He tricks them by arranging for Benjamin—the next youngest, and his father's new favorite—to be put in jeopardy. But Judah puts himself in Benjamin's place, refusing to let another be expelled, thus indicating the extent to which the Bible's story of Joseph and his brothers commends a conversion of heart (Gn 42–45).[18]

The Jesuit theologian Leo Lefebure, attempting to discredit Girard on religion in general and Judeo-Christian distinctiveness in particular, insists that the Joseph story does not represent a distinctive breakthrough. He points to the nonpersecutory attitude evident to him in a much earlier Egyptian myth—one acknowledged to have influenced the Genesis text.[19] The "Tale of Two Brothers," dated around the early second millennium B.C.E., has Bata, the younger brother of Anubis, blamed by his sister-in-law for making advances when in fact Bata had resisted advances from her. Pursued by Anubis for his supposed betrayal, Bata pleads his innocence, cutting off his penis as a sign of good faith and feeding it to the fish. Convinced now of Bata's integrity, Anubis kills his lying wife. Bata himself is killed incognito three times as the story progresses, thanks to his own angry and unforgiving wife, twice involving the felling of trees by teams of men and once when slaughterers are sent to sacrifice a bullock. But like a trickster Bata is reborn each time. Finally, Bata becomes Pharaoh and promotes Anubis.[20] No founding murders or subsequent divinizations here, Lefebure decides, and proof positive of a victim being counted innocent apart from the Bible. He concludes that "the Egyptian tale had vindicated the scapegoat long before the birth of Israel."[21]

Applying Girard's method of reading, however,[22] one might conclude that Bata was indeed sacrificed (thrice in person, once "in penis"), judged innocent *retrospectively*—as befits an established Egyptian deity in this, his "prequel"—then resurrected, divinized (i.e., in becoming Pharaoh), and hence treated no differently from other pagan myths. The story of Joseph and his brothers in Genesis has an entirely different feel to it, with its persistent emphasis on innocence and forgiveness, including its intentional renunciation of scapegoating. I may be wrong about this. Girard does indeed acknowledge instances of victim innocence discerned in pagan antiquity (e.g., Socrates, Antigone)[23] and in the Vedas,[24] though never sufficient to influence and transform a whole society. So even if Lefebure is right about Bata, this isolated example does not prove Girard wrong on the Bible's distinctiveness.

The Ten Commandments

Girard addresses the Ten Commandments (Ex 20:1–17) in the context of mimetic rivalry and the public risk of violence, insisting that they represent anything but the hatred of freedom that today's libertarian spirit condemns in religion. On the contrary, such prohibitions began entirely pragmatically, because "indifference to the threat of runaway conflict is a luxury that small ancient societies could not afford."[25] Thus the Commandments about killing, adultery, stealing, and false witness are best understood as necessary warnings against behavior that heightens violence by awakening jealous rivalries and vendettas. In general, then, Girard finds the Decalogue consistent with primitive religious prohibitions, though more lucid.[26]

The key to his interpretation, and to the Decalogue's distinctiveness, is the Tenth Commandment, addressing the heart of the matter, mimetic desire for objects belonging to the likeliest potential model of desire, and hence rival, our neighbor: "You shall not covet your neighbor's house; you shall not covet your neighbor's wife, or male or female slave, or ox, or donkey, or anything that belongs to your neighbor" (Ex 20:17). Girard:

> In reading the Tenth Commandment one has the impression of being present at the intellectual process of its elaboration. To prevent people from fighting, the lawgiver seeks at first to forbid all the objects about which they ceaselessly fight, and he decides to make a list of these. However, he quickly perceives that the objects are too numerous: he cannot enumerate all of them. So he interrupts himself in the process, gives up focussing on the objects that keep changing anyway, and he turns to what never changes. Or rather, he turns to that one who is always present, the neighbour. One always desires *whatever belongs to that one,* the neighbour.[27]

Getting at the root of destructive desire is the aim here, anticipating Jesus' attention to right desiring rather than to prohibitions that can give it only partial expression. Hence Jesus' advice—regularly misunderstood but in fact not at all egotistical—to imitate him. What we truly imitate is his *desire,* which is to do the will of his Father. Because in so doing, we are freed from models of desire who will lead us into rivalry and violence.[28] I return to this in the conclusion to this volume.

The Prophets

Girard's brief discussion of the prophets in *Things Hidden Since the Foundation of the World* emphasizes their significant advance on earlier books of the law, which retain (alongside a number of breakthroughs already noted) elements of standard prohibitions typical of archaic religion. In particular, Girard mentions fear of undifferentiation and mixed states, on which the anthropologist Mary Douglas writes so insightfully (though Girard thinks that she misses the crucial motive for these concerns, which is fear of the escalating violence that such uncontrolled undifferentiation suggests).[29]

Girard's main commentary on the prophets concerns the so-called Servant Songs of Isaiah (Isa 42:1–4, 49:1–6, 50:4–9, 52:13–53:12), in particular, the fourth song with its enigmatic figure of the Servant whose sacrifice God allows, yet whose innocence is emphasized and whose killing at human hands is declared to be undeserved. This is contrasted with a more usual mythological assessment, as reflected in Isaiah 53:4b: "yet we accounted him stricken, struck down by God, and afflicted." "In other words," explains Girard, "this was not so. It was not God who smote him; God's responsibility is explicitly denied."[30] Some years later Girard developed his insight into Isaiah's text as exposing the horror of mimetic crisis and founding murder. The flattening and undifferentiating of Isaiah 40:3–4 (in words made famous by Handel's *Messiah*, about valleys lifted up, mountains and hills made low and the rough places plain) actually refers to a violent mimetic crisis, subsequently resolved in Isaiah 52–53 by lynching the suffering servant.[31]

Other Girardian writers also address this fourth servant song. Williams, for example, finds that the servant offers himself knowingly to pacify a society in crisis,[32] concluding memorably that "it is not the will of God to bruise him, but it is the will of God to use him."[33] According to the Austrian Jesuit Raymund Schwager, whose theological work on Girard influenced Girard himself, the suffering servant is a signal breakthrough in understanding the nature of biblical revelation in comparison to the archaic sacred. "If sacred ideas and concepts develop from aggressive projections," Schwager writes, "then the true God will reveal himself most clearly where the world of violence also is most decisively contrasted to him. If the gods are the product of human mechanisms, then he must appear most clearly in that world of violence as a person where this mechanism is most radically unmasked."[34] Yet Girard acknowledges the continuing ambiguity about sacred violence even in these most advanced Old Testament texts. It is never fully gone, as nearby texts like Isaiah 53:10 make clear: "Yet it was the will of the Lord to crush him with pain."[35]

Further insights on the prophets emerge elsewhere in the Girardian conversation. Williams highlights Amos 5:21–24 as the first explicit prophetic denunciation of sacrifice, calling Israel to a preferential option for the poor and needy—an antisacrificial posture that Hosea presents in terms of rejecting false gods (Hos 4:12–13).[36] Ezekiel actually condemns the earlier state of statutes and ordinances (Ez 20:25–26), while Jeremiah points beyond the heteronomy characteristic of the archaic sacred, with its externalized means of control, toward a true theonomy—an internalized law of the heart (Jer 31:33).[37]

Alison pays close attention to three prophetic texts, showing how personal anger in the prophet and a punishing God in the prophet's proclamation go together. He charts a climb down on the part of God's self-appointed enforcer, Elijah (1 Kgs 18–19), beginning after his bloody triumph against the sacrificial priests of Baal.[38] For Alison, all such aspects of Elijah's dramatic and violent public career are disavowed by God, who appears thereafter as a still, small voice, with no more grand tasks for Elijah. He must begin again after the collapse of the sacred, and Jerusalem's exile, with a new view of God as one who is not a violent sacred competitor with Baal or with anyone else. "At the end of his undeceiving," Alison concludes, "Elijah is more Yahwist, more atheist, less of a shaman, less of a sacrificer, because God is not like the gods, not even so as to show himself superior to them. The cave at Horeb was, for Elijah, the theological space for a cracking of heart."[39] The still, small voice is a sign of the real God's silence among the clamoring mimetic voices of this world, disavowing their human-only agenda of making life secure and meaningful that always involves unacknowledged victims.[40] Alison also writes about Jonah overcoming his anger against Nineveh, having to catch up with God's forgiveness. Jonah's period in the belly of the great fish is a symbol of his being held in being by God in a place of deep personal transformation while his own theological "cracking of heart" takes place.[41]

Alison's third example is Ezekiel, who undergoes the exilic Yahwistic revolution in his own person. Ezekiel abandons the temple and its religion of sacrifice, along with his own angry projection of spurned love onto God. Thus he arrives eventually at a life-giving vision for Israel beyond loyalty to a system that God is abandoning.[42] The Ezekiel 37 vision of a valley filled with dry bones, on which God's Spirit moves to rehabilitate history's slain multitude of unacknowledged victims, is the positive image with which Girard concludes

Things Hidden Since the Foundation of the World,[43] looking forward to the New Testament for a fuller revelation of this vision.

The Psalms and Job

In an article on the notoriously violent language of payback found in the Psalms, Girard admits its presence. But with C. S. Lewis he contrasts such hot-blooded explicitness with the cold cruelties and brutal insensitivities of pagan texts.[44] This violence is often deplored in enlightened modern circles (Anglican prayer books typically list the most offensive verses for ease of leaving them out), but Girard notes that the actual persecution that inspires the angry psalmic responses is never singled out for criticism, as if the persecution to which the Psalms refer were some sort of hallucination. Yet the commonness of mob violence in mythology prompts Girard's belief that it must have been far more common in archaic societies than anthropologists typically acknowledge. So the Psalms reveal what was really going on. Girard is reminded by Schwager that in 100 of 150 psalms we encounter a victim at the center of a group of persecutors.[45] Israel's psalms of malediction and execration are the first texts in history in which this victim actually speaks out, reclaiming the voices of victims formerly reduced to silent cogs in a mythological machine.[46]

As for the sharp contrast that this anger poses to the serene harmony of persecutors, as heard for instance in Greek myth—"who maintain that they did the right thing in lynching their victims"— Girard insists that "in the Bible we hear from the victims themselves who do not see lynching as a nice thing, and tell us so in extremely violent words."[47] Hence we learn the truth about mythology and the primitive sacred. "The victim of the Psalms is disturbing, it is true," Girard wryly acknowledges, "and even annoying compared with an Oedipus who has the good taste to join in the wonderful classical harmony."[48] He certainly agrees that we should resile from such violent tirades, having acknowledged the reality of the victim—not because we moderns are more advanced and spiritually discerning, however, but because the Bible has taught us to do so.[49] Jesus calls us to forgive such persecutors, "for they know not what they do."

Girard points to the Book of Job as an enormously enlarged psalm of malediction, adding that if Job were a myth the only viewpoint we would have would be that of his friends.[50] In *Job: The Victim of His People,* Girard views Job as a fallen public figure scapegoated in some brouhaha whose friends sacralize their persecuting violence by metamorphosing their insults and meanness "into the grandiose accomplishments of a supernatural mission."[51] But Job is a failed scapegoat because he reveals the mythology striving to envelop him, scorning the show trial where he was meant to capitulate and confess.[52] According to Girard, "What is most important in the book of Job is, not the murderous conformity of the multitude, but the final audacity of the hero himself, whom we see hesitate at length, vacillate, then finally take hold of the mimetic contagion and defeat it. In doing this, Job not only resists totalitarian contagion but wrests the deity out of the process of persecution to envision him as the God of victims, not of persecutors. This is what Job means when he affirms, 'As for me, I know that my Defender lives' (19:25)."[53]

Hence the real God emerges to trump the social god of *vox populi, vox dei,* who is what we always get from the scapegoat system—a god who does our human dirty work for us.[54] This is the false god to whom Job's three friends cling (Job 3:1–31:40), and who ultimately takes the stage in a long concluding monologue (Job 38:1–48:6). Here Job is confronted with a grand ecological and providential vision to which many theologians are still drawn, as if the question were primarily one of theodicy. Yet the real God is not a metaphysical proposition about how suffering and death can be reconciled with meaning and purpose. This philosophers' god is another fabricated deity of persecution, erecting stability and meaning over the graves of victims.

Girard insists that if there is only the mob and the victim, then the real God must be found suffering alongside the victim. Of this God, a God not made with human hands, Girard says, "If the logic of this God shares nothing in common with that of the God of persecution and its mystifying mimesis, the only possible means of intervention in the world is that illustrated by the Gospel." To which I will presently turn.

For now, I close this section on the Hebrew Bible with a brief comment on the unfinished transformation we find there. A struggle remains between the mesmerizing power of sacred violence and an emerging God beyond all such projections.[55] Schwager delineates four series of texts in the Hebrew Bible that chart the development of human religious sensibility along the direction Girard has identified.

1. God appears as an irrational being killing or wanting to kill without apparent reason.
2. He reacts to evil deeds perpetrated by humans, and himself takes revenge.
3. He punishes evildoers by delivering them in his anger to other (cruel) human beings.
4. The wicked are punished by their deeds' recoiling on themselves.[56]

Schwager clarifies the latter points by reminding us that Hebrew thought does not always distinguish (i.e., in the Aristotelian manner) between active causing and passive letting-be, such that what *we* know to be wholly human violence is still ascribed to God.[57] Williams offers some further mitigation by suggesting that the new thing invariably suffers by being expressed in the language and thought-world of the old.[58] But in the end Girard sits with the unresolved problem, the unfulfilled promise, of these new developments coexisting with echoes of the old violent sacred. "In the Hebrew Bible, there is clearly a dynamic that moves in the direction of the rehabilitation of the victims," he insists, "but it is not a cut-and-dried thing. Rather, it is a process under way, a text in travail; it is not a chronologically progressive process, but a struggle that advances and retreats."[59]

CHRIST, THE BONFIRE OF THE VANITIES

René Girard is causing a revolution in how the New Testament is read. Through his own writings and those of his dialogue partners Robert Hamerton-Kelly, James G. Williams, Gil Baillie, Raymund Schwager, and James Alison—as well as Sunday-by-Sunday and text-by-text compilations of these insights by Paul Nuechterlein on the preaching website girardianlectionary.net—the New Testament emerges as thematically coherent, mimetically self-aware, deeply culturally and psychologically savvy, and positively catastrophic for every pretense of the false sacred. Girard provides a powerful and fruitful hermeneutical strategy. No Christian priest or minister who catches on will be content with preaching shallow platitudes: a pallid pietism, a conventional moralism, a reactionary conservatism, a stubborn biblical literalism, a demythologizing rationalism, a Jungian spirituality, or a soft-left social gospel. Whether in presenting Jesus' teaching and praxis, his definitive clash with the powers and principalities at Easter, his life-changing impact on Paul and other canonical witnesses, or his apocalyptic unraveling of culture's sacred protection against violence, the New Testament reveals a semirealized dream called the Kingdom of God.

In the remainder of this chapter I propose to state Girard's case for Jesus' apocalyptic impact—a secularizing tide sweeping the West toward modernity and which, perhaps in time, will bring the end of history to a world shorn of archaic sacred protection. My first stop is Girard's brief overview, in *Things Hidden Since the Foundation of the World*, of what was then a new breakthrough. Next comes Girard's discussion of Jesus' cross and resurrection, looking chiefly to *The Scapegoat* and *I See Satan Fall Like Lightning*. Finally, I introduce Girard's insights on Jesus' secularizing impact, which, ironically, Nietzsche was the first to really understand.

Gospel, Sacrifice, Apocalypse

In *Things Hidden Since the Foundation of the World*, Girard argues that the Gospels supply what was left incomplete by Hebrew Scripture.[60] Jesus curses the Pharisees for all prophets, wise men, and scribes murdered since the foundation of the world, from Abel to Zechariah—"the A–Z of false religion," as Giles Fraser calls it.[61] Of course, it is not just Israel and its Pharisees, but the whole violent mechanism of culture and religion that Girard calls to account.[62]

This scapegoat mechanism is what Jesus means when he refers to Satan, as Girard argues. Satan is not the horned figure of popular imagination, or the personal supernatural antagonist of fevered fundamentalist dualism. *Satan* is a *technical term*, signifying the mimetic charade, with its lies, rivalries, and obstacles. Satan is the destructive escalation of scandal, the reliance of human world-making on violence and its false sacred repression, and therefore "all the forms of lying order in which humanity lives." This is why Satan can tempt Jesus with world dominion in the wilderness (Mt 4:8–10; Lk 4:5–8), because such dominion belongs to this "transcendent source of falsehood that infiltrates every domain and structures everything in its own image."[63] Hence Satan, the "murderer from the beginning" (Jn 8:44), is more malign and dangerous as an interdividual sociocultural force than as an actual supernatural individual.

Typically, all such surrogate violence at the root of culture is violently disavowed, as Jesus reveals in his repeated emphasis on tombs and the concealment they signify (e.g., Lk 11:44).[64] As for the whited sepulchers to which Jesus compares the scribes and Pharisees (Mt 23:27), Girard explains that "the rotting corpse inside and the beautiful structure around it resemble the entire process of human culture in its relationship to the original victim."[65]

It is preeminently in the passion narratives that Jesus reveals the surrogate victim mechanism as the basis of religion and culture, whereby a stone rejected by the builders becomes the cornerstone (Lk 20:17).[66] Jesus is himself sacrificed outside the holy city to avoid contamination in a way very familiar from archaic religion, establishing his representative solidarity with every surrogate victim. This is reiterated in the account of Stephen's martyrdom, in case we missed the point (Acts 7:51–58).[67] Thus Jesus makes possible the building of a new structure, on a new cornerstone. And instead of yet one more tomb becoming the sacred shrine of a sacrificed and divinized victim,[68] Jesus' empty tomb is a sign "that the new beginning constituted by Easter reaches so deep that the ultimate foundations of human culture itself, until now veiled, are laid bare."[69]

Girard takes pains to clarify the nature of Jesus' sacrifice, in particular, just how God is *and is not* involved in it. The violence against Jesus is a necessary step in God's revelation of the truth of things to humanity. By "submitting to violence," as Girard explains, "Christ reveals and uproots the structural matrix of all religion."[70] Here the divinity typically ascribed to the scapegoat in mythology reappears but in a way that does not issue from the scapegoat mechanism. "God willingly becomes the scapegoat of his own people not for the purpose of evacuating internal violence through the old mythical understanding but for the opposite reason," Girard explains, "for clearing up . . . all such misunderstandings and raising humanity above the culture of scapegoating."[71]

But Jesus' death is not God's doing, let alone any sort of price exacted by God. Such misguided Christian (and atheistic) readings of the passion texts are dismissed by Girard as just one more chapter in the history of sacrificial religion. They have cost Christianity its proper distinctiveness, and its appeal in the eyes of many modern people of goodwill.[72] Girard identifies as central for understanding his take on Jesus' death a Deutero-Pauline text in Colossians 2:13–15. Here Jesus' cross erases the record standing against humanity and overcomes the principalities and powers (named in this text as the world's rulers and authorities), thus achieving a triumph—also described as a revelation—in the form of their disempowering exposure to public ridicule. "The bond that stood against us with its demands is human culture, which is the terrifying reflection of our own violence," explains Girard. "By dissipating all this ignorance, the cross triumphs over the powers, brings them into ridicule, and exposes the pitiful secret of the mechanism of sacralization."[73]

In chapter 1 I noted Girard's use of apocalyptic language to describe modernity's mimetic descent into ontological sickness. Apocalypse is culture's natural fate once deprived of the old false sacred protection. And this has nothing to do with divine violence. Rather, it is and always was about strictly *human* violence, as Girard highlights with a powerful insight into Jesus' apocalyptic vineyard parable about the destruction of unjust tenants who have murdered the owner's son. This punishment is *proposed by the hearers* but never ascribed to God: "*they say* to *him*, 'He will put those wretches to a miserable death'" (see Mt 21:40–41).[74] If there is terror in apocalyptic, then, Girard insists that it is human, not divine, terror. It is the demystifying of divine punishment, which is revealed as a figment of the punishing human imagination.[75] So, for Girard, "if men turn down the peace Jesus offers them—a peace which is not derived from violence and that, by virtue of this fact, *passes human understanding*, the effect of the Gospel revelation will be made manifest through violence, through a sacrificial and cultural crisis whose radical effect must be unprecedented since there is no longer any sacralized victim to stand in the way of its consequences."[76]

Jesus' kingdom of peace entails a share in his self-sacrifice as the cost of renouncing complicity in sacrificial violence, and hence a share in God's life—of which Jesus' share is preeminent, because he transcended the false sacred in his own person.[77] From his birth marked by a heavenly portent (Mt 2:1–2), Jesus is set against typical human cultural dynamics as the bringer of countertranscendence.[78] Jesus' birth according to the Gospels of Matthew (1:18–2:23), Luke (1–2), and, from a different perspective, John (1:1–18) is described in terms quite different from those of heroic miracle births in archaic and classical mythology. For Girard, "Saying that Christ is God, born of God, and saying that he has been conceived without sin is stating over again that he is completely alien to the world of violence within which humankind has been imprisoned ever since the foundation of the world."[79]

Easter, the Turning Point of History

In *The Scapegoat*, Girard looks in detail at the passion narratives and other gospel texts that illuminate them. He deepens earlier insights into the nature of mimesis, mythology, and world making by showing how Jesus begins their unraveling. In *I See Satan Fall Like Lightning*, Girard's exploration of Jesus' historical impact focuses on the triumph of his cross, part of which of course is the resurrection.

Crux Probat Omnia

Jesus' passion narratives confront the world of myth by internal subversion rather than external assault. Girard believes that their use of typical mythic themes such as victim immolation to reestablish order allows mythical illusions to be discredited point by point.[80] Because the text informs its audience that Jesus is innocent, his universal condemnation and calls for his sacrifice reveal the extent of their deluded blindness. The mimetic crowd and its sacred violence is formidable, however, co-opting even Peter and overcoming the rationality of Roman law whereby Pilate had declared Jesus innocent (most explicitly in Lk 23:4)—even converting to friendship such old enemies as Pilate and Herod (Lk 23:12).[81] Jesus states (with precise technical intent, Girard insists) that his persecutors do not know what they are doing (Lk 23:34), a conviction later echoed in a sermon of Peter (Acts 3:17). This constitutes for Girard a first-ever definition of the human unconscious, though understood in terms of intersubjective mimetic entrapment rather than the depth dimension of individual minds familiar from Freud and Jung.[82] This *méconnaissance,* shared by the whole crowd, extends to the fact of the whole scapegoating mechanism itself, not just to the individual so designated.[83] But *we readers* know what is going on, as Jesus is named "lamb of God" and the high priest matter-of-factly states that one man needs to die for the people (Jn 18:14).

Emphasizing the continuity between Jesus' death and the universality of mimetically driven surrogate victimage, Girard then shows how the execution of John the Baptist parallels Jesus' passion in Mark (6:17–29). This verifies "the systematic character of evangelical thought on the subject of collective murder and its role in the genesis of non-Christian religion."[84] All the mimetic dynamics are there: the rivalrous brothers; the twinned names (Herod/Herodias); that virgin magnet of mimeticism, the dancing daughter, who borrows her desire for the Baptist's death from her mother; the mimetic intimidation of Herod by the dignity of a powerful crowd assembled; the Baptist as an obstacle on whom Herod and Herodias were fixated; and finally the ritual nature of Herod's birthday celebration, providing a lens for intensifying mimesis to the point of sacrifice.[85] Here Girard introduces in passing a new thematic connection between mimesis, obstacle fascination, and sacrifice, seeing the first of these as inevitably spawning the last once a particular point of intensity has been passed.

> The diffusion of mimeticism at the height of its intensity guarantees the absence of any real object for the desire. Beyond a certain threshold hate exists without . . . need of cause or pretext; there

remain only intertwined desires, buttressed against one another. If these desires are divided and set in opposition as they focus on the object they wish to preserve—alive, in order to monopolize it, as in Herod's case, when he imprisons the prophet—then by becoming purely destructive these same desires may be reconciled. This is the terrible paradox of human desires. They can never be reconciled in the preservation of their object but only through its destruction; they can only find agreement at the expense of a victim.[86]

Girard illustrates the other aspect of mythology, the divinization of the victim shown in the belief of Herod and some in the crowd that Jesus is the slain Baptist resurrected (Mk 6:14–16). The gospel text is having none of it, however: Peter explicitly denies this allegation (Mk 8:27–30).

But the mechanism is not done with. Girard again emphasizes the stubborn intractability of mimeticism and its escalation toward scapegoating in his account of Peter's denial (Mk 14:66–72). Like Pilate and Herod, now Peter too is weak, eager for acceptance as part of the crowd gathered around that highly symbolic fire in the High Priest's courtyard. A mimetically adept servant girl tries to exclude Peter, but the deserter typically seeks to reestablish his belonging at the expense of disavowing former friends. Peter's obsession with success, which caused Jesus to name him Satan (Mk 8:31–33), and the rivalry he demonstrated even when claiming to be Jesus' most reliable champion (Mk 14:30–31)—hence the virtual indistinguishability of Peter's commitment to Christ and his commitment to being on the winning team—shows how deep, uniform, and intractable the Gospels recognize mimetic dynamics to be.[87]

Girard identifies another gospel example of this intractability of mimesis and sacrifice in the narrative about demons at Gerasa (Mk 5:1–20). There we find a neat false sacred system in which regular expulsion of its tame demoniac unifies the community, with the victim even joining in the stoning by doing it to himself. The mimetic twinning on which this convenient arrangement hangs is emphasized in Matthew's version where there are two demoniacs (Mt 8:28–34). The stoning which Jesus heads off (that of the woman taken in adultery: Jn 8:1–12) and his own risk of being edged over a cliff at Nazareth (Lk 4:29) are called to mind by this story, as the Roman pigs plunge to their deaths in place of the human victim and hence reveal *by its reversal* the universal mechanism by which societies everywhere establish their stability.[88] Imagine, with Girard, if only the *pharmakos* survived while all the Greek philosophers and mathematicians went over the cliff. Or picture it in a Roman context: "Instead of the outcast being toppled from the heights of the Tarpeian rock it is the majestic consuls, virtuous Cato, solemn juriconsults, the procurators of Judea, and all the rest of the *senatus populusque romanus*. All of them disappear into the abyss while the ex-victim, 'clothed and in his full senses,' calmly observes from above the astounding sight."[89] The expulsion that Jesus brings is not on a par with such typical satanic or false sacred expulsion, which propagates the system. Rather, the pigs and the demons are gone for good, and the Gerasenes, with their former demoniac, must face the alarming prospect of a new future beyond the mimetic surrogate victimage of their uneasy but stable past.

So Jesus is God's great advocate for the defense of victims, and after his ascension the Holy Spirit of God takes on the same role. Girard mentions Paul's conversion as an instance of this Paraclete at work, turning the heart of a young enforcer to the realization that his beloved law, with its exclusive righteousness, was really a system of *self-righteousness* secured at the expense of innocent victims who were actually at one with Christ himself (Acts 9:1–22). This is the Paraclete's message for every witch-hunter and totalitarian bureaucrat thereafter, says Girard—though while such as these maintain the system by unwitting violence, those who learn the Gospels' lesson must forgive them, as Jesus did.

The Triumph of the Cross

In *I See Satan Fall Like Lightning* Girard considers the triumph of Jesus' cross in a more theological, less scripturally based discussion, looking first at Jesus' resurrection. Its difference from the pagan resurrections of mythology is pointed out. Jesus is not declared divine by a murderous crowd miraculously unified by his death but by a dissident minority in an outcome without parallel in mythology.[90] Luke indicates his awareness of such pagan resurrections stemming from the collective murder with two examples: Herod and Pilate reconciled and Herod's fascinated dread of John the Baptist coming back to life.[91] Girard explains elsewhere that "just as the revelation of the Christian victim differs from mythical revelations because it is not rooted in the illusion of the guilty scapegoat, so the Christian resurrection differs from mythical ones because its witnesses are the people who ultimately overcome the contagion of victimization (such as Peter and Paul) and not the people who surrender to it (such as Herod and Pilate)."[92]

Likewise, the resurrection is God's great testimony to Jesus' innocence, and as *God's act*, it is precisely *not* the act of any crowd, or of Israel as a whole: "God has made him both Lord and Christ, this Jesus whom you crucified (Acts 2:36)."[93] So Jesus' divinity is not the product of mythical snowballing but rather its decisive critique.[94]

What the cross conquers, according to Girard, is paganism's way of organizing the world. It deprives the victim mechanism of the concealment it requires to operate.[95] The powers and principalities are defeated expressly by being put on display in this way, so that Satan can no longer cast out Satan—so that the evils of violent escalation no longer succumb to the real but unacknowledged evils of the surrogate victim mechanism, producing the deviated transcendence that stabilizes society.[96] Girard puts it in terms of Satan being duped by the cross—a theme found in Paul's comments on the ignorance of the powers (1 Cor 2:7–9) and in Origen and the Greek fathers, though it is typically discounted in modernity.[97] Yet a mimetic reading can illuminate this theme from Christian antiquity. "Since the 'princes of this world' were not in communion with God," Girard explains, "they did not understand that the victim mechanism they unleashed against Jesus would result in truthful accounts. If they had been able to read the future, not only would they not have encouraged the Crucifixion, but they would have opposed it with all their might."[98]

Hence Jesus' claim not to bring peace but a sword (Mt 10:34), which Girard understands as Jesus' refusal to serve as a prop for the status quo in society. This Jesus enacts by hastening the collapse of all pagan means for social protection.[99]

The Gospels do everything that the (Old Testament) Bible had done before, rehabilitating a victimized prophet, a wrongly accused victim. But they also universalize this rehabilitation. They show that, since the foundation of the world, the victims of all Passion-like murders have been victims of the same mob contagion as Jesus. The Gospels make the revelation complete because they give to the biblical denunciation of idolatry a concrete demonstration of how false Gods and their violent cultural systems are generated. This is the truth missing from mythology, the truth that subverts the violent system of this world. This revelation of collective violence as a lie is the earmark of Christianity. This is what is unique about Christianity. And this uniqueness is true.[100]

This is a very practical approach to divinity on Girard's part. Though it does not disavow supernatural and metaphysical claims, it adheres by preference to the cultural-historical facts of human existence, so that "no appeal to the supernatural should break the thread of anthropological analyses."[101] Thus he acts to save the supernatural from becoming a religious idealism.[102] To this end, Girard boldly claims that his conclusions do not require faith's validation, because common sense suffices. He insists that "the superiority of the Bible and the Gospels can be demonstrated scientifically."[103] Girard's claim for Christian uniqueness is absolutely convinced but also absolutely *from below:* "The biblical revelation (exposure) of mythology ... rests on commonsensical observations. It requires no religious commitment to be understood. Far from being an ethnocentric prejudice in favour of our own religion, the Judeo-Christian claim to unique truthfulness, almost universally reviled and ridiculed these days, is objectively, verifiably true."[104]

The important corollary for Girard is that Christians must handle these momentous truths respectfully, to avoid making them appear parochial and self-justifying and hence drawing attention away from their crucial world historical significance. "If the intellectual independence of the mimetic theory is obscured," Girard insists, "if it is perceived as a mere servant of this or that theology, *ancilla theologiae,* its effectiveness is nullified."[105] I want to conclude this chapter by considering the nature of that effectiveness—how these Judeo-Christian truths changed the Western world, driving it toward secular modernity.

CHRIST AND CULTURE

For Girard, the death of Jesus is the end of the archaic sacred, revealing the truth of surrogate victimage. The temple veil is torn on Good Friday (Mt 27:51), exposing the place of sacrifice for what it is, and the graves are opened. "These are the victims who have been assassinated since the foundation of the world," Girard explains, "who begin to return upon this earth and make themselves known."[106] Furthermore, Jesus' resurrection is not a phoenixlike rebirth from the ashes of violence—not just one more "pagan resurrection" confirming that religion based on sacrifice is working to specifications—but a gift from God, leaving behind an empty tomb on the way to a quite different future.[107] Thus the Gospels slander and undermine archaic religion,[108] ushering in what Alison calls "the time of Abel"—the last day of history, the postsacrificial world.[109]

Jesus' resurrection brought about for Saint Paul the death of what Michel Serres described as his "libido of belonging," comprising the religious nexus of Jewish monotheism, Greek cosmos, and Roman law. Paul's former secure place of mastery was thus replaced by a markedly rootless, homeless, and individual existence.[110] Hence a comparatively benign secularity and nonreligious holiness begins to replace what Alison calls "cheap togetherness and junk goodness."[111] Girard understands this desacralizing process, unleashed by the Gospels, as the truest meaning of Western culture's much-vaunted "death of God," but this death refers to the old gods of sacrifice rather than the Christian God who has nothing to do with them.[112] From a mustard seed, which represents a very small start indeed, Christ's historical impact grows like a spreading tree, with many secularizing birds nesting in its branches (Mt 13:31–32).[113]

But world history in general, and church history in particular, shows this transformation to have been neither straightforward nor uncontested. The Christian revelation, which disrupts cultures, was soon enlisted in forming a culture of its own, involving accommodation with the sacrificial past. And this even though the new wine was not supposed to be put into old wineskins (Lk 5:36–39)[114]—even though the gospel is a force for the undoing of systems, so that we should never presume to make it into one.[115] Girard sees the rot setting in with a sacrificial interpretation of Jesus' passion and the redemption it brings.[116] The outcome, according to Hamerton-Kelly, is clear, and lamentable, but the gospel challenge remains: "As just another religion Christianity is a more or less satisfactory amalgam of Greek philosophy, Jewish moralism, pagan enthusiasm, and Roman bureaucracy, misappropriated and reapplied. Its record as a religious machine is the same mixture of self-deception and sublimity as the other great religions. But as the hermeneutic of the Cross, it is the first and most radical insight into the pathos of the human enterprise, credible precisely because of its incredulity."[117]

For Girard, the effect of this Christian hermeneutic on culture is real, however, even when diluted and undermined. In what follows I consider with him the growth of victim consciousness, some insights into the collapsing false sacred, and the emergence of secular modernity. I then note some modern attempts to expel the Christian impulse and restore the false sacred—particularly that of Friedrich Nietzsche, who named what was going on with the Christian rehabilitation of victims and fatefully set about discrediting it.

Modernity and the Collapsing Sacred

Girard observes the old victimizing sacred collapsing under the impact of Christ and his gospel, beginning with perhaps the last gasp of ancient paganism, Philostratus's third-century life of the second-century pagan guru Apollonius of Tyana, whose miracles vied in popularity with those of Jesus. The episode in question has Apollonius saving Ephesus from the plague (naturally, a mimetic crisis) by encouraging the crowd to stone a poor blind beggar, who in dying is revealed to have been a demon all along. Girard notes that the Ephesians were reluctant to cast the first stone. He credits this to the effect of Jesus' warning in his encounter with the woman taken in adultery (one of Jesus' few successes in overcoming the dynamics of crowd violence) (Jn 8:2–11).

Apollonius had to lobby vigorously before the crowd gave in and took up stones, unleashing the single-victim mechanism. Jesus on the other hand had restrained such violence by depriving an ugly crowd of its impetus for stoning, initially by discouraging anyone from going first and thereby providing a mimetic model that others would follow. Next, Jesus stooped to write in the dust, thus refusing to meet anyone's eye. This avoided inflaming the situation by edging somebody in the mob toward mimetic rivalry with Jesus, whereupon a first stone would have been thrown and a mimetic frenzy unleashed. Jesus' miracle of peaceful resolution is countered almost literally by its opposite in Philostratus's pagan version. So by the time of Constantine Jesus' own crucified solidarity with the likes of that persecuted Ephesian beggar had begun to ruin the empire's appetite for pagan victimage.[118]

From the Middle Ages the rights of individuals in law and the protection of victims grew, and we see also the arrival of the charitable foundation l'Hôtel-Dieu. For Girard, "Inventing the hospital meant dissociating for the very first time the idea of victim from all concrete ethnic, regional or class identity. It is the invention of the modern victim concept."[119] This is the first hint of coming globalization, as closed local worlds held in being with victimage began their decomposition.[120] Emerging human rights began to put a brake on mimetic snowballing, as the West became alert to occasional persecutions and long-entrenched injustices.[121] Girard sees modernity emerging with Shakespeare in the Renaissance.[122] Plainly, such a working out of the gospel in concrete historical terms was a lengthy process, as "true Christianity" mixed with the sacrificial, culture-making sort that still saw witches, Jews, lepers, heretics, and other stereotypical victims hounded for the sake of social cohesion in the face of various disasters.[123] Christianity's accommodation with violent control— from Caesaropapism to just war theory to the Crusades to support for colonialism, slavery, and militarism in modern times—shows that the gospel has yet to fully convert even its adherents from sacred violence.[124]

Of course there remains ample victimization in the modern world, though it is not as straightforward. As noted in the preceding chapter, it is first necessary to overcome today's widespread mood of resistance by resorting to subterfuge, with persecutors claiming to be victims while victims are cast as persecutors. As Girard ruefully observes, "Never before in history have people spent so much time throwing victims at one another's heads as a substitute for other weapons. This can only happen in a world that though far from Christian to be sure, is totally permeated by the values of the gospels."[125] For example, modern dictators typically wave the victim flag. Before his downfall, Libya's Colonel Gaddafi lamented his oppression by the freedom fighters challenging his regime while blaming the NATO air campaign for bringing harm to his people. His own disregard for civilian lives was not mentioned, however—so obviously the victim, how could he be a persecutor? This tragicomic state of affairs demonstrates how seriously problematized the making of victims has become.

The need for maintaining all such mechanisms of sacred violence through myth and ritual has been established by Girard, as has the way these mechanisms can tire and slacken, so that having begun to lose their grip on the group imagination they need the infusion of fresh sacrificial blood. Gil Baillie recounts an example from the voyages of James Cook, who observed a Tahitian human sacrifice aimed at heading off a local war. What he witnessed was a practice in decline, with no evidence of sacred dread or even respectful deportment among participants. It appeared that the victim had been knocked on the head in advance and was dead during a ceremony meant to climax with his immolation, while the willingness of shamans to answer Cook's skeptical questions and explain the rite's efficacy showed that the mechanism had already been emptied of its sacred aura to become something technically explicable and hence matter-of-fact. Furthermore, the sacrifice failed to reunite factions in the village who disagreed over the war.[126] Clearly there would be no chance of this sacrificial culture reviving once Cook's Christian worldview made its consolidated arrival in Tahiti with European traders, settlers, and missionaries.

Girard addresses this phenomenon in his reflections on the sacrifice of Shakespeare's Julius Caesar, where the hope that "great Rome shall suck reviving blood" was not realized.[127] Rather, Caesar's untidy assassination became a bad omen, and a mimetic incitement to further violence. Girard:

> When sacrificial cultures understand their own rites too well, they can no longer practice them innocently as their ancestors had, and the institution must evolve in the direction of non-violent mysticism on the one hand and political manipulation on the other. As sacrifice loses its sacred power a few holy men flee to the desert, leaving the sacrificial altar to many ambitious leaders who turn it into a political stage upon which the Caesars, Brutuses, and Mark Antonys of this world play sacrificial politics, each one trying to sell his own brand of "good violence" to the mob.[128]

Baillie gives two further striking examples. One concerns nineteenth-century public hangings, seen as an act of barbarity in the service of civilized values. Despite encouraging the public excoriation of victims and a measure of mob catharsis in times of social disquiet, however, such sacrifices failed to restrain mimetic escalation of violence and to unify the society in numbed awe of its sacred foundations. Coventry Patmore revealed all this in his poem, "A London Fête."

> The dangling corpse hung straight and still.
> The show complete, the pleasure past,
> The solid masses loosened fast:
> The thief slunk off, with ample spoil,
> To ply elsewhere his daily toil;
> A baby strung its doll to a stick;
> Two children caught and hanged a cat;
> Two friends walked on, in lively chat;
> And two, who had disputed places,
> Went forth to fight, with murderous faces.[129]

His other example is of an event quite tellingly symbolic: Bob Dylan's 1990 concert at America's elite West Point Military Academy, from whence emerge national security advisers and other chief priests of America's official militaristic cult. Like Captain Cook in Tahiti, the presence of an antiwar singer before a delirious crowd of officer cadets in their dress grays shows that the times, they are a changin'. Baillie writes, "At Tahiti, Western culture, infected with a gospel-inspired empathy for victims, invaded a sacrificial cult ill prepared to repel the Western ethos. At West Point, the empathy for victims at the heart of Western culture was overtaking one of the more formidable of its own cultural institutions."[130]

The Girardian literary scholar Cesáreo Bandera notes that Dante in *The Divine Comedy* could incorporate contemporary Florentine life into his sacred allegory, while Milton could not conceivably have included the life of Puritan England in his *Paradise Lost*.[131] "A sudden heightening of the sensitivity to the 'mixing of the human and the divine,' as happened during the Renaissance," Bandera explains, "could only mean that the sacrificial mechanism was not working as smoothly as it used to. When the breathing space between the sacred and the profane is felt to be in need of restoration, we must assume that the effectiveness of the sacred expulsion of the danger is also at stake. The process no longer commands the solid unanimity it used to."[132]

Bandera argues that widespread medieval emphasis on Christ's passion helped finally turn the cultural tide, so that from the Renaissance the West fully awoke to the role of sacrificial violence.[133] Desacralizing the persecuting crowd freed fiction from its traditional burden of helping sustain such closed, sacrificial cultures, leaving the responsible modern individual center stage, as evident in the first works of modern fiction from Cervantes, Calderón, and Shakespeare. Don Quixote's painful emergence from delusion points the way.[134] Here are the roots of a familiar novelistic struggle, with the modern individual existentially cast beyond the nexus of a social belonging that is ultimately rooted in a violent compact.[135]

Thus just as preserving the old sacred from anything profane had been necessary before the shift, the emerging modern would deemed a similar separation necessary so it could retain access to the archaic sacred. The new secular realm created as the archaic sacred collapsed at the hands of Christianity was no longer compatible with the sacrificial literature of that former world. It represented what was no longer a socially useful version of the sacred.[136] As Bandera argues, "Christian mythology is basically unfit for poetic fiction, especially for poetic fiction of the highest kind, epic poetry; because it is inspired by a logos or spirit that undermines the setting up of a human being on a pedestal, because it has discovered that such a pedestal is the altar on which the sacrificial victim is immolated."[137]

But this newly deregulated, secular spirit was now free enough to opt for a return of the older sacred, which Bandera finds in the Renaissance revival of interest in pagan antiquity.[138] Because the more limpid and self-aware Christian vision was proving incompatible with the old tragic epics of heroes and villains, of healing sacrifice and an implacable sacred, many felt the need to recover a bygone literary world that provided a vehicle for such fancies. As Bandera observes, "Desacralization can actually be turned by an unrepentant old sacred into a new way of keeping itself alive. Art, and in particular poetic fiction, can become an ideal refuge for the old spirit. Once again, a secular appearance is no guarantee of a desacralized heart."[139]

So modern secularism in its irreligious form can be seen as an expulsion of the sacred in its transformed Christian manifestation in order to keep paganism alive covertly.[140] This is certainly what Girard sees happening. "At the time of the Renaissance and later," he explains, "modern intellectuals substituted ancient culture for the Judeo-Christian scriptures. The later humanism of Rousseau and his successors has excessively glorified primitive cultures, and it is also against the Bible."[141] Hence the irony that paganism has regularly been made to seem healthy since the Renaissance while Christianity has been undersold. "No one ever detects in the myths the stench of corpses badly buried,"[142] Girard ruefully concludes. This is an old state of affairs, now busy renewing itself. Girard writes:

> During the first centuries of its existence, Christianity stirred up adversaries—Celsus, for example—who called attention to [the Gospel's equivalence with mythology]. There is in the Gospels a series of phenomena recalling the sequence of events in many earlier cults. Celsus made early use of these resemblances to contest the Christian form of singularity. The Middle Ages interrupt the

little game of comparisons that recommences in modern times, provoking such an interest that academics made it an independent discipline—the comparative study of religion, which has no interest, ultimately, but to demonstrate the banality of the Gospels in the context of world religion.[143]

Here it is timely to mention Nietzsche's central role, according to Girard, as a champion of the modern neopaganism that is reasserting itself in, with, and under the gospel's secularizing impact.

Nietzsche, the False Sacred, and Its "Eternal Return"

Nietzsche has a place of honor in Girard's work for opposing the nineteenth-century positivistic blurring together of Christianity and myth. Nietzsche knew that Christianity was unique,[144] yet he chose to be its opponent rather than its champion. He correctly identified Christian distinctiveness in its commitment to the victim, compared to the pagan sacrificial mechanism with its Dionysian taste for therapeutic violence that is "beyond good and evil." Girard reads Nietzsche's "eternal return" in terms of his belief in the permanent necessity of this mechanism. Christianity disavows such cathartic sacred vengeance in favor of an embittered slave morality, according to Nietzsche, which he calls *ressentiment,* favoring instead the return of real vengeance with his triumphant "overman."[145] To this end Nietzsche proclaims not the "death of God"—not the kind of weary natural expiry that we meet in much sociological talk of religious decline in today's West,[146] but quite explicitly the murder of God, in his famous Aphorism 125 uttered by a madman in *The Gay Science.*[147] This is gospel fruit, the destruction of the old false sacred. The next eternal return will have to be of the archaic sacred past that Christianity has abolished,[148] according to Girard's reading of Nietzsche's aphorism: "What festivals of atonement, what sacred games shall we have to invent? Is not the greatness of this deed too great for us? Must we ourselves not become gods simply to appear worthy of it?"

Girard believes that Nietzsche was driven to madness "by the folly of deliberately siding with the violence and deceptiveness of mythology against the non-violence and truthfulness of the biblical attitude."[149] In this conscious choice made by Nietzsche, and in its consequences, lies a clear lesson for the West, according to Girard. "His was not chit-chat in a café," Girard insists, but "he literally became mad. Nietzsche's greatness is that he perceived the abyss that lies beyond humanism, and that he did his best to get lost in it."[150] He chose what we might call *a preferential option for the persecutors*, thinking that in Dionysian excess he was escaping the herd mind, whereas it is Christ who most truly liberates us from control by the herd mind.[151] Nietzsche lost his sanity attempting to evade the grandeur of the gospel's claim for the sake of something misguided, nasty, and predictable. He indirectly urged Europe to do the same, pointing the way to some of the twentieth century's worst abominations.[152]

It occurs to me that the event triggering Nietzsche's final collapse into madness—seeing a horse savagely beaten in a Turin street and rushing forward to protect it—might have signaled that he could no longer sustain his grandiose indifference to the suffering of victims that his philosophy demanded. Perhaps this unexpected eruption of Christian concern for an innocent victim terminally compromised Nietzsche's Dionysian worldview, so that acquiescing to madness proved his only alternative to repentance and conversion.

The National Socialist way of being Nietzschean was "to bury the modern concern for victims under millions and millions of corpses,"[153] albeit masking the extent of these crimes for tactical reasons—a compliment paid by the false sacred to the gospel, much as hypocrisy is the compliment that vice pays to virtue. According to Bandera, Marxist totalitarianism worked in a similar way. It opposed the "open society" with a mythically charged return to the old security of the tribe and the "closed society."[154] Marx subordinated modern individuals to a system deemed to account for their violence and alienation, postulating a real archaic or ontological violence as the principle of history, hence ensuring that the victimizing sacred made its inevitable return—"a regression to the terrors of Acheron in secular and bureaucratic form but no less oppressive."[155] It gripped the world as only a religion could, and Marx tried to manipulate the religious impulse once shorn of "ideology." Communism proved less efficient than the old sacred, however, so that innumerably more victims were required. Bandera concludes, against the failed Marxist experiment, that "the only way to undermine the old sacrificial mechanism is to avoid it as much as possible."[156]

Girard goes on to explore aspects of Nietzsche-inspired Western neopaganism surviving today: "an intelligentsia, whose sole common ground and binding theme—*religio*—has become the systematic expulsion of everything biblical, our last sacrificial operation in the grand manner."[157] Among this intelligentsia we find today's so-called new atheism. However, insists Girard, "modern atheism is incapable of bringing the victimage mechanism to light; its empty skepticism about all religion constitutes a new method of keeping these mechanisms invisible which favors their perpetuation."[158]

This mentality seeks to outflank Christianity on the left by borrowing the Bible's concern for victims, then insisting on its own moral superiority, making much of Christianity's many historical failures. Wherever the prohibitions of traditional Christian morality are deemed oppressive and in urgent need of abolition, and wherever hedonistic consumerist excess is identified with happiness, neopaganism is at work promising ultimate liberation for victims. Girard is absolutely unsparing in his assessment of this "other totalitarianism," describing it as Satan trying to make a new start in the world by annexing Christian distinctiveness: "The New Testament evokes this process in the language of the Antichrist. To understand this title, we should de-dramatize it, for it expresses something banal and prosaic. The Antichrist boasts of bringing to human beings the peace and tolerance that Christianity promised but has failed to deliver. Actually, what the radicalization of contemporary victimology produces is a return to all sorts of pagan practices: abortion, euthanasia, sexual indifferentiation, Roman circus games galore but without real victims, etc."[159]

Summing up: "In Girard's telling, modernity as a whole is the final movement of apocalyptic revelation—the disclosure of the truth of Christ through the self-annihilation of the regime of violence."[160] Yet he sees secular modernity taking fifteen hundred years to emerge as the gospel asserted its claim on the West by degrees.[161] We have noted counterpressure since the Renaissance, of which Nietzsche proves the linchpin, whereby the false sacred seeks to roll back the real thing and reestablish its violent antihumanism. Consequently, having been a secularizing and modernizing force in history, Christianity is now labeled antimodern by a purportedly secular mood of militancy that is more accurately described as antisecular. This is the latest festival of atonement called for by Nietzsche's aphorizing madman, witnessing the archaic sacred being murdered and calling up the forces of eternal return. Girard does not believe the claims of this militant pseudosecularism. It is a betrayal of the real thing, which affronts the avant-garde by its gospel provenance.

So, like John Milbank,[162] Girard sees Christianity and its global impact for good as under threat today not from secularization but from neopaganism—"not an archaic form of the sacred, but a sacred that has been 'Satanized' by the awareness that we have of it."[163] It will encourage the eternal return of sacrificial religion if Christianity lacks the will to resist. "The decisive break which Christian rationalists, then deists, and then atheists have thought they recognized in . . . the history of the modern West," Girard concludes, "is but an insignificant fold in the gown of Maja."[164] It is as if seven devils worse than the first have reoccupied our home in the West, having seen it swept clean of its former occupant by the gospel (Mt 12:43–45). In the next chapter we see how secular modernity and its major institutions represent a holding operation against mimetic crisis in a world shorn of false sacred protection—also some examples of mimetic escalation and of sacrificial violence persisting in secular modern dress.

CHAPTER 4

Modern Institutions and Violence

Modernity, according to Girard, is a shift from hierarchy to equality, from differentiation to undifferentiation, from external to internal mediation. It is the social shift to a more level playing field, but it also increases the mimetic risk of envy, rivalry, and violence. The available mimetic models proliferate, their proximity awakening desire and encouraging its escalating rivalry. Secularization for Girard begins once the false sacred starts to unravel, its violent foundations having been revealed. Thanks to the Judeo-Christian Scriptures in general and to Jesus Christ in particular, innocent victims no longer serve unproblematically as cannon fodder for maintaining social order. So, putting the two things together—modernity and secularization—you get a formula for increased risk of violence with reduced protection. This is secular modernity according to Girard.

If sacred violence provided the necessary social glue in traditional societies, then modern institutions that prevent social collapse into crises of conflictual mimesis might be assumed to carry over at least some aspects of archaic religion. Such survivals can be traced from the early compromises of Christian culture to medieval persecutions and crusades to Renaissance fascination with antiquity and finally to two centuries of worsening horrors "from Napoleon to Bin Laden,"[1] with Nietzsche as apologist in chief. Yet all such attempts to "suck reviving blood" for the preservation of culture are well past their use-by date. This is why traditional sacrificial remedies for containing human violence today call for an increased dosage, "immolating more and more victims in holocausts that are meant to be sacrificial but are less and less so."[2] Indeed, one might date modernity's definitive onset from the Peace of Westphalia in 1648, at which the sacrifice of a significant proportion of Europe's population during the Thirty Years' War demonstrated its failure to produce any unity beyond the agreement to differ.[3] So, for Girard, "Satan" is still with us, though today only as a force of disorder. The other satanic dimension of the false sacred, the reestablishment of order at the expense of victims, can no longer found or even reliably maintain a culture.[4]

In this chapter I consider how these forces of disruption have been kept from tearing our modern world apart. Girard's answer is that major modern institutions have provided restraint but that these can no longer be relied on. Functioning premodern societies preserved themselves from constant violent disruption by limiting internal mediation. These societies included India, with its rigid caste system, and Europe by and large until the Renaissance. Secular modernity in the modern West has relied on the nation-state and, more recently, the market, with its accompanying consumer culture, variously to out-threaten, divert, distract, and dilute conflictual mimesis. Let me now consider how this might be so according to Girard, noting in particular that this temporary state of affairs coexists with various survivals and mutations of sacred violence—from civil religion to consumer culture; from anorexic self-immolation to abortion and capital punishment.

VERSIONS OF THE *KATÉCHON/KATÉCHŌN*

Saint Paul gives us τὸ κατέχον, "that which restrains" (2 Thes 2:6), and ὁ κατέχων, "the restrainer" (2 Thes 2:7). This more or less personalized usage refers to the preservation of human societies from violence and chaos until the reign of Christ is finally revealed.[5] In 2 Thessalonians 2:6–7 we read about God restraining the pretender, the lawless one, the Antichrist, in the following terms: "And you know what is now restraining him, so that he may be revealed [i.e., to be destroyed by Christ] when his time comes. For the mystery of law-lessness is already at work, but only until the one who now restrains it is removed [i.e., by Christ's return at the end of this interim period]."[6] Such restraint, for Girard, represents "the peace which the world gives" rather than "the peace of God which passes all understanding"; such tactical deployment of violence, whether threatened or actual, is all too understandable.[7] Girard offers examples of the *katéchon* holding off the risk of human self-destructiveness in modern times, listing democratic ideology and judicial institutions, enhanced technological capabilities, mass media, market society, and the objectification of individual relationships.[8] What might he mean by these?

I suggest that *democratic ideology*, for Girard, must refer to the responsible citizenship and commonality of purpose that form the heart of civic virtue. Without this principled adherence, the trust and mutual respect necessary for maintaining justice, equity, and the rule of law is absent, as Francis Fukuyama shows.[9] While the modern democratic experiment as it is analyzed by Tocqueville introduces potentially disruptive "internal mediation" to the heart of social dynamics, in a marked departure from the more hierarchical ancien régime, nevertheless democratic statecraft and the habits it disseminates can be seen to apply a countervailing force. They help counter the obsessive isolation of mimetic competition with strong models of desire representing civil society–type values and cooperation. A less high-minded assessment is offered by the Girardian social scientist Jean-Pierre Dupuy, who likens voting in a democracy to Carnival in Brazil. This annual mimetic safety valve allows a controlled experience of social undifferentiation, just as the regular opportunity in democratic societies to vote down the government allows a significant amount of spleen venting in a managed way.[10]

Judicial institutions, aided by police forces, represent a collectively subscribed secular transcendence granted power to detain, interrogate, try, condemn, and imprison, with the right to do violence as necessary for enforcing order and restraining worse violence. In effect, the judicial system and its agents hold a monopoly on violence. The majesty of the law—the special dress of jurists, the substantial public buildings devoted to its exercise, the blind figure of Justice herself wielding not only scales but a sword as well, and judicial independence under the Westminster system—adds mimetic weight to the discouragement of offending. Chiefly, however, it provides tolerably reliable redress for the victims of offense, so that payback by family or clan is both less necessary and less likely (given the penalties against it). Likewise, the presence of uniformed and armed police in the community mimetically reinforces communal standards of good behavior, but chiefly it stifles dangerous excesses of "acquisitive" and "conflictual mimesis." It does this by denying access to inappropriate objects of desire and by separating conflicted mimetic rivals through implied threat or active intervention. Together, democratic and legal institutions help protect modern societies from the mimetic violence that deals with frustration and offense by payback, vendetta, and blood feud.

Enhanced technological capabilities and *market society* allow a proliferation of desirable goods to be readily available, as we shall see in the discussion below of late capitalist economics, producing overall a better standard of living. All this helps keep mimetic rivalry at bay. The *mass media* diverts us with a steady diet of sport, entertainment, and gossip. It presents us with a wide range of mimetic models beyond those available in the close quarters of small traditional communities, so that internal mediation is less likely to invade our private space and bring about conflictual mimesis. It also ensures that misuse of power is regularly exposed, albeit at the expense of much prurience and disingenuousness, with the effect that frustrated powerlessness is less likely to fester and then flare up mimetically. In this sense, the mass media shares a safety valve function with our democratic and legal institutions. As for *the objectification of individual relations,* I read this as referring to a further isolating effect whereby individuals are decoupled from the older kinship networks that were so well suited to storing up, channeling, and unleashing violence.

The Girardian theological ethicist Wolfgang Palaver identifies some past manifestations of the *katéchon.*[11] The Egyptian god Horus, for instance, was described in these terms. We find echoes of Horus's mission in the divine monologues at the end of Job, particularly with reference to a divinity restraining the watery chaos that was symbolized for Egyptians by the Nile-dwelling hippopotamus and crocodile (Job 40:15–41:34). As noted in chapter 3, this is a divine voice that

Girard dismisses as a continuation of the false sacred perspective of Job's friends rather than the authentic voice of Israel's covenant God. The Roman Empire and the Roman Catholic Church have also been identified with the *katéchon*. So has a sacrificial culture representing Christianized paganism, with Dostoyevsky's Grand Inquisitor (from *The Brothers Karamazov*) providing a fine example of this. The Grand Inquisitor's eagerness to get rid of Christ represents a complete departure from the New Testament, which culminates in a plea for Christ's return.

Yet for all their numerous and readily identifiable faults, these various *katéchon* functions retain a God-given role. Girard:

> Le *katechon* se situe dans un monde chrétien, dans un monde débar-rassé du règne de Satan, qui n'en veut plus. En même temps, le *katechon* retient encore un peu l'ordre ancien, sans lequel s'ouvrirait la porte à la violence absolue. Le *katechon* retient la violence, c'est-à-dire ce qui reste alors que Satan a été roulé, dupé. Il faut admettre que, pour empêcher la violence, nous ne pouvons nous passer d'une certaine violence. Nous sommes donc obligés de penser en termes de moindre violence. Mais, au fond, il est difficile de cerner précisé-ment leur différence.[12]

> ---

> (The *katéchon* stands in a Christian world, in a world cleared of Satan's rule, which doesn't want any more of it. At the same time, the *katéchon* still retains a little of the old order, without which the door to absolute violence could open. The *katéchon* restrains violence—that is to say, that which remains after Satan has been rolled, duped. One must admit that, for preventing violence, we are not able to do without a certain violence. We are therefore obliged to think in terms of the lesser violence. But, in fact, it is difficult to precisely define their difference.)

THE SECULAR MODERN STATE AND THE SACRED

The modern nation-state is one of two major *katéchon* functions on which I focus in this chapter, the other being late capitalist market economics. In early modern times Thomas Hobbes realized that the church could no longer fulfill this purpose once Europe's religious house acrimoniously divided during the Reformation. So, instead, a sovereign Leviathan, presiding over a nation-state with an essentially privatized religion, took over the *katéchon* function. Dietrich Bonhoeffer identified the *katéchon* with state power to establish and maintain order, declaring it not to be guiltless, and certainly not to be God, but a necessary expedient nonetheless.[13] This is what Luther meant by God's "strange work," compared to God's "proper work" of salvation, and by describing the hangman as God's minister. Anglicans traditionally celebrated the same conviction liturgically, praying at Holy Communion for the sovereign, "that under her we may be godly and quietly governed"—a *katéchon* function meant to ensure "the punishment of wickedness and vice and the maintenance of Thy true religion and virtue." In American Episcopalianism the Evensong versicle "God save the King" actually becomes "God save the State."

At the cost of some sidelining of the gospel and attenuation of reason, the founders of modern Western political thought strove for the maximizing of individualism and the minimizing of disorder—in effect, for the optimal management of mimesis. The American theologian Fred Lawrence points out that "Hobbes, Locke, and Rousseau fallaciously eliminated the light of faith and truncated the light of reason into a merely calculating faculty in order to establish the foundations of civil society on the 'low but solid basis' of damage control: people can pursue mimetic desires without killing each other."[14] But despite this trend, no fully sacrificial political system emerged, according to Palaver, because Hobbes allowed inner reservation in religious matters. Hobbes was too committed to the worth and dignity of all people because he had been influenced by the Bible.[15]

The nation-state thus brings an interesting modern secular version of the old intertwining of religion and society. The widespread official version is one of separation, because religion is no longer able to bear the weight of preserving public unity. Religion is relegated to the heart and the private realm, whereas the state goes for public reality, seizing for itself the high metanarrative ground and the restraining function formerly provided by religion. The historian John

Bossy is surely right, then, that "the object of inventing the term Religion with a capital 'R' was to make it possible to invent the term Society with a capital 'S,'"[16] so that society and state could henceforth take over formerly religious functions. Hence today's prevailing rhetoric of secularization, focused on the dwindling of institutional Christianity in the modern West, underestimates the covert resacralization of society and state. It helps to think of this resacralization as having two forms: civil and political.[17]

So-called civil religion is the more widespread form, coexisting with traditional religions in democratic modern societies and using elements of these for its own purpose. The sociologist Robert Bellah talks of American civil religion as broadly Unitarian (i.e., a doctrinally spare monotheism), providing a sense of national calling, of American sacrificial leadership for the sake of the nations, all underpinned by biblical archetypes: "Exodus, chosen people, Promised Land, New Jerusalem, Sacrificial Death and Rebirth. But it is also genuinely American and genuinely new."[18] Visiting Arlington National Cemetery on a Good Friday gave me a taste of this civil religion, and of its roots in a sacrificial reworking of Christianity—for instance, the crowds seeking to "suck reviving blood" at the graves of Jack and Bobby Kennedy, who had of course been murdered by fellow Americans. I had the same sense at Washington's Lincoln Memorial—also nearby at "the Wall," which commemorates around 58,000 Americans sacrificed in Vietnam.

Civil religions range from anticlericalism (France) to an official role for the church (England). The Afrikaner regime in South Africa provided an interesting variant, aiming (probably unwittingly) to limit the spread of internal mediation by a system of racial segregation endorsed by the Dutch Reformed Church, though apartheid, maintained by violent repression, was condemned by such Anglican saints as Father Trevor Huddleston and Archbishop Desmond Tutu as antithetical to the gospel.

The other version we can call political religion. This flourished in a twentieth century marked by dogmatic ideologies, personality cults, and implacable hatred in the name of nation-states. Fascist and communist alternatives proliferated, and any countervailing Christian influence was firmly repressed. Indeed, pagan imagery from the Roman past (Italy under Il Duce) and Northern myth (the Nuremberg vision of Hitler and Albert Speer) was consciously revived, revealing the incompatibility of such aspirations with gospel Christianity. Emilio Gentile thinks political religions will recede in the twenty-first century,[19] though I believe Girard is arguing that a new sacrificial cult of this sort is arising under the banner of radical Islam (more of this in the final chapter). An obvious reason that political religions might no longer seem so necessary is the rise of a new sacred, with market forces increasingly defining and dominating our times.

LATE MODERN CAPITALISM AND THE SACRED

The *katéchon* can also be seen at work in the market and the economy, rallying for good the self-interest of individuals. Blaise Pascal remarks that humanity transforms its concupiscence, "d'en avoir su tirer un règlement admirable, et d'en avoir fait un tableau de la charité [knowing how to pull from it a wonderful rule, and making an image of charity out of it]."[20] Bernard Mandeville's discussion of "private vices, public benefits,"[21] makes a similar point, with the Enlightenment economist Adam Smith going on to theorize "the invisible hand," whereby everyone's pursuit of his or her private interest yields the unintended outcome of heightened prosperity for all.[22] The neoliberal guru Friedrich Hayek reads this as a moral imperative for unfettered consumption and luxury living, declaring inevitable and necessary the elite few enjoying superior benefits in the present so that these same benefits can one day be manufactured more cheaply and hence become more widely available. Restricted wealth and comfort today ensures prosperity for tomorrow's multitude, with the trickle-down effect of unequal domestic and international wealth distribution most reliably delivering continuous growth in prosperity.[23]

There is surely a sacrificial dimension to this famously cold logic of neoliberalism. The Girard-inspired liberation theologian Jung Mo Sung points out that secularization now means this transfer of sacrificial religion to the market, and of eschatology to a paradise of endless consumption for the well-off here on earth, at the expense of the third world poor and the environment. All this constitutes a victim mechanism of sorts, supported by a sacrificial reading of Christianity.[24] Thus the market becomes the meeting place of secularization, so that the mimetic yearning for "being" constitutive of "metaphysical desire" is channeled into consumer culture and elements of a new sacrificial religion. This is the other version of modernity, replacing the nation-state–based version, with its stable institutions, rule of law, and organized social reform. It leaves only minor roles to the state: limited repair of damage caused by an unfettered market,[25] along with police functions to preserve the free flow of global capital.[26] "Satellized by the market, the State is increasingly auto-abolishing itself as guardian of the common good and as support for the needy," the Girardian theologians Michel Beaudin and Jean-Marc Gauthier unsparingly conclude; the state "longs to reduce itself to a mere guarantor of a legal framework favourable to the market."[27] How do mimesis and sacrifice function in the market? And has the market become a religion?

Gift Exchange, Scarcity, Aspiration, Consumption

Girardian writing on the origins of markets and money begins with the gift exchange of primitive societies, understood as a pacifying ritual ringed about with prohibitions for keeping envy and rivalry in check and for nipping the cycle of vengeance in the bud.[28] Such a communally based approach to economics goes unappreciated among advocates of a more rationalist take on the gloomy science, severed from its original role of maintaining social cohesion. Put more technically, it is a highly *substantivist* version of economics that Girardian writing emphasizes rather than a *formalist* one.[29]

The mutual obligation of gift exchange helped take the mimetic sting out of scarcity and inequality in premodern societies, maintaining a solidarity whereby "obligations and prescriptions restrain the desires of those who have, by imposing upon them a duty to give, and of those who have not, for they must be satisfied with what they get. Thus 'abundance,' so to speak, is achieved at the same time that existing hierarchies of wealth and power are reproduced."[30] Market-style

exchange was reserved for outsiders, who could be cheated and victimized to the actual benefit of peaceful relations for those inside the
community.[31] Alternatively, when a community was faced by external
enemies, gifts could serve to pacify a possibly threatening foreign god.
Here Girard identifies the beginning of foreign trade in the conflict-
restraining dynamics of archaic religion,[32] just as he located the beginnings of politics in sacrificial kingship, of animal domestication in
keeping animals for sacrifice, and of technological breakthroughs in
ritual practice.

The link between capitalism, scarcity, and envy championed by
the veteran Girardian thinkers Paul Dumouchel and Jean-Pierre
Dupuy has become part of contemporary social theory.[33] Following
the collapse of the older solidarity, and the sacred violence that helped
secure it, scarcity became individualized, today prompting a lifetime
of aspirational acquisitiveness. In addition to providing enough mass-
produced goods to satisfy this acquisitiveness, however, late capitalist culture isolates these units of aspirational scarcity and preoccupies
them with meeting their own mimetic needs, thus ensuring indifference to others and especially to "losers" in the global economy. Further, these consumers rarely find their personal conflicts lining up with
those of others similarly isolated and preoccupied, so that any wider
mimetic crisis is short-circuited.[34] This represents what the Austrian
economist Erich Kitzmüller calls "anonymous victimization," "manufactured unawareness," and "systematic blindness."[35] And of course the
house always wins, as the economic system itself remains effectively
beyond question. This is because the desire to achieve a certain fictive
middle-class identity drives the pursuit of status as today's leading
Western metanarrative, so that "to indict the economic system would
be to negate this identity."[36]

Hence middle-class aspiration emerges as the mimetic key to
understanding today's economy. It is clearly not the "rational self-
interest" of economic formalism that accounts for this but rather one
of the "animal spirits" that Adam Smith recognized. For middle-class
Westerners, this essentially mimetic dynamic underwrites a keeping
up with (or ahead of) the Joneses life project of them-and-us scenarios, success and failure, dignity versus shame, matched by boom-
and-bust cycles in the economy as a whole.[37] And none of this is

primarily about *objects*. Rather, the consumer culture expressing these aspirations becomes a "positional arms race."[38] In a society where basic needs are met and where traditional hierarchies and distinctions are largely gone, our mimetic need for differentiating ourselves now brings a "social construction of scarcity," requiring a brisk trade in prestige goods.[39] As Eric Gans points out, from the age of Madame Bovary "goods began to be marketed to compensate for resentments of the middle classes." And it extends beyond goods; the body itself has become a commodity and a sign. In many Western countries today that self-differentiation manifests in the "somatic commitment to semiosis" of body modification,[40] which includes many sacrificial excesses undergone for the sake of obtaining status markers such as slimness (on which more shortly).[41]

As Jean Baudrillard argues in his classic study of consumerism, our life in nontraditional, democratically undifferentiated modern societies is one of immanence in an order of signs. Objects serve primarily as markers of difference rather than as creature comforts and ends in themselves, so that consumer culture is best understood as the unconscious discipline of learning and inhabiting a code for the maximizing of self-differentiation,[42] with advertising providing the major training vehicle.[43] Baudrillard is clear, like Girard, that whichever object one desires is best understood as a reification of interpersonal forces.[44] But Baudrillard's French structuralist account of how desire flows into culturally mandated channels lacks the simple directness of mimetic theory to explain these dynamics via models of desire and internal mediation. Baudrillard certainly seeks such a straightforward, comprehensive account, however, registering how

> all the positivity of desire passes into the series of needs and satisfactions, where it resolves itself in terms of managed aims; all the negativity of desire, however, passes into the uncontrollable somatization of the acting out of violence. This explains the profound unity of the whole process: no other hypothesis can account for the disparate phenomena (affluence, violence, euphoria, depression) which, taken together, characterize the "consumer society" and which we sense are all necessarily inter-linked, though their logic remains inexplicable within the perspective of classical anthropology.[45]

But not within the perspective of Girardian anthropology, which accounts for the negatives in terms of ontological sickness, the affluence in terms of mimetic rivalry driving aspiration, and the violence contained by limiting internal mediation. What are some examples of how these socioeconomic but actually mimetic dynamics play out in practice today?

In the United States there is a relentless upward pressure on expectations so that one does not fall behind, leading to measurable increases in terms of house size and number of swimming pools, with longer work hours and commuting time, as well as lower savings, greater debt, and hence higher risk of financial trouble, stress, and consequent health issues. A major result of this was the subprime mortgage crisis. The economist Robert Frank would affirm Baudrillard's semiotic approach to objects of consumption, seeing this escalation in terms of standards rising overall rather than individuals becoming more prone to envy.[46] Though a mimetic understanding of motivation—based on the fact that we are not self-contained individuals and therefore that we "leak being" and must replenish it—can account for phenomenon whether it be structural or individual.

The importance of these considerations for understanding contemporary social problems in the United States and Britain cannot be underestimated. Inequalities surviving into our brave new posthierarchical world mean enhanced burdens of shame, envy, and disappointed reaction whenever this "inequality among equals" is perceived.[47] To put it plainly, now that Jack is as good as his master he resents his master and his neighbors for every sign that this is not true.

Demographic research gathered by Richard Wilkinson and Kate Pickett shows that we cope badly with the modern double bind of equality as a pillar of self-belief in a post-traditional society while some are plainly more equal than others in terms of income. Comparison with other modern countries and between U.S. states shows that societies such as those in Scandinavia, with better social services, a higher sense of worth for all citizens, and less flagrant wealth disparity, are less plagued by the dysfunction that comes from angry self-assertion and desperate self-medication. They are happier, healthier, and more peaceful. Typically, however, high scores for self-esteem in the United States and Britain accompany high scores for "social evaluative threat." This is an example of whistling in the dark. Wilkinson and Pickett offer an illuminating, statistics-based conclusion.

> The relationships between inequality and the prevalence of health and social problems ... suggest that if the United States was to reduce its income inequality to something like the average of the four most equal of the rich countries (Japan, Norway, Sweden and Finland), the proportion of the population feeling they could trust others might rise by 75 per cent—presumably with matching improvements in the quality of community life; rates of mental illness and obesity might similarly each be cut by almost two-thirds, teenage birth rates could be more than halved, prison populations might be reduced by 75 per cent, and people could live longer while working the equivalent of two months less per year.
>
> Similarly, if Britain became as equal as the same four countries, levels of trust might be expected to be two-thirds as high again as they are now, mental illness might be more than halved, everyone would get an additional year of life, teenage birth rates would fall to one-third of what they are now, homicide rates would fall by 75 per cent, everyone would get the equivalent of almost seven weeks extra holiday a year, and the government would be closing prisons all over the country.[48]

All this could be achieved by containing internal mediation via the active promotion of social alternatives, with strong communitarian and humanitarian models of desire. Otherwise we can continue to divert anger generated by shame into an ultimately dispiriting consumer lifestyle that drives an endlessly growing economy, while social isolation ensures that frustrations remain unfocused. Or, at worst, it can continue to be channeled into manageable social disorder. One example is widespread family breakdown, generating extensive but largely private acrimony. Another is the criminal dysfunction of social underclass communities, which is typically contained within isolated demographic pockets. Indeed, the drug and gang crimes associated with such mimetic festering among the disadvantaged can be seen—from the perspective of the archaic sacred—as perversely and deplorably beneficial, providing something like our own late capitalist class of *pharmakoi* (more on this shortly). No doubt with such evidence of socioeconomic distress in view, Girard dismisses "the ideas of a Locke or an Adam Smith which [argue that] free competition will always be good and generous. That's an absurd idea, and we have known it for a long time."[49] It is a tribute to the successful *katéchon* function of our late modern economy, however, that so much personal and social dysfunction does not prompt major social crises.

Where the global poor take matters positively into their own hands, a more encouraging outcome can emerge from the dynamics of mimeticism. In Latin America and South America, China, India, the Middle East, and Europe, the mimetic phenomenon of aspiring to middle-class status is driving what may prove to be the world's last and greatest migration. It leads from the village and the poverty-ensuring past of subsistence agriculture to a new future in which urban middle-class living could become nearly universal, supported by efficient, large-scale agriculture in significantly depopulated rural areas. The intermediate stage occupies today's in-between world of favelas, barrios, and shantytowns on the periphery of major urban centers. Such "arrival cities" are meccas of aspiration, at their best teeming with unregulated commercial enterprise, in which the first generation to leave the village embraces a life of rigorous frugality in drastically reduced circumstances so that their children and grandchildren might have a future beyond anything conceivable by yesterday's rural poor. The arrival city thrives if properly empowered, if not overregulated, and if given some support in terms of infrastructure, education, and policing. Apart from which it can become a festering site of despair, crime, and terrorism. At best, however, its mimetic energy channeled productively could foster a transformed global future.[50]

Is Late Capitalism a Religion?

Girard points out that money originated to facilitate the business of sacrifice, with most ancient coins unearthed in the vicinity of temples. Indeed, the Roman goddess Juno Moneta gave her name to money, and coins were minted near her temple. Perhaps understandably the early Christians preferred the basilica, a neutral space for public business, over the temple as the most suitable style of building in which to meet for worship (though they were also aware that money used even in day-to-day affairs retained a connection to the false sacred).[51]

Hence Jesus's cleansing the temple of its moneychangers represents symbolic protest against the monetary dimension of sacrificial practice (Jn 2:13–22). His deescalation of a mimetically charged situation (Mt 22:15–22) when presented with Caesar's coin (the image of a false god, shown to Jesus in the precincts of a sacrificial temple) and his airy dismissal of Peter to go fishing and thus to reel in a coin for the temple tax (Mt 17:24–27) further demonstrate his aloofness from sacred violence. In the latter case Jesus stands apart from mimetic contagion, represented by the watery chaos from which the coin-bearing fish would come, likewise from society's sacrificial control of chaotic violence that the temple tax represented.

The association of modern economy with religion is not a new idea. Max Weber famously linked the Protestant ethic to the spirit of capitalism, seeing the focus of religiously motivated self-sacrifice shift from the medieval monastery to a disciplined development of the market in early modern Calvinism,[52] and Walter Benjamin noted the transfer of many calming religious functions to capitalism.[53] Girard's own views on the market in religious terms are summarized in a mid-1990s interview.[54] Here the market with its mass production of desirable goods takes on the *katéchon* function, restraining mimetic rivalry by allowing people to have the same objects of desire by purchasing replicas of them.[55] This helps us manage our envy by keeping up with the Joneses rather than killing them. The market's similarity to a violent sacred order is evident in the limited life span of the satisfactions it delivers, in its ability to renew itself coupled with its instability (e.g., in fostering twentieth-century totalitarian reactions against severe market downturns), in the presence of many "losers" who are its victims, and in the amount of used goods constantly being sacrificed to new consumer enthusiasms. Girard notes that this unbridled mimetic escalation of consumerism is sustainable only at the cost of environmental damage, which he likens to the production of human victims.[56]

In sum, Girard believes "that the market, fundamentally, like all modern institutions, is a complex combination of an archaic sacrificial basis combined with aspects of Jewish-Christian revelation.... [I]t's better than anything we had before, and I don't want to sell it short. But at the same time it constantly shows signs of crisis."[57] In particular, its capacity to use mimetic rivalry positively by encouraging nonviolent economic competition constitutes late modern capitalism as a new stage of civilization. Girard finds this capacity inconceivable apart from the cultural dissemination of moral rules that come ultimately from Christianity.[58] He argues this on the basis of a distinction between the global economy and globalization more generally. The latter he sees collectively as the end of older, local, enclosed social orders of the violent sacred type, and hence as the spreading influence of Christianity into every sphere of human activity—including aspects of its subset, the global economy.[59]

So, for instance, Girard is confident that such elements of Christian sensibility as are retained in the culture of markets, and in the "Christian atmosphere" of the Western world more generally, make it unlikely that neoliberal economic theory will progress unchallenged.[60] But, then, he is no left-wing critic cursing the G8. Girard aims to steer between two poles: "What I want to make clear is that I am not an advocate of globalization or the so-called new international order. I am trying to see the complexity of the contemporary situation without reducing it either to an irresponsible collaboration or to a complete condemnation."[61]

One pole, represented by Dupuy, denies victim status to those sidelined and struggling under global capitalism because he thinks that this entails a formal discrepancy with Girard's theory of sacred violence. "The 'excluded' are not sacrificial victims because," he argues, "far from being the focus of general fascination, they succumb to the indifference of everyone else."[62] In other words, they are not Girardian victims because the system disregards rather than deifies them. One could counter, however, that nowhere according to Girard can modern quasi-survivals of archaic sacrificial systems succeed in divinizing their victims. Furthermore, the contemporary phenomenon of political correctness, whereby society takes over concern for victims from Christianity—fêting them but also weaponizing them in an assault on everything prohibitive that is deemed victimizing—means that the excluded get more attention than Dupuy acknowledges.

The alternative critique from the left was brought home to Girard by Michel Serres and in dialogue with liberation theologians.[63] A strong version is offered by Erich Kitzmüller, for whom "market society is a mutant of sacrificial order which mobilizes mimetic energy into technopathical expansion and contains violence inside the market."[64] In *Abiding Faith* I appealed to Girard in mounting a scathing modern victimology, drawing also on left-wing voices from Foucault to Fanon to feminism to queer theory to animal liberation.[65] Now I note Girard's reticence about painting the global economy as a sacrificial cult, in light of how much worse things would be if not for the gospel, of how restrained all this looks compared to the archaic sacred, and remembering the many who are actually saved from suffering and who prosper thanks to today's global economy. Girard:

> I don't think we can fully equate the victims of a system as complex as the global market with the deliberate slaughtering of a human being by other human beings involved in sacrificial rituals. The market is not a technical apparatus devised to kill people in the same way as the gas chambers were in the Nazi camps. As I say, the *Kathecon* of these systems still relies on false transcendence, and they are inevitably bound to produce injustice and violence, but we live in a world where the Satanic power of the mimetic mechanism is unleashed, so we have to take into account that this system is also protecting us, albeit temporarily, from the explosion of even greater violence. As a matter of fact, if it is true that inequality is growing between First and Third World countries, this is bound to become explosive. At some point they may try to turn the tables, and we already have clear signals that something of the sort is happening today. We certainly must have a compassionate adjustment of free market society, and we have to criticize its injustice on the basis of Christian ethics.[66]

Anyone suggesting the presence of a reactionary conservatism in this passage will surely pause over the returning apocalyptic note, which so radically relativizes and judges every system, threatening an end to the *katéchon* in its modern institutional guises of nation and market. As the Girardian thinker Mark Anspach asks, "What is the violent outburst of religious fervor afflicting so many nations today if not a backlash against the religion of the market at the very moment of its planetary triumph?"[67]

It is clear, then, that Girard points beyond typical liberal and conservative views, and certainly beyond characteristic modern confidence in human progress and perfectibility whatever its ideological stamp.[68] All this is far too naive. Instead, what we find is "a synthesis of violence and globalization in which all boundaries on violence are abolished, be they geographic, professional (for example, civilian non-combatants), or demographic (for example, children). At the extremes, even the distinction between violence inflicted on oneself and violence inflicted on other people is in the process of evaporating, in the disturbing new phenomenon of suicide murderers."[69]

I now intend to explore some expressions of violence *within* the secular modern West, with this blurring together of violence against both self and other in mind. Such problems close to home are linked to wider developments in modern warfare, as well as to today's global terrorist impasse. These particular issues I will save for the final chapter, however, discussing them there in conversation with Girard's now complete apocalyptic account of modern history.

SELF-HARM AND THE BODY POLITIC

We can begin to unpack mimetic violence afflicting self and other in the secular modern world by revisiting Girard on self-sacrifice. Here I do not refer to the appropriate, life-giving sort but to the "ontological sickness" canvassed in chapter 1. "Girard . . . has not just one but two theories of sacrifice," as Stephen Gardner sums it up, "the second (and chronologically the first) being that of romantic self-immolation, the self-defeating and ultimately self-destructive character of modern 'romantic desire.'"[70] Hence so many obstacle-addicted, self-destructive modern people who reach beyond their own private torment to afflict others (as in the cruelty that Dostoyevsky's underground man turns on the kindhearted prostitute Liza, displacing the hurt caused to himself through his own mimetic folly).

The "Anorexic Logic" of Modernity

Girard offers a straightforward account of eating disorders as an accelerating mimetic epidemic. His explanation is more enlightening than Freudian talk about girls needing to please their fathers or feminist denunciation of patriarchal culture. Anorexic starvation, with its bulimic variant achieving the same goal through habitual violent purging, accompanies today's widespread obsession with exercise, which Girard wryly calls *"gymnastica nervosa,"* along with the use of smoking for weight loss—a practice confirming that ordinary, boring, nonmimetic good health is not the issue.[71] All this provides an illuminating example of mimesis and sacrifice in secular modernity.

Girard points to Dostoyevsky's prophetic realization that "the new, liberated man, would generate cruel forms of asceticism rooted in nihilism" and provides a number of modern literary examples where radical fasting served a Dionysian cult of the body.[72] The initial models for today's eating disorders, according to Girard, were Elizabeth of Austria—the fashionable dieting gymnast popularly known as Sisi—and her mimetic rival for thinness, Empress Eugenie of France. The first clinical descriptions of anorexia (in 1860 and 1873) came at the height of both women's influence. Their rivalrous trend escaped aristocratic confines to saturate the West after World War II.[73]

Anorexia is a symbol of secular modernity in microcosm, according to Girard, reflecting the minimalist movement—a progressive radicalism that begins with undoing the past, then continues to efface every previous wave of radicalism. Likewise, he equates bulimia with postmodernity's indiscriminate ingestion and vomiting up of the past in ever new forms while according that past no objective worth.[74] He considers how mimetic pressure toward thinness is channeled among girls but also among a new breed of wan, skinny youths mimetically rejecting traditional masculine models of robust stability in favor of models offering a leisure class insouciance. Among young women there is the mimetic counterpressure of voluptuousness in the trend to artificially accentuate lips and breasts—a practice, we note, in which syringe and knife are wielded against women's bodies.

Girard likens anorexic and bulimic self-sacrifice in pursuit of ideological thinness with suicide bombing, concluding that "l'existence des *fashion victims* est sans doute le signe d'une crise sociale" (the existence of fashion victims is without doubt the sign of a social crisis), representing "une espèce de retour à l'archaïsme dans notre monde" (a type of return to archaism in our world).[75] He addresses the question of why some women and not others succumb to eating disorders, suggesting, "Les individus sont plus ou moins rivalitaires, il n'en va pas autrement dans le cas de la minceur que dans d'autres domaines. Les femmes anorexiques veulent être championnes de leur catégorie" (Individuals are more or less rivalrous, it's no different in the case of thinness than in other areas. Anorexic women want to be champions of their category). None of this is any more mad than today's widespread mimetic competition over wealth, as Girard concludes.[76]

I once conducted the funeral of a sixteen-year-old girl who starved herself to death—or, more exactly, who died of heart failure due to a dietary potassium deficiency caused by anorexia. The onset of her fatal condition was triggered by a boyfriend telling her (rightly or wrongly) that she was fat. It may seem far-fetched to describe anorexia as a phenomenon of mimesis and sacrifice, but such mimetic pursuit of thinness really does kill young women. Like that sad girl who I laid to rest, whose fatal fascination with a mimetic obstacle had given her no rest.

I want to go on now to some Girardian thoughts on being overweight, which is widely considered shameful for anyone who is not a member of the underclass.[77] Being overweight is a matter of social and economic discrimination, demonstrating for Girard how "the anorexic ideal of radical emaciation affects more and more areas of human activity."[78] Elena Levy-Navarro highlights the link between modernity, rationality, and control, which ensures that fat becomes a symbol of undiscipline, excess, and breakdown. The requirement of thinness on the part of professional and political elites is an early modern development, overturning a fatter view of worthiness from agrarian and feudal times. The lean figure of Hal, in Shakespeare's Henry plays, had to "banish plump Jack"—Falstaff being reassuringly round, generous, lenient with the poor, not mean and "lean-witted." Rather, he was "fat-witted" in his openness to a fuller vision of reality,[79] whereas Hal and all his lean, utilitarian, puritanical kind eat up the poor, as the lean cattle in Pharaoh's dream consumed the fat cattle (Gn 41:4): "If to be fat is to be hated, then Pharaoh's lean kine are to be loved" (*King Henry IV* 2.4). The "predatory nature of Hal's trim regime" is unforgiving, representing a power-driven construction of reality whereby "certain bodies are presumptively virtuous."[80] "The privilege of the few elite is secured, their overconsumption allowed to be virtuous," concludes Levy-Navarro, "precisely because the fat body of the underclass is made into the emblem of our collective overconsumption."[81]

Here are many echoes of Girard on mimeticism and sacrifice, with a class of overweight *pharmakoi* fattened up for public ridicule while Western consumption spirals out of control and the competitive individualism of our hypermimetic society shows signs of pending crisis. Meanwhile the mimetic will-to-power pursues thinner models of desire—like yonder Cassius with his lean and hungry look (*Julius Caesar* 1.2)—in a competitive way, which also consigns many female fashion victims to sacrificial deaths.[82]

Abortion on Demand

As an adopted person who only escaped the abortionist's curette thanks to my unwed natural mother changing her mind on the way to the clinic, I claim a privileged perspective on the practice of abortion. Today's culture of abortion struck me as a survival of archaic sacrifice from my first comprehending encounters with Girard's work. In an unsparing Girardian essay titled "Abortion as a Sacrament," Bernadette Waterman Ward identifies the crisis facing unwillingly pregnant women in secular modern culture as a symbolic one, rendering rational practical options such as pregnancy help and adoption largely irrelevant. If women typically prefer abortion to adoption, it is because the fetus is viewed as an invader threatening their being.[83]

Abortion thus resembles a cult of child sacrifice, with today's absolute ethical imperative to fulfill one's own desire as the new Moloch.
Such thinking is so entrenched, says Ward, that if desire's mimetic
nature became widely known, it would upend American culture.[84]
Ward likens the sacrificial role abortion plays in contemporary life to
the immolation of Hindu widows: "The assertion that women's sexuality can be just like men's, however sincerely proclaimed, is deeply
mimetic and biologically oppressive. Such an unstable belief system
requires sacrifice for its maintenance. If pregnancy is death to self,
and sexual intercourse is required for self-fulfilment—both culturally conditioned notions—abortion seems to provide the only escape
from the terrors of living in a woman's body. The breakdown of that
sacrificial system threatens a woman with the emptiness that drives
Hindu women to *suttee*."[85]

Abortion is an example of violence directed toward both self and
other. I now touch on some linked examples of other-directed violence with a particular sacrificial role in modernity.

Crime and Punishment

Earlier in the chapter I mentioned sacrificial aspects of American
civil religion.[86] At the level of popular cultural imagination expressed
in characteristically American genre films—western, gangster, horror,
sci-fi—social cohesion is still celebrated at the expense of victims cast
in the role of monsters and publicly put to death, offering reassurance in the face of widespread concern that justice is being delayed,
or denied.[87] The Girardian literary theorist Andrew McKenna unerr-
ingly identifies the mimetic and sacrificial origin of such monsters in
their cultural, literary, and cinematic manifestations. They externalize
our own violence, allowing both its disavowal and its control.

Yet no one can believe in monsters, at least no one who has read
works like *Don Quixote, A Midsummer Night's Dream,* and Dostoyevsky's novels, which artfully and knowingly dispel such creatures. We cannot believe in monsters for we know what they
are. They are sacred, and like the sacred, they are not. When
they threaten us, they are nothing but the form violence takes in its

indifference to difference, the form our own violence takes when we disown it. When vanquished, they are surrogates for the victim, the form violence takes when we sacralize it, the form the victim takes when its destruction reconciles the community. The sacred and the monster are proof of a false reconciliation among violent rivals, and it is wrong to believe in them.[88]

This is true of fictional monsters like vampires who, as plague causers accused of the worst atrocities and set upon by stake-wielding mobs, can be understood as pointers to the victim mechanism.[89] The popular *Twilight* series of novels and films is compatible with this reading. A new category of monster in American culture is the serial killer and his variant the shooting-spree killer, whose limited existence in reality is matched by his overrepresentation in American movies and police procedurals. These up-to-date versions of Dostoyevsky's underground man[90] also resemble suicide bombers in their regular refusal to be taken alive. Jean-Michel Oughourlian describes serial killers as most likely to emerge in a modern society in which prohibitions have drained away. Unchecked mimetic envy leads some into murderous rivalry against each and all so that, in a reversal of direction within the same sacrificial pattern of violence, the victim-minded individual kills the crowd.[91]

The American Lutheran theologian Jon Pahl provides a compelling analysis of civilly religious America as a sacrificial culture. Examples he cites are Puritan Boston hanging Quakers, the punished bodies of black slaves as a handy repository for displaced white Protestant anxieties, capital punishment prosecuted ideologically, and the many young people slain programmatically in American movies—also as real casualties in the military service of American nationalism. All these are necessary sacrifices for containing social disorder.[92]

I highlight two of these themes. Slavery is linked directly to continuing racial tensions at the heart of American life, which in turn are connected to capital punishment. Frederick Douglass, author of the first and best slave escape narrative, indicted slave-owning Methodists as the cruellest masters, typically insisting that their slaves perform the role of dissolute other—forbidding their literacy and church attendance and consigning them to Sunday debauchery. He excoriates the slave-owning South for maintaining a sacrificial distortion of Christianity, in an excruciating meditation on Jesus' words, "Woe to you, scribes and Pharisees, hypocrites" (Mt 23).[93] White resentment at the cultural destruction of the antebellum South continued the scapegoating of blacks via burning crosses and lynch mobs, while more recently the sacrificial role of African Americans is evident in crack cocaine addiction and ghetto shootings, where the sacrificial violence is turned inward, and in newer resistance to affirmative action and adequate welfare provision from the white community.[94] I have already mentioned the fat issue, which in America is significantly a race issue.

Capital punishment is also largely a racial matter in America, as Hispanics and underclass whites make up the numbers. The function of this barbaric practice was exposed in the iconic film *Dead Man Walking*, showing capital punishment "as a quasi-religious 'ritual of killing' or as a secular liturgy of death,"[95] by comparison with the victim-revealing Christianity represented by Sister Helen Prejean. Girard agrees: "Capital punishment is already ritual murder, and the proof of it is the stoning in Leviticus."[96]

James McBride argues that the 1993 U.S. Supreme Court *Herrera* decision—that a prisoner on death row in Texas who claimed that new evidence proved his factual innocence had no recourse to the Supreme Court since no constitutional issues were involved—reveals a sacrificial motive lurking beneath the legal argument. Regardless of Herrera's likely guilt, this six-three decision of the Court, with a minority dissenting opinion from Justice Blackmun expressing a degree of moral outrage, warrants careful consideration. The Court's confidence that executive clemency remains a reliable last resort—a provision which followed the British royal prerogative into U.S. law[97]—offers insufficient reassurance that justice will be served. British sovereigns are not elected on a strong law-and-order ticket, unlike Texas governors.

McBride is convinced that many poor blacks are kept on death row essentially as *pharmakoi*, regardless of guilt, as necessary sacrificial victims for the calming of white anxieties. "A Girardian reading of the death penalty," he concludes, "demonstrates the numinous character of public execution, embraced by the state for the expiation of violence in the American body politic. As such, the death penalty is an establishment of religion which violates the First Amendment."[98] Once again, as with a Victorian-era public hanging in the aforementioned poem by Coventry Patmore, we note the failure of modern capital punishment to provide an entirely satisfying and efficacious sacrifice. This is why a regular supply of such deaths is necessary—though not too many in case that were to give the game away. Here is a further example of secular modernity demanding more sacrificial victims now that the archaic sacrificial mechanism has been exposed and rendered increasingly ineffective.

As a final word on crime and punishment, and with the necessary *katéchon* function of legal systems in view, I mention an intriguing observation by the Girardian philosopher Stephen Gardner on the necessary pacifying role of crime itself in American culture. He notes that F. Scott Fitzgerald presents Jay Gatsby's crimes as continuous with the American dream of self-betterment. Much as global markets restrain violent escalation by isolating individuals in their own mimetically competitive corners, hence short-circuiting wider social disruption, Gardner argues, "criminality plays its lubricating role, absorbing the surplus of democratic passion, as desires and ambitions expand more quickly than the system can satisfy. Far from undermining it, it affords it a steam-valve. Criminality vents class antagonism on the politically harmless level of individualism. In Europe, class war in the last century spawned revolution, genocide, world war or social paralysis. Europeans preferred to commit crimes collectively, whereas Americans favour the 'criminal enterprise.'"[99]

So, in all these examples of crime and punishment we discern traces of the sacrificial mechanism surviving to distract and divert violence from erupting into mimetic crisis. The examples thus far have been personal and domestic. In the next chapter the issues are strongly related, but the scale is broader—both globally and historically. I reflect on today's wars in general and terrorism in particular, against the backdrop of Girard's now-complete apocalyptic account of modern history. This involves attention to a variety of sources major and minor but especially to Girard's last major work, *Battling to the End*.

CHAPTER 5

War, Terror, Apocalypse

All the great political thinkers of modernity, including those receiving most Girardian attention (Hobbes, Tocqueville, Carl Schmitt),
"recognized the fearful creakings coming from the machinery of the
modern state at the time when it was still being developed and established."[1] Those creakings reveal the *katéchon* already under strain.
Today this problem has jumped the boundaries of nation-states, with
globalization erasing cultural differences to threaten a worldwide mimetic crisis.[2] Elements of that crisis are evident in the way warfare has
changed and in modern terrorism. Rather than today's conflict between radical Islam and the modern secular West representing what
Samuel Huntington famously called a "clash of civilizations"—with
Western values of human rights, equality, liberty, the rule of law, democracy, free markets, and the separation of church and state differentiating the West from other cultures, including but not limited to
Islamic ones[3]—it is better understood as a global *civil war* based on
the *erasure of difference*.[4]

This is the stuff of internal mediation, conflictual mimesis, and,
finally, mimetic crisis. "This is the genie let out of the bottle by the rise
of democracy, the emancipation of 'mimetic desire' from traditional
constraints, *mimetic rivalry*, moving inevitably toward Clausewitz's
absolute war, nations like individuals striving to annihilate each other

in obsessive mutual hatred."[5] The Clausewitz reference is to the Prussian general's military classic of 1832, *On War,* which in Girard's late major work, *Battling to the End,* is drawn upon to complete a mimetic account of history in terms of escalating violence. Girard's rendering of this is now unsparingly apocalyptic, as we will see later in the chapter.

TODAY'S WARS AS CIVIL WARS

Warfare is gaining an intoxicating normalcy in our world as conflicts multiply beyond the measured military operations of nation-states. The mimetic descent of ordinary populations into bloodlust, the manipulation, mythifying, and forgetting which allow every side to claim the victim status that alone today justifies victimizing others—likewise the scapegoating of those defying the collective psychosis—are all well documented. Chris Hedges, in his illuminating book *War Is a Force That Gives Us Meaning,* as a long-term correspondent in the world's hot spots, confesses his personal addiction to war. He reminded me of the Best Picture Oscar–winning film *Hurt Locker,* which I saw in a packed downtown Manhattan cinema not far from Ground Zero, its sad hero counting the days of boredom during home leave with his young family, craving his return to the intensity of army bomb disposal work in Baghdad.

The universal claim to victim status as the license for committing atrocities is a strange fruit of the gospel, proving necessary to justify the worst excesses of modern bloodlust. For example, the Girardian scholar Giuseppe Fornari connects the uniquely extensive violence of modern totalitarianism with the personal stories of its two worst protagonists: "The biographies of Hitler and Stalin both document the fact that the totalitarian chief is a victim who has escaped his persecutors and succeeded in taking over the persecutory system . . . in order to become the principle of vengeance itself. The leader is the supreme embodiment of the victim and of the persecutory system that produces victims, a real Christ stripped of his divine nature and transformed into a living, operative image of Satan."[6]

The characteristic modern war is a civil war, overcoming the state's *katéchon*. Such wars have replaced the single transcendent defining enmity of the Cold War. In its place are local enmities fueled by internal mediation—by shame, envy, and humiliation seeking redress—all supercharged by the mimetic elixir of media coverage. As Hans Magnus Enzensberger shows, gang warfare provides the typical pattern, in which "it is the case of the have-nots shooting at each other."[7] This mirror doubling typical of the blood feud extends to police death squads, indistinguishable in their violence from the drug gangs they pursue, and armies behaving just like the insurgents they confront.[8] The Sri Lankan army, in its 2009 cleanout of Tamil Tiger territory, mirrored the savagery of its recently defeated enemy in the murderous ferocity it displayed against Tamil Tiger prisoners of war and civilian noncombatants. The Northern Ireland conflict exemplified all this, too, with the mirror doubling of Protestant and Catholic factions. In a Girardian reflection during the troubles, Duncan Morrow noted, "Each group imitates the other in uncanny fashion. As the groups become more and more alike, each also becomes more and more convinced of its own distinct and contrary qualities. As the similarities increase, the rivalries multiply."[9]

The World War II–era German political theorist Carl Schmitt had an answer to the threat of violence following upon modernity's increasing undifferentiation. He advocated the intentional embrace of "official" enemies and purposive yet dispassionate warfare—a principled commitment to *impersonal* national enmity, which comes close to becoming a new defining purpose for nation-states. This meant engaging in one great conflict in order to restrain all the lesser conflicts that were taken too personally, right down to the individual enmities that Hobbes had sought to contain with his Leviathan.[10]

Schmitt's new "nomos (law) of the earth" is a self-defining militarism representing a further *katéchon* function. I am reminded of perpetual wars in the background of perceptive modern fictional dystopias—from George Orwell's *1984* to Margaret Atwood's *The Handmaid's Tale* to the *Terminator* films. Schmitt finds a proof-text for this in Genesis 3:15, which establishes humanity's defining enmity with the snake. He feared that nothing less could restrain the extent of destructive personal hatred characteristic of modern wars, criticizing modern liberalism and pluralism as useless in this regard and denying transcendent reasonableness its claim to prevent violence—from Reformation-era theology via metaphysical rationality and moral humanism in subsequent centuries to economy and technology today. Wolfgang Palaver sees Schmitt's proposal resurfacing in Huntington's clash of civilizations thesis, which he views as an attempt to consolidate and so to limit global violence.[11] But this reliance on managed warfare as the last *katéchon* among modern societies will no longer deliver.

Wars of Religion?

It does not help to blame war and violence on religion, as if secular modernity were a natively tranquil condition if left alone by fanatical believers. Neopagan revival of the archaic sacred, as discussed at the end of chapter 3, is how Girard views this widespread, popular, but also misguided claim. The American theologian William T. Cavanaugh puts paid to it in his important book, *The Myth of Religious Violence*. He understands what Girard is trying to do, pointing out that "whatever one thinks of the merits of Girard's theory, the subject of his argument about religion is not some set of beliefs and practices composed of the world religions: Buddhism, Christianity, Sikhism, etc. Girard's argument is about the violent preservation of social orders including secular ones. Girard's solution to the problem of violence, therefore, is not [what is typically called] secularization. . . . Girard's theory cannot be employed to advance the secularist argument that religion is linked to violence without equivocating on the term religion."[12]

Cavanaugh's case centers on the so-called wars of religion, which did so much harm to seventeenth-century Europe. They are widely appealed to for proof that as religion is inherently violent it is better off privatized, and kept on a leash in the public square. But there was an ulterior motive to this conclusion. The reification and retreat of religion from its functional role as the key agency of social control into a timeless, universal, private, and apolitical human impulse actually served the interests that created modern states, with their drive to annex religion's former social power.[13] Hence this supposedly secularizing move actually served a covert resacralizing—of the state.[14] The wars of religion, on closer examination, *actually involved much violence within particular religious groupings, and collaboration between religions,* as rivalrous state-building elites eager to consolidate their power waged a secular war under the cover of religious differences.[15]

Recalling the illuminating thesis of Edward Said in his classic *Orientalism,* Cavanaugh shows how "the myth of religious violence is a form of Orientalist discourse that helps to reinforce a dichotomy between the rational West and the other, more benighted cultures— Muslims especially—that lag behind."[16] He criticizes writers on contemporary terrorism who overlook postcolonial trauma or widespread Muslim anger over America's Middle East policies, mistaking political motives for religious ones.[17] This sort of thinking supports a Western, clash of civilizations style of argument that allows reasonable, targeted, peacemaking secular violence to claim the moral high ground over irrational, divisive, uncontrolled religious violence.[18] But this solution is wrongheaded, hampering proper Western understanding of present enmities. As Cavanaugh concludes, "Understanding the theopolitical project of Muslim radicals is not a matter of understanding the timeless essence of religion, but rather requires analysis of how different theologies have been formed in encounters with modern forms of power."[19]

TERRORISM: MIMESIS AND SACRIFICE

Terrorism has erupted during Girard's publishing career, especially so-called religious terrorism in general and Islamic-affiliated terrorism in particular. In 1968 none of the eleven terrorist groups operating worldwide labeled themselves as religious, compared to twelve of fifty groups active in the mid-1990s. By 2004, however, thirty-seven of the forty *religious* terrorist groups identified themselves as Islamic—as many as there were nonreligious terrorist groups in the same year.[20]

Girard before 9/11

Girard's first contribution on the subject, in his early 1960s reflections on Dostoyevsky, concerned the revolutionary behavior that he already saw as mimetically mediated.[21] Jean-Pierre Dupuy explores this Dostoyevskian connection, highlighting the crucial mimetic factor of masochistic obstacle fixation: "The underground hero is a being who pitifully and tragically crashes into every obstacle on his path—like a moth drawn to the flame that consumes it, or like two Boeings that crash into towers of power—and this, *because they are more focused on removing the obstacle than on reaching the object*."[22]

Mimetic and sacrificial dimensions were central to Girard's early 1990s reflection, with Mark Anspach, on the emergence of religiously themed terrorism. They show how the mimetic entanglement of terrorists with the modern states they oppose leads to their becoming what Shakespeare in *Timon of Athens* calls "confounding contraries," whereby "unconscious mimetic rivalry operates ... as a desperate search for and espousal of views, attitudes, and actions antithetical to those of the model. It operates, therefore, as a search for independence that produces an impoverished opposite of the model's attitude."[23]

With both dimensions of the victim mechanism in view—demonization, then divinization—Girard and Anspach note that suicide bombers, who are "sacrificed in the guise of cannon fodder," are subsequently sacralized as martyrs. But perhaps they were first suspected and feared, too, in that they are typically young unmarried men, at a loose end, socially liminal, and hence potential figures of disorder who are best disposed of ritually.[24] Here is the main reason that Girard denies Gauchet's thesis that secular modernity represents an inexorable disenchantment, because the archaic sacred is so obviously resurgent.[25]

In the year before 9/11 Girard offered a further assessment of Islamist terror: "The hatred of the West and all it represents is not due to its spirit being truly foreign to these people, or because they are really opposed to the 'progress' we embody for them, but because the *competitive spirit* is as familiar to them as it is to us. Far from turning away from the West, they cannot help but imitating it, from adopting its values without admitting to themselves what they are doing; and that they are as consumed as we are by the ideology of individual or collective success."[26] Girard's early approach to terrorism as a mimetic entanglement with modernity, acknowledging also a resurgent sacrificial dimension, is developed in his responses to 9/11.

Girard since 9/11

Since 9/11 Girard has undertaken a major apocalyptically themed study of modern history from the perspective of warfare, all understood mimetically. Perhaps 9/11 provided a catalyst for this broader account of violence in modernity, now escalating to extremes, in which he sees today's Islamist terrorism as a not fully explicable late flowering. Neither in his first response to 9/11, in a *Le Monde* interview of 6 November 2001, nor in his mid-2007 *Battling to the End* "Epilogue"—which he devoted to the theme of Islamist terrorism— does Girard claim to be an expert or to have fully worked out the nature of this confronting new development. Indeed, that Girard excerpted most of his comments on terror from the main body of *Battling to the End* and put them in an epilogue might be a demonstration of the care he wants to take here, perhaps to avoid what he calls today's "fraudulent propaganda against Muslims."[27] Hence it seems appropriate to give the theme of Islamist terror in Girard's post-9/11 writing separate attention, before looking more closely at the bigger historical picture set out in *Battling to the End*. I also want to canvass a limited range of wider views after considering his own. This will show that Girard, while remaining more tentative in his conclusions about Islamist terrorism than some other commentators, is not out on a limb.

Most notably in the *Le Monde* interview, coming on the heels of 9/11, Girard declares Islam the new Communism—the banner under which "we find a will to rally and mobilize an entire third world of those frustrated victims in their relations of mimetic rivalry with the West."[28] Yet this is not poor versus rich, or purely an Islamic-Western clash of civilizations, as much as a contest over prestige within *one world*. In support of this assessment, Girard mentions three things.

First, there was early rhetoric from a triumphant Bin Laden about the 9/11 attacks also avenging America's nuclear first strike on Japan in 1945. This suggested to Girard that Bin Laden represented a planet-wide reaction, not just an Islamic one. That is to say, he focused victimary rhetoric within a newly unified global consciousness.[29] Second, Girard addresses the personal animus of Bin Laden himself, who was a rich Saudi with no personal need to envy anyone's wealth yet like many Muslims saw America as the symbol of their disempowerment and humiliation. Third, Girard notes the sheer American-style know-how and efficiency of the plotters, as well as their familiarity with America through residency there, asking, "Were not the authors of the attack at least somewhat American?"[30]

Girard then raises the possibility that Islam retains a more antiquated sacrificial dynamic, though not the whole panoply of sacrificial mythology. The "Muslim kamikazes" of 9/11 were certainly a model intended for emulation in the project of transforming the world politically, whereas "the martyr is for Christians a model to accompany them but not a model for throwing oneself into the fire with him."[31] Muslim rehabilitation of the victim is thus militant rather than cruciform, though since *Violence and the Sacred* Girard has acknowledged *some* prophetic insight in Muslim tradition into the role of sacrifice—for instance, in an (unreferenced) traditional Muslim version of two familiar stories from Genesis, according to which the ram sacrificed by Abel (hence avoiding murder, as the nonsacrificing Cain was unable to do) is the same ram sent to Abraham for preventing the killing of Isaac.[32]

What is clear from the *Le Monde* interview in the immediate aftermath of 9/11 is that Girard was not entirely clear on how to read the attacks, or on the precise role played by Islam. But his two main points—about mimetic rivalry within one world and the role of sacrifice within Islam—reappear in subsequent work. I will refer chiefly to the aforementioned mid-2007 "Epilogue" in *Battling to the End,* devoted to Islamist terrorism,[33] then to a 2008 interview with Robert Doran—mentioning also some remarks in three other contemporaneous interviews.

Girard begins the "Epilogue" by naming today's "war on terror" as the thoroughly mimetic rivalry of two crusades,[34] though the ongoing

crusade of Muhammad is declared more powerful for its explicitly religious underpinning.[35] We find repeated his mention of Bin
Laden's wealth from the post-9/11 *Le Monde* interview, suggesting
that the gathering up of a whole world's frustrations and directing
them against America cannot simply be a matter of resentful poverty.[36] However, some envy of Western wealth remains as a motive;
Girard seems to equate terrorist motives with the sort of competition
familiar between internally mediated Westerners beset by middle-
class rivalry. Indeed, Girard's return to wealth disparity as a motive
is matched by a renewed sense that here is a problem *interior* to the
dynamics of Western culture. This subtlety is evident when Girard
identifies post-9/11 extremism as "one of the last metastases of the
cancer that has torn the Western world apart."[37]

A related suggestion concerns direct mimetic entanglement of
radical Islamist terrorists with their Western model-rival. The very
fact of sleeper cells able to operate incognito within Western populations suggests at least some undifferentiation. But the 9/11 plotters
took this even further. Girard asks who these men *really* were, and
who they *actually* represented, in light of the FBI's discovery that Atta
and his accomplices spent their last nights before the attacks in bars.[38]
Jonathan Raban, in a post-9/11 article for the *New Yorker*, fills out
this picture of how the 9/11 attackers "left a forensic spur of brand
names across the length and breadth of the United States." "We know
them best," he writes, "as efficient modern consumers—of Parrot-Ice,
Tommy Hilfiger, Econo Lodge, AAA Discounts, Starbucks, Cyber
Zone, Golden Tee '97 golf at Shuckum's Raw Bar and Grill, Salem
cigarettes, Heineken and Budweiser, Chinese takeout from Wo
Hop III, lap dancing at Nardone's Sports Go-Go Bar and the Olym-
pic Garden Topless Cabaret."[39]

This leads to the second of Girard's points from the earlier *Le
Monde* interview, about Islam's role in all this and the place of archaic
sacrifice within Islam. For Girard, "it is a given that terrorism is a
brutal action that hijacks religious codes for its own purposes," yet
Islamist terror's religious element contributes to its broad appeal—
beyond that of Leninism, for instance, which shared some of its features but was not a religion.[40] Girard declares this phenomenon to
be opaque both psychologically and in terms of classical Islam. It is

something new, exploiting Islam for its own purposes—a modern attempt "to counter the most powerful and refined tool of the Western world: technology," and which, with regard to its host religion, is "both linked to Islam and different from it."[41] In light of the fuller perspective charted throughout *Battling to the End*, Girard offers "the tentative hypothesis that the escalation to extremes now uses Islam as it used to use Napoleonism and Pangermanism."[42] I will explain this Clausewitzian notion of an escalation to extremes, which Girard makes his own with *Battling to the End*, in the final section of this chapter.

Girard then argues that Islam does not share Christianity's awareness of the founding murder.[43] Around this time he expanded on this point in two interviews. To Wolfgang Palaver (Ottawa, 2006) Girard explained that Islam is very different from Christianity in its handling of violence, lacking the struggle with sacred violence that he uncovers in the Bible and most clearly in Jesus' passion (which is declared blasphemous by Islam).[44] And to Guilio Meotti, in *Il Foglio* (March 2007): "In Islam the most important thing is missing: a cross. Like Christianity, Islam re-enables the innocent victim, but does it in a militant way."[45]

Yet the expansionist Islamic impulse toward assimilating the West continues from of old.[46] And within that a new manifestation of the archaic sacred is returning unresisted, in what Girard sees as a more powerful form than all the others because the Bible and Christianity are being enlisted in support. Or at least transformed versions of them are enlisted,[47] which I suspect must refer to denatured, sacrificial versions and to biblical apocalyptic read in terms of divine violence. What is returning is not traditional Islam, then, but a political-religious hybrid of terroristic form which Girard sees as "something both very new and very primitive . . . internal to the development of technology,"[48] in the sense of occupying a place in the modern world's technologically supported escalation of conflict.[49] Militant Islam is further implicated as an insider to modernity's dynamics via its link to modern totalitarianism, with Mao and Lenin apparently referenced by Al Qaeda—a link that has not gone unnoticed in the wider assessment of Islamist terrorism today.[50]

In an interview with the Canadian media theorist Phil Rose (conducted in August 2006 and May 2007), Girard concludes that "the existence of terrorism is literally a monstrous problem.... It shows that history is as dangerous as ever, because the most archaic barbarian types of violence seem to be back with us at the same time as the most sophisticated means of destruction which face mankind in this situation which is without parallel in the past."[51]

In his 2008 interview with Robert Doran, Girard begins to broaden the suggestion, made in *Le Monde* after 9/11, that all this is simple resentment by the mimetically disaffected. He now speaks of a reaction under way against the loss of prohibitions once secured under the archaic sacred. Hence "9/11 represents a strange return of the archaic within the secularism of our time"—yet this archaism uses modern weapons, and we can anticipate militant Islam deploying nuclear weapons someday.[52] Here Girard is prepared to say that this is a form of archaic religion, divinizing violence in opposition to the Bible while preserving a strongly self-defining position within the orbit of modernity: "What the Muslim really sees is that religious prohibition rituals are a force that keeps the community together, which has totally disappeared or is on the way out in the West. People in the West are united only by consumerism, good salaries etc. The Muslims say: 'their weapons are terribly dangerous but as people they are so weak that their civilization can easily be destroyed.' This is the way they think, and they may not be totally wrong."[53]

Finally, Girard admits that the chief antipathy of radical Islam is Christianity itself, rather than secular Western modernity, over whether God is violent or not. He acknowledges that "the Muslim religion has copied Christianity more than anything, it is not openly sacrificial. But the Muslim religion has not destroyed the sacrifice of archaic religion the way Christianity has. No part of the Christian world has retained pre-Christian sacrifice. Many parts of the Muslim world have retained pre-Muslim sacrifice."[54]

In all these comments on Islamist terrorism since 9/11, it may appear that Girard is offering a clash of civilizations view after all, though we must remember that the chronic instabilities of conflictual mimesis are most fully at work precisely where everyone is really too alike, so that differentiation has to be restored. We note the redress and also the prestige craved by Bin Laden, and the 9/11 plotters "going native" even as they prepared to dash themselves against their American model-obstacle. These and the annexing of archaic sacred elements by a new "political religion" badged as Islam—a more amenable host nowadays than Christianity because it has not offloaded the false sacred as extensively as has Christianity—all add up to a mimetic struggle within globalized modernity rather than a clash of civilizations. As Dupuy concludes:

> Resentment unites the very actors who mutually excommunicate each other. It is now on a planetary scale that the game of mimetic rivalry will play itself out, a game that binds the rivals all the more compulsively and tightly together even as they claim to have nothing in common. The image that appears to emerge—in place of the "clash of civilizations" slogan invoked by those who do not understand the state of the world—is that of a civil war within a single global civilization, which has come into being kicking and screaming. It is within this framework that we must analyse the stunning mirror games in which Al Qaeda and the West have become entangled.[55]

The fact of this mirror doubling was clear in the execution of an unarmed Osama bin Laden by U.S. Navy SEALS. America's relentless payback exercise after 9/11, wrong-footed given the failure to unearth any WMDs in Iraq, has at least now found a plausible target. President Obama's insistence, in the light of criticism—including some from Christian leaders, among them the archbishop of Canterbury—that no one in their right mind would question this action is certainly true according to the wisdom of conventional statecraft. The question is, however, how do we understand the dynamics of such conventional right-mindedness? And the answer (of course) is, *mimetically, sacrificially.*

Wolfgang Palaver finds Charles Taylor's reading of secularization helpful in interpreting the post-9/11 Girardian texts. Taylor's account is of reforming, mobilizing modernity disembedding many people from clan, family, and community, who then find a new identity with the help of religion (especially if it is sufficiently us vs. them). Hence what emerge are neo-Durkheimian identities akin to those found in modern nationalism.[56] Militant Islam seems most clearly explicable along these lines, resembling one of the aforementioned "political religions." This suggestion is supported in other contemporary writing on terrorism and militant Islam, as I will illustrate, before a closer look at *Battling to the End* where all this is put in a larger context.

Girard and the Wider Debate on Islamist Terrorism

Girard's assessment of jihadism is broadly consistent with key conclusions in the wider debate. I want to consider four areas of compatibility.

1. *Jihad is only one version of Islamic modernity.* Another face of Islam today is literate, commercial, and media supported, with its own alcohol-free resorts, fashion boutiques, civil marriage and women's rights, student activists, and feminists—though often hijab wearing. For the Turkish French feminist Nilüfer Göle, this distinctively Islamic form of modernity is not anti-Western, though different from the Christian West in its Islamic need for a public visibility that women's dress provides. A new generation is not persuaded by radical Islamist rhetoric, preferring to carve out its own place in the sun and be modern in its own way.[57] Thus, as Dale Eickelman points out, the real clash of civilizations is not the West versus a homogeneous other but between rival carriers of tradition in Islam's own sphere.[58]

2. *Islamic militancy reflects Western themes and influences.* Jihad emerges in tandem with modern Western currents, and in response to Western provocations—Girard would say, mimetically. Roxanne Euben takes the example of Sayyid Qutb, one of three key mid-twentieth-century Islamist ideologues, showing how his writings are parasitic on Western modernity. Qutb introduces modern Qur'anic interpretations (e.g., advocating equality for women) while insisting on Islamic and not Enlightenment reason (reflecting the sovereignty of God), all aimed at reenchanting the modern world. As Euben shows, Qutb is in step with many Western critics of modernity, especially regarding reenchantment. "The Western and Islamist critique of modernity ... is thus perhaps best characterized as an attempt

simultaneously to abolish, transcend, preserve and transform modernity," concludes Euben, "a dialectical *aufhebung* of modernity rather than an a priori rejection of it."[59]

Qutb's distaste for supposedly decadent Truman-era America certainly stiffened his Islamist-infused cultural nationalism. But it was the decadent Islam, tribal infighting, and lack of political will stalling the progress of Egyptian nationalism that ignited his radicalism.[60] Several such failures of Islamic nationalism in which local corruption and incompetence were exacerbated by Western hypocrisy—in supporting dictatorial regimes while overthrowing secular and progressive governments—sparked the outbreak of today's militant Islam. Radical groups also gained followers by providing necessary support and infrastructure when governments withheld them, while also suppressing secular providers (e.g., communist ones). So the West is deeply implicated in the emergence of this new enemy, but the dynamic is equally intra-Islamic. In any event, what Hafaid Gafaiti calls the "hyperculturalization" of this issue in the Huntington manner is not helpful, as it overlooks both Western mendacity and intra-Islamic provocations.[61]

A further dimension emerges from the intertwined history of Islam and the West. Laurent Murawiek identifies a shared patrimony in ancient Gnostic antiworldliness and late medieval notions of absolute divine sovereignty that (nominalist-influenced) Christianity shared with Islam, all fueling a utopianism extending from medieval Christian apocalyptic via Islamic expectations of the Mahdi, and nineteenth-century nihilism spawning twentieth-century totalitarian utopianism, to today's jihadism. "The world as it is has to be destroyed and reconstructed according to the conceit of the autistic sectarian," reports Murawiek,[62] in all forms of this one murderous modernity. "For the lovers of death of radical Islam," he concludes, "the unbelievers are what the *Untermenschen* were to their fellow Gnostics the Nazis, what the 'exploiting classes' were to their fellow Gnostics the Bolsheviks; what the educated were to their fellow Gnostic Pol Pot."[63]

Modern complicity in spawning radical Islam extends from Marxist anticolonial rhetoric via Algeria to the 1979 Iranian Revolution and from Red Army training of Muslims in the terror methods of Soviet statecraft to the grooming of Palestinian extremists by Cuban State Intelligence. One and all were enlisted to destabilize the West. Likewise, World War I incitement of Muslims against England by Germany took a darker turn under the Nazis, with the Grand Mufti of Jerusalem helping found a training school in Dresden for Muslim SS chaplains and receiving a tour of the Auschwitz gas chambers from Eichmann.[64] I add the related example of America supporting the Taliban against the Soviets in Afghanistan, helping to create their own enemy.[65] And, from an earlier century, the totalizing concept of war brought to the attention of Egyptians by Napoleon. Murawiek finds no pure, hermetically sealed Muslim culture in this shared history.[66] "Jihadis of all stripes in the modern age share the same highly toxic mix of messianism, revolution, and the cult of blood and violence. Modern jihad is the tapestry resulting from the weaving together of different warps and woofs: Pan-Islamism and Bolshevism, Nazi and fascist ideology and practices, and Gnostic-Manichean beliefs within Islam."[67]

As for the actual phenomenon of suicide bombing, which shocks so many as a barbarity far removed from Western values, Girard has described it as a scarcely comprehensible inversion of primitive sacrifice[68]—rather like Oughourlian's assessment of the serial murderer as a victim killing the crowd of persecutors. But the violent archaisms surviving in modernity extend beyond terrorism. We might consider the lemminglike mass slaughter of World War I, and subsequent Western obliteration of civilians in carpet bombing, fire bombing, nuclear bombing, and video-arcade bombing by pilotless drones. Talal Asad highlights the similarities, suggesting that "the suicide bomber belongs in an important sense to a modern Western tradition of armed conflict for the defence of a free political community. To save the nation (or to found its state) in confronting a dangerous enemy, it may be necessary to act without being bound to ordinary moral constraints."[69] Asad does, however, effectively recognize the role of rivalrous model-obstacles described by Girard, observing, "Suicide bombing is an act of passionate identification—you take the enemy with you in a deadly embrace."[70]

3. *Jihad registers frustrated aspirations.* Disappointed rivalry is a widely acknowledged motive. Girard's insight about the collapse of community-preserving prohibitions in the West encouraging militant Islam appears also in Mark Juergensmeyer, for whom religion symbolically empowers alternative ideologies of public order.[71] We would expect to find mimetic envy and rivalry in the background of this combination of religion, violence, and social control, and Juergensmeyer does not disappoint, describing typical young recruits to terror groups in terms similar to Girard. These young men, unemployed and hence unable to marry, whose "marginality in the modern world is experienced as a kind of sexual despair that leads to violent acts of symbolic empowerment,"[72] call Frantz Fanon to mind, from *The Wretched of the Earth,* with his doctor's prescription of postcolonial violence for restoring potency.

The Irish political scientist Louise Richardson links the psychological and the structural in her account of terrorist motivation based on envy and rivalry, supporting my earlier conclusion that relative socioeconomic position rather than absolute poverty is the truer mimetic marker of shame.[73] She shows that terrorism is primarily reactive (in Girard's terms, obstacle-directed), evident when the leaders of five terrorist movements proved unable to describe the sort of society they wanted to create.[74] Drivers of terrorism include unequal access to the benefits of modernization (e.g., education but no jobs), a loss of traditional social controls, and globalization experienced as colonization, with religion providing a focus for dissent and the recovery of lost control. Thus religion mixes with social, economic, and political factors in the mind-set of terrorist groups, helping to forge an all-encompassing ideology capable of attracting recruits and legitimizing violence.[75] Richardson concludes with simple directness: what terrorists want is *revenge, renown,* and *reaction.* The mimetic theory accounts for all three.

4 *The jihadi as a typical modern type.* Girard identifies Dostoyevskian underground psychology at work in the revolutionary. Andrew McKenna takes this up, reflecting on Dostoyevsky's own flirtation with political radicalism after his early writing efforts met with rejection. This resulted in a period of imprisonment that proved to

be a sobering and broadening experience of the human condition for Dostoyevsky, helping him overcome the black-and-white moralism of his former radical posture. So it was that "Dostoyevsky's failure as a terrorist made him a novelist."[76] McKenna thus links terrorist psychology with Girard's account of scandal, so that "the object of desire, as designated by others, is an occasion of offence, or scandal, whose magnetic force is multiplied by the limitless number of models designating it, and where, as a result, the taboo operates as an incentive."[77]

All this reminds McKenna of American campus radicalism and its resentment-fueled vocational craving.[78] He refers to a very good analysis of this mind-set presented autobiographically in a *New Yorker* article by the journalist Jonathan Raban, the son of an English vicar, reflecting on his own youthful embrace of atheist student radicalism. Raban understands the terrorist's "dissident religious creed, full of furious conviction, and an inchoate, adolescent hunger for the battlefield."[79] Raban compares the radical Islamist thinker Sayyid Qutb—studying in Truman-era America and finding even the model community of Greeley, Colorado, seething with indecency and spiritual dissoluteness—with Mohamed Atta, the 9/11 cell leader, while he was in Germany: sexually repressed, awkward, and adrift in the wilderness of outer Hamburg. The Islamist ideology on offer at the radical Al-Tauhid mosque helped Atta glamorize his disappointments, fueling his petulant adolescent aggression and personal bitterness, and strengthening an obsession to avoid ritual impurity.[80] The same hint of "intense, prurient disgust"[81] evident in Qutb's writing obviously boiled over in Atta's American sojourn,[82] as he and his co-conspirators took the lifestyle of their model-rival for a test drive in the fleshpots of Las Vegas, Nevada, and Elizabeth, New Jersey.

For Raban, "the call to jihad answers so resonantly the yearnings of clever, unhappy, well-heeled young men from Mill Valley and Luton as well as from Cairo and Jidda." He provides a good example, referring to John Walker Lindh, a young American captured by his own countrymen while fighting alongside the Taliban in Afghanistan and now serving a long sentence in a U.S. federal prison. Raban reflects on how we might imagine Lindh as "different" from other Americans, an outsider, someone "other," as he must *surely* have been.

Raban concludes rather to the contrary, recognizing that "this son of Marin County is a dark and extreme version of a classic American type, of the kind who might have been found on the road to Marrakech or Ludakh, or hanging out with Peruvian revolutionaries."[83]

Another former activist is Ed Husain, who abandoned and later reclaimed the devout, meditative, scholarly Islam of his family tradition.[84] As a student he was caught up in the Hizb-ut-Tahrir group in London, sharing their contempt for ordinary Muslims in a way of life he now describes as power obsessed, manipulative, and, significantly, riven with internal conflict (hence needing enemies to maintain cohesion). His fellow activists disdained prayers, attending the mosque, and Qur'anic recitation, in favor of activism. They preferred too-fast cars, used pornography, and also lied barefacedly to Kuffar—since without the express command of a sovereign God something cannot be wrong, and because unbelievers deserve no quarter. It was while studying Arabic in what he describes as the racist, misogynist, unspiritual, Wahhabist-influenced culture of Saudi Arabia that Husain realized he had lost touch with the truth of Islam. His account from beginning to end is about a succession of mimetic models, with plenty of Dostoyevsky's underground psychology identified in others and sacrificial archaism under cover of Islam—yet all within a thoroughly modern profile.

Throughout we find Girard's major insights confirmed, though the various writers I have studied lack the clear focus of his mimetic theory and his distinction between modern religions *tout simple* and the archaic sacred—because, of course, Girard is not criticizing traditional Islam but, rather, radical Islamist terrorism.[85] This jihadism is best understood as a new political religion, mimetically driven, and implicated in today's wider return of the archaic sacred within secular modernity. Its commitment to the utopian expulsion of perceived evil is an example of how Girard reads Jesus' teaching about those who enter or take the Kingdom of God by force (Lk 16:16).[86]

In the range of short pieces and interviews that have formed the mainstay of Girard's responses to 9/11, he offers a nuanced reading of Islamist terror along mimetic lines. But he offers it tentatively, refusing to single out Islam for particular blame, though acknowledging the particular liability of Islam in serving as the religious backdrop for an ideology of violence. Perhaps the accustomed Girardian clarity was being held in reserve during this period because its appearance was pending in a fuller form. Hence to the last major piece of the Girardian picture in *Battling to the End*.

ACHEVER CLAUSEWITZ

Girard's apocalyptic sensibility was present from his early writing on Dostoyevsky and ontological sickness, with the universe of Dostoyevsky's characters always in danger of being engulfed.[87] This peril, first identified in mimetic personal relations, revealed its fuller extent once Girard had discovered the scapegoat mechanism and its gospel undoing, which left the world exposed to violent mimetic escalation. He has come to see history as accelerating toward a denouement,[88] so that a choice is called for between a military and environmental apocalypse of our own making or a personal and cultural conversion reaching deep enough to avert it.[89] Apocalypse for Girard is *not* about unleashing divine violence on the unrighteous, for which the mythically minded fundamentalist longs. Rather, it concerns our own self-destructiveness, which could lead us via nuclear, genocidal, and environmental disasters to the likely extinction of human and much other life on Earth. Such an end of the world can also be seen as Christ's coming, according to Girard,[90] though I suggest that this is best understood in terms of the belated vindication of Jesus' teaching about the nature of sin and the need for repentance.

In an extended conversation with the French philosopher Benoît Chantre, which appeared as *Achever Clausewitz* (Completing Clausewitz) and was translated into English as *Battling to the End*, Girard brings this picture frighteningly up to date. He recognizes in its apocalypticism the unique prescience of Christianity, accurately predicting its own failure to sufficiently change the world.[91] Humanity does not want to hear the gospel truth of its own mimetic entrapment in violence, so that in our own time Heraclitus's conviction that war (*Polemos*) is the father and king of all is now being visibly confirmed.[92] As Girard puts it in an interview, "The era of wars is over: from now on war exists everywhere."[93]

The key breakthrough belongs to Carl von Clausewitz, the brooding Prussian general and military theorist who, in the first chapter of his much-studied (and much misunderstood) work *On War*, identified an irrational, escalating, and theoretically unstoppable mimetic *duel* as the real law of warfare.[94] Clausewitz's German word is not the *duel* with pistols, however, which is over quickly whatever the outcome, but the *zweikampf* of one-on-one wrestling, or perhaps fighting for possession of the soccer ball so you can score.[95] In lighting on this, Girard has in mind the conflictual mimesis between rivals whose clash over a particular object soon leaves that object behind. All their mimetic fascination is transferred to the conflict, until they become mirror doubles who feed off one another's heightened enmity and lose all perspective. In military terms, the equivalent trend is what Girard, following Clausewitz, calls an escalation to extremes.

For Clausewitz, in the seminal first chapter of *On War*, the "extreme" in question is "a clash of forces freely operating and obedient to no law but their own."[96] He describes three extremes, which are really three ways of stating the same impetus to the ramping up of warfare: first, the simple reciprocation, from side to side in conflict, of the amount of force brought to bear, which in theory will lead to extremes;[97] second, the threat of greater counterforce from the opponent while conflict endures, felt equally by both sides as a dangerous atmosphere of mutual fear;[98] and third, the calculation of how much force is needed to defeat an enemy whose strength you have sought to gauge, while the enemy does the same, potentially resulting in competitive escalation.[99] But more than any automatic or systemic process is at work here. Central to Girard's understanding of this escalation in its modern form is an unleashing of the passions to annex the business of war—until "naturalistic hatreds" and "hostile feeling" overtake the more containable "hostile intention" that marked an earlier era of disciplined, rational enmities (of the Carl Schmitt sort).[100]

Clausewitz views the carrying through of this escalation to extremes, while intrinsic to the *abstract* nature of war and present wherever the stakes and the level of belligerence are high enough,[101] as unlikely to erupt given the checks and balances typically imposed by the constraints on military endeavor before the era of faster-paced modern warfare and the "telegraphic ultimatum."[102] Here we recall the restricted pace of premechanized armies and their communications, the inevitability of stalled action, and the wisdom of resting troops and capitalizing on an enemy's delays, along with the restraints inherent in sober, self-interested statecraft. So supervening on his initial prophetic insight about war as a duel comes this attempt to reassert the countervailing force of reason. "Were it a complete, untrammelled, absolute manifestation of violence (as the pure concept would require)," Clausewitz writes, "war would of its own independent will usurp the place of policy the moment policy had brought it into being; it would then drive policy out of office and rule by the laws of its own nature."[103] This unthinkable possibility, from which Clausewitz resiles, is the very thing that Girard says has happened. The Clausewitzian escalation to extremes has ceased to be an unpalatable theoretical possibility and has become a verifiable historical actuality, as the age of restraint and ritual in warfare yields place to the military hell on earth that modernity has unleashed.

It is evident, for instance, in the involvement of whole populations, conscripted into armies or engaged in desperate partisan struggles. In this spirit, Tito's partisans in Yugoslavia tied up whole German divisions. Equally, it suggests high civilian casualties, suffered as "collateral damage" in the prosecution of warfare by "legitimate" means (which are in fact becoming illegitimately more violent and indiscriminate). All this registers an all-or-nothing mood that escalates toward the use of biological and nuclear weapons. The same mood is manifest in the venting of real or manufactured ethnic hatreds in mass killings of innocent scapegoats, which we have witnessed from the Armenian genocide to the Nazi Holocaust and the Cambodian killing fields, to Rwanda, to the siege of Sarajevo, and the massacre of Srebrenica.

Of Clausewitz, Girard reports: "His ideas enabled me to finally articulate the broad lines of my mimetic theory in its relation to history,"[104] referring in particular to the Napoleonic period as a cusp on which Clausewitz was poised. From the Napoleonic era warfare inexorably lost its former character as a matter of rules and customs and the limited exercise of violence. Battles had been noble undertakings led by gentlemen and bound by codes of dignified gallantry. They served the ends of statecraft, and were centered on ritualized shows of force. They shared in the *katéchon* function. With Napoleon, however, Clausewitz discerned a sea change in the escalation of warfare to a higher, all-inclusive pitch. Hence war as a manageable tool of statecraft threatened to give way before a totalizing bloodlust and will to power.[105] Accordingly, observes Girard, "reciprocal action, which used to suspend the escalation to extremes in the time of 'the wars of gentlemen' accelerates now that it [i.e., the mimetic principle] is no longer hidden."[106] Clausewitz resiled in alarm from this insight, attempting thereafter to get warfare back into its former box as "the continuation of policy by other means"[107]—as if the escalation to extremes that he had intuitively grasped could remain a mere theoretical possibility.[108] So Girard sets out to "*complete* Clausewitz by taking up the route he interrupted and following it right to the end."[109]

Girard sees this modern escalation to extremes as beginning with the extent of forces marshaled by Napoleon, conscripting the population and waging total war for the first time,[110] and with the aforementioned mobilization of partisans in desperate defensive struggles waged by occupied countries—the logical end point of which is today's terrorism.[111] The likely extremes of this more totalized concept of war became plainly evident for the first time in World War I; Girard concludes that the apocalypse began at Verdun.[112] Such escalation emerged from the reciprocity of mimetic doubles, though manifested by nations rather than individuals. The model of desire possesses something desirable and is attacked for it, responding subsequently with a hunger for war that is modeled on the attacker's desire but which is stronger than that of the attacker. The attacker would be content with peaceful possession of whatever the model possesses, while, in a Clausewitzian paradox that Girard resolves in terms of escalating internal mediation, "the attacker wants peace but the defender wants war."[113] As an example he points to Napoleon lamenting on the eve of his Russian campaign that he did not want war, while Kutusov let Moscow burn to prepare a defeat for the Grande Armée.[114] So a vigorous defense, equally an obsession with maintaining defenses, virtually ensures the escalation rather than the restraint of violence.[115]

An essentially mimetic reading of post-Napoleonic relations between Germany and France is identified by Girard in the nineteenth-century writer Germaine de Staël,[116] and in *The Passing of an Illusion* by François Furet, about World War I.[117] This enmity was symbolically laid to rest when de Gaulle and Adenauer met at Reims in 1953, the place where French and German armies had paraded peacefully together at the baptism of Clovis in 496. As an earlier but linked example Girard points to the feud between pope and Holy Roman emperor which led John Paul II to visit Reims for the fifteen hundredth anniversary of Clovis's baptism, hence symbolically healing the breach between Charlemagne and Leo III.[118]

And the mimetic baton is passed along. The German nation, consolidated as the mimetic legacy of Napoleon, locked horns with Bolshevism, which in turn fought with Nazism (Ernst Nolte, in *The European Civil War*, helped Girard see this mimetically).[119] Next, Nazism fought mimetically with Stalinism, after which erupted Soviet-American mirror doubling in the Cold War.[120] Girard also mentions the Yugoslavian and Rwandan tragedies, and the Sunni-Shiite conflict throughout the Middle East since the Bush administration succeeded in "demolishing a form of co-existence more or less maintained between brothers who have always been enemies."[121]

It is in this whole escalating history of violence that we find the bigger-picture perspective on terrorism that I flagged in the previous section. Girard:

> We have indeed entered into an era of ubiquitous, unpredictable hostility in which the adversaries despise and seek to annihilate each other. Bush and Bin Laden, the Palestinians and the Israelis, the Russians and the Chechnyans, the Indians and the Pakistanis: the conflicts are all the same. The fact that we speak of "rogue states" proves how far we have left behind the codification of inter-state war. Under the guise of maintaining international security, the Bush administration has done as it pleased in Afghanistan, as the Russians did in Chechnya. In return, there are Islamist attacks everywhere.
>
> The ignominy of Guantanamo, the inhumane American camp for presumed terrorists who are suspected of having ties with Al Qaeda, demonstrates the contempt for the laws of war. Classical war, which included respect for the rights of prisoners, no longer exists.[122]

Next will come a dirty bomb, Girard thinks, involving the (of course mimetic) copying of American miniaturization technology by Islamist terrorists.[123]

Another thing that Girard predicts is conflict between China and the United States, though he does not think it will be a military conflict at first.[124] As in all mirror doubling the rivals have become indistinguishable (though the Chinese differ in a long strategic history of using the enemy's strength against him). This will not be a "clash of civilizations" between communist and capitalist, therefore, but between rival versions of modern capitalism. "The Chinese will not stop; they want to beat the Americans," insists Girard, "they want there to be more cars in China than in the United States."[125] The prophetic nature of this 2007 prediction became clear at the 2009 Global Climate Summit in Copenhagen. China held out against any cap on its heavy pollution despite intense international pressure, insisting on preserving its strong economic growth regardless of the environmental cost.

Girard sees globalization today as a planetary amplifier of violent reciprocity whereby the slightest event can cause unpredictable repercussions—consequently, "from Napoleon to Bin Laden . . . attacking and defending have been promoted to the rank of the unique engine of history."[126] The law of violence that we now have to grasp is that violence will always return. There is no scapegoat mechanism anymore that will stop this from happening.[127] Unless the whole of humanity emerges as scapegoat, and destroys itself. "This is something that the genocides in the twentieth century and the massacres of civilian populations have been telling us," suggests Girard, adding that "today's massacres of civilians are . . . simply sacrificial failures, proof that it is impossible to eliminate violence through violence, to expel reciprocity violently."[128] And not just humanity is at risk, but all life on Earth. "There is an indissoluble link between global warming and the rise in violence," Girard argues. "I have repeatedly emphasized the confusion of the natural and the artificial, which is perhaps the strongest thing in apocalyptic texts."[129]

Girard's confronting message in *Battling to the End* is ultimately direct and simple: "Sooner or later, either humanity will renounce violence without sacrifice or it will destroy the planet."[130] For the out-come of history to be any different, Girard says that we must learn "to fight a violence that can no longer be controlled or mastered"[131] in the name of reconciliation rather than mimetic rivalry, yet do so in a mimetic tangle that he now regards as inescapable. Because this will require skillful maneuvering in morally, politically, and interperson-ally murky waters, and in ever more treacherous conditions, Girard seems stunned by the enormous *difficulty* of the task ahead. For this reason, I think, and not just for his Clausewitzian insights into the likely escalation of violence, he utters a chilling lament: "More than ever I am convinced that history has meaning and that its mean-ing is terrifying."[132] I look more closely at Girard's modest Christian prescription for averting global catastrophe in the conclusion that follows.

Conclusion

I have traced the three elements of Girard's vision—mimeticism, sacrifice, and their gospel overcoming—to reveal the wellsprings of secular modernity at a level deeper than ideological and functional definitions of secularization and modernity typically place them. A shift to internal mediation without sacred protection is the long and short of it. The seeds of secular modernity are to be found in the Bible and in the ministry of Jesus rather than where they are usually sought: in the late medieval period, the Renaissance, and the Reformation. They become visible from there, but their genesis is much earlier. The Judeo-Christian vision undermined the archaic false sacred and its prohibitions, rituals, and myths—though that earlier stage of human evolution made our world possible, and we can see God at work in it, protecting humanity until we were ready for a bolder vision.

Yet even the church has failed to live up to that bolder vision, as Dostoyevsky's Grand Inquisitor reminds us. Likewise, human history reveals persistent if diminished reappearances of the false sacred. In secular modernity, the nation-state, market economics, and "war as the continuation of policy by other means" have served a *katéchon* function, restraining the escalation of mimetic dissatisfaction into violent social breakdown. But this is now increasingly tenuous, as the world veers toward an apocalypse of self-destruction and environmental devastation—of enormous sacrifice but without the unifying, pacifying outcome that the archaic sacred delivered.

Girard's is a provocative and unique voice. In a subsequent project I aim to engage more fully with Girard's philosophical work—especially his treatment of violence in philosophy from Heraclitus and Plato on to Nietzsche, Heidegger, Derrida, and his philosophical conversation partner and Christian convert, Gianni Vattimo—as part of a comprehensive theological discussion. In that context I would also like to answer Girard's various critics: postmodern relativists, angry feminists, Catholic-minded theologians concerned that he ontologizes violence, Protestant-minded ones declaring him inadequate on the atonement, and religious pluralists deploring his emphasis on "Christ alone."[1] For now, with the Girardian picture complete since *Battling to the End,* I want to take stock of our options. This entails a more explicitly theological tone in my reflections, because this is where Girard has left us: with the apocalypse, and with no future for humanity apart from repentance and conversion. What might be possible for us beyond Girard's apocalyptic prophecy, and how might we be best placed to seize hold of it?

THE KINGDOM GROWING IN SECRET

In *Battling to the End,* Girard argues that humanity will destroy life on earth if it continues in thrall to a mimetic *zweikampf* that is now escalating beyond control for want of adequate restraints. The escalation to extremes of violence now that no scapegoat has the power to deflect it is Girard's prediction, confirmed since the Napoleonic Wars as murderous, tit-for-tat hatred reveals itself as the new and tragically simple law of history.

Girard has shown that more violence is not the answer, as it will only redouble mimetically. Indeed, there may not be an answer in history, as the Christian vision that reveals the lie of sacred violence and begins to undo its effect is not a religion of God's Kingdom coming on earth. "Fundamentally, it is a religion that announces the world to come; it is not about fighting for this world," as Girard reminds us in a 2008 interview. "It is modern Christianity that forgets its origin and its real direction," he continues. "The apocalypse at the beginning of Christianity was a *promise,* not a threat, because they really believed in the next world."[2] Yet he still suggests that through Christ a choice remains for humanity—a conviction he discerns also in the poet Hölderlin, whom he quotes: "But where danger threatens / That which saves from it also grows."[3]

The Need for Conversion

The choice is primarily to undergo a conversion beyond the morally black-and-white thinking that typifies entrapment in mimetic rivalry. This is what being Christian entails: coming to share mimetically in Christ's nonrivalrous desire, which uproots self-definitional hatred against the despised other and the violence that follows. The resultant profile is, paradoxically, one of powerlessness, which alone proves able to truly change the world, providing a more reliable *katéchon* than those currently on offer. Let me set out this Girardian footnote to apocalypse that regularly surfaces in his published work, though most completely in *Battling to the End.*

The original French title of Girard's first book (published in English as *Deceit, Desire, and the Novel*) highlights the choices: *Mensonge romantique et vérité romanesque,* which literally means "romantic lie and novelistic truth." The typical novelist is dualistic, black-and-white in presenting heroes and villains, whereas sensing that this vision is a false construct and moving beyond it is how great writers emerge. They are demystified of the pride and vanity of mimeticism and hence undergo a so-called novelistic conversion.[4] Proust serves as an example for Girard. He learned that mimetic desire is circular and will not provide satisfaction, abandoning his mimetic fascination for the salons and his *snobbisme* for a life of withdrawal in his *appartement* on the Boulevard Haussmann, where he spent his last twelve years exploring the converted imagination through his five-volume masterwork, *À la rescherche du temps perdu* (In Search of Lost Time)—the time Proust had wasted on mimetic folly before his conversion.[5] Though Proust did not become a Christian, Girard discerns a Christian form in this conversion that "seems to be present in Western literature whenever the hero-creator is saved from an idolatrous world by a spiritual metamorphosis which makes him able to describe his former position."[6]

For other literary figures it *was* an explicitly Christian conversion, for example, Dostoyevsky, who showed Girard that "to the humble imitation of Jesus Christ is opposed the prideful and Satanic imitation of the possessed,"[7] in an experience essentially similar for Augustine, Dante,[8] and, closer to our own time, the mimetic fox-hunting man and reformed wartime avenger, Siegfried Sassoon.[9]

Conversion is to the truth, especially the truth about our selves and our mimetic entanglements, which we know from Girard's work on "metaphysical desire" and "ontological sickness" is really a desire for the substantial being that mimetic creatures cannot attain. The being we lack can only come as a gift from God, as Girard testifies in his reflection on the statue scene concluding Shakespeare's *The Winter's Tale*—the bard's own farewell to the theater.

> One thing alone can put an end to this infernal ordeal, the certainty of being forgiven. This is what Leontes is granted when he finally sees that Hermione is being returned to him alive. This is the first such miracle in Shakespeare. . . . The model for this conclusion can only be the Gospel itself. . . . Shakespeare must have recognized in the Gospels the true revelation not only of God but of man, of what his mimetic imprisonment makes of man. His genius, and more than his genius, enabled Shakespeare to recapture in this conclusion something that belongs exclusively to the Gospels, the non-magical and yet nonnaturalistic quality of their resurrection. The more we examine the statue scene, the more we are reminded of what that resurrection is supposed to be, a resurrection *of the flesh*, in contradistinction to the vaporous world of spirits conjured up by mimetic idolatry.[10]

The comprehensiveness and yet the typical slowness of this conversion are both emphasized in a number of James Alison's writings,[11] with James G. Williams describing conversion as inconceivable apart from religious and contemplative practice via the *agon* of a lifetime's struggle, even after moments of original insight and liberation.[12] It is not only intellectual, or purely formal, and it is not a quick fix.

Girard's Conversion

Girard's personal experience provides a significant example of such a conversion, with a literary as well as a specifically Christian element. In a French interview with Mark Anspach, Girard confesses to having been an autodidact from boyhood who struggled with institutional belonging in school and university (though as a child he had his first significant encounter with *Don Quixote* and later recognized the mimetic and sacrificial elements in his beloved *Jungle Book*).[13] Reflecting on his early academic life, Girard mentions his traumatic mimetic relationship with America after its liberation of France in 1944, his surely cathartic doctoral project on wartime American perceptions of France, then an extreme dose of *"le snobbisme littéraire,"* resentfully rejecting avant-garde literary theory—whereas, to the contrary, as a younger student in France he had "filled [his] head with the farcical, with the stupid, simple mediocrity of the avant-garde."[14] This cashed out for Girard in an intellectual paralysis that cost him his job at Indiana University, so that he only narrowly avoided professional disaster by landing a job at Duke University. There, in the pre–civil rights South, working on Perse and Malraux for his early publications, Girard developed a sense of purpose and began to find his own distinctive method of approaching texts. He clung to the possibility of an absolute truth in these writers, as denied by the literary avant-garde. Girard's discovery of the mimetic theory followed, through reading the French novels that he had to teach during the 1950s, though he wryly adds, "Je conservai tout mon dégoût pour l'érudition et aussi pour toute langue désincarnée, abstraite et philosophique" (I retained all my disgust for erudition and also for all discarnate, abstract philosophical language).[15]

In 1959, at the age of thirty-five, while writing the conclusion of *Deceit, Desire, and the Novel* and while the aforementioned recovery from mimetic literary snobbism was no doubt in train, Girard found himself undergoing a Christian conversion. He was attracted by how the ultramimetic character Stepan Verkovensky in Dostoyevsky's *Devils* turned to the Gospels before his death: "So I began to read the Gospels and the rest of the Bible. And I turned into a Christian."[16]

He mentions weekly return train journeys on the Baltimore-Philadelphia line—though based at Johns Hopkins, he gave a class at Bryn Mawr—during which the weakest winter sunlight on a bleak industrial landscape would spark a spiritual ecstasy in him. Yet one morning on that train another dimension of his conversion fell into place with the discovery of a lump on his forehead. This potentially cancerous growth, and some unsparing medical advice given at the time, ensured a focused Lenten discipline for Girard while test results were awaited. When the all-clear came it was during Holy Week, 1959. Girard went thankfully to confession and rejoined the worshiping church of his childhood for Easter, and subsequently had his sons baptized.[17] And so he has continued as a Catholic layman going regularly to mass, declaring, "I am an ordinary Christian."[18] "Mine is a search for the anthropology of the Cross," Girard summed up his subsequent sense of a Christian vocational calling, "which turns out to rehabilitate orthodox theology."[19]

Imitatio Christi: Redeemed Mimesis

Yet the conversion that he declares necessary is not a conversion away from mimetic desire as such. Girard admits that sometimes he confuses things by saying "mimesis" as shorthand for "mimetic rivalry," insisting that while mimetic rivalry is bad, mimesis itself constitutes an openness to others that is intrinsically good.[20] It is mimesis that elevates us beyond animal instinct, too; otherwise our desires would be fixed forever on predetermined objects.[21] In *Battling to the End*, Girard says that we cannot get outside of mimesis, as he had once thought possible.[22] We do, however, need to learn its rules in order to overcome its destructive aspect.[23] Girard concludes, "There is no solution to mimeticism aside from a good model."[24] The right model is preeminently Christ himself.

The important truth here is that *there will be no mimetic rivalry with Jesus as the model of our desire*, since Jesus' desire is to do God's will, which includes blessing and honoring every other person. We are not called to renounce our mimetic nature but to imitate Christ as little children, without rivalrous fascination—apart from which Jesus does indeed become an obstacle,[25] as we see in Nietzsche and among his heirs both philosophical and political. With Jesus as model, however, our desire follows the generosity of God in dealing with others, reducing the likelihood of our falling into mimetic rivalry with them[26]—"so that you may be children of your Father in heaven: for he makes the sun rise on the evil and on the good, and sends rain on the righteous and unrighteous" (Mt 5:45). Alison emphasizes that Christ is not the typical other of mimetic entrapment but an "other other" who is bigger than we are (i.e., not internally mediated; not our competitive equal), so that imitating Jesus' nonrivalrous desire paradoxically establishes us as free people.[27]

This conversion process involves spiritual disciplines of renunciation, as Girard points out, referring to Jesus' teaching about plucking out your right eye and cutting off your right hand if they cause you to sin (Mt 5:29–30)—images of drastic self-limitation and sensory deprivation to avoid the mimetic vortex, to which we have to become at least somewhat "blind" (and, as it were, hands-off).[28] Jim Grote interprets the traditional seven deadly sins in such terms, as variously to do with craving the being of others while despising our own limited state (lust, gluttony, etc.).[29] As habituated pathways for living beyond mimetic entrapment, three traditional Christian options present themselves.

One is monogamous marriage, understood as a counterpractice in the contemporary Western culture of hypermimetic sexual deregulation.[30] In response to an interview question about mimeticism promoting sexual promiscuity, Girard replied, "I read the monogamous relationship as the greatest achievement of human culture and, in regard to your question, the only 'solution' to the sexual dilemma that is potentially free of gender discrimination and discrimination against persons as such."[31]

Another traditional Christian practice is contemplative prayer, which Grote reinterprets in terms of mimetic desensitization, concluding that "the stilling of the mimetic process is the essence of silence."[32] It is as if the silent focus of contemplative prayer decouples us from the mimetic matrix that runs our imaginations, so we can step out of our mimeticism and really become more "free," more "individual," and all the other things that modern people crave. This is because our incessant mimetic connectedness is being calmed by an alternative model of desire who engenders no envy or rivalry, so we find ourselves drawing down "being" through "good mimesis." God does not even necessarily intrude, so nonrivalrous and non-self-assertive is God, which is why this contemplative experience is often imageless and contentless.

After years of daily prayer in the college chapel or my study at home, I recognized the nonmimetic nature of this silence for the first time while saying my daily offices on the wooded bank of a Minnesota lake on sabbatical in spring 2010—Elijah's "sound of sheer silence" indeed (1 Kgs 19:12). I suspect that the natural setting, overwhelmingly *not* of human making, further occluded the mimetic pressure of human otherness. Likewise, devotional focus on an icon, a candle, a cross, or the eucharistic Host, even in worshipful public gatherings—in addition to the liturgical participation and collective hymn singing that can create unity without violence—acts to shift mimetic attention away from less worthy models of desire.

A third traditional option is life in a monastic community, about which Abbott Andrew Marr, an Episcopalian Benedictine, writes in Girardian terms. He commends the ancient Rule of Saint Benedict as the key to how life can be lived at close quarters, though beyond internal mediation. The careful handling of status and offices within the community, reverence for the abbot, particular concern for the young and the old, and a respectful attitude toward food and the various goods of the monastery (lifting objects out of the mimetic current) all foster a pattern of redeemed desire.[33]

Renouncing Violence and Fighting for Peace

But it must not be thought that this conversion is purely inward and God-ward. Girard's consistent theme is that conversion to Christ means the renunciation of our own violent posture toward others.

This is the Kingdom of God, Girard says: to give up disputes when mimetic rivalry is beginning to take over, to help victims, and to refuse all violence.[34] With Shakespeare's *Hamlet* in mind, and the retaliatory violence typical of so-called honor societies, Girard insists that "to all previous religious laws, the Gospel substitutes a single command: 'give up retaliation and revenge in any form.'"[35] In *Battling to the End*, this is presented as a new ethic, dealing soberly and rationally with the looming fact of catastrophe.[36] Though Girard concludes, "Like Hölderlin, I think that Christ alone allows us to face this reality without sinking into madness."[37] In perhaps his most comprehensive statement about conversion and what is at stake, Girard writes in *Battling to the End*:

> The Biblical and Christian tradition was the first to upset the supremacy of the crowd, to see violent unanimity from the other side, and to pinpoint the principle of reciprocity. Christ, the last prophet, then places humanity before a terrible alternative: either continue to refuse to see that the duel is the underlying structure of all human activities, or escape from that hidden logic by means of a better one, that of love, of positive reciprocity. In this respect, it is striking to see how closely negative and positive reciprocity resemble each other: almost the same form of undifferentiation is involved in both cases, but what is at stake is the salvation of the world.[38]

Significantly, despite much in Girard tending in the direction of pacifism, his position does not necessarily entail it. Girard suggests, for example, that France could have headed off Hitler by ignoring Britain and the United States and invading the Rhineland in 1936, early in the period of Germany's rearming when resistance would have been minimal.[39] Elsewhere, Girard declares that he is "inclined to believe there is a just war on terror."[40] Indeed, he argues that pacifism can be the mirror double of oppression, allowing it to flourish.[41] The use of limited military force in defense of victims, however, represents a wholly new and laudable historical development because it is not about mimetic rivalry. This is fighting for peace but without the mimetically escalating personal hatred that marks the wars that become crusades.[42]

This rejection of nonviolence—an example of Girard's "sensibly conservative politics, his political realism," to which Stephen Gardner draws attention[43]—is surely a confronting admission on Girard's part. It shows how much capitulation to the *katéchon* function of violence he still deems necessary despite having discovered its overtaking and radical recontextualizing by the gospel. Perhaps the master could learn from the disciple here, following Walter Wink in his unsentimental, pragmatic embrace of strategic nonviolence based on a historically informed awareness of its genuine power to bring change in the world of Realpolitik.[44]

Divine Withdrawal and Self-Effacement

The conversion away from the romantic lie, from mimeticism's moral self-delusion, ultimately from rivalry and violence is, as we have seen, about discovering new models of desire. Optimally, these are Christ and his saints. Yet Girard introduces a qualification in *Battling to the End*, about imitation of Christ settling neither for triumphalism nor institutional captivity. Hölderlin's conversion, and his healing from the mimetic back-and-forth of his bipolar disorder, was evident in his withdrawal from active life into solitary reflection and writing, which Girard sees as an appropriate sharing of God's desire.[45] Girard:

> Christ . . . withdraws at the very point when he could dominate. We in turn are thus required to experience *the peril of the absence of God*, the modern experience par excellence. . . . To imitate Christ is to refuse to impose oneself as a model and to always efface oneself before others. To imitate Christ is to do everything to avoid being imitated. . . . The death of the gods, which so frightens Nietzsche, is simply the same thing as an essential withdrawal in which Christ asks us to see the new face of the divine. Mimetic theory has allowed us to conclude that the purpose of the Incarnation was to finish all religions, whose sacrificial crutches had become ineffective.[46]

This is a subtle point, and I take it to resemble the messianic secret in the early part of Mark's Gospel where Jesus disavows acclamation as Messiah. He will not fulfill the expected role; his Messiahship is embarked on *deconstructively*, marked by loving solidarity with the victims rather than triumphalistic payback against the oppressor. Girard is distancing Jesus from the false gods whose day is done, with his incarnation marking the death of religion. Hence the mimetic grandiosity of the false sacred gives way to self-effacement, whereby Alison's "other other" becomes, if you like, "the nonmodel model."

Girard's picture of desire according to this nonmodel model is of absence, silence, withdrawal, nonpresence—the aforementioned "sound of sheer silence" amid the world's mimetic clamor. This is why Christianity is closer to atheism than to anything resembling the archaic sacred, and why the secular imagination cut off from every sense of sacred power is actually *appropriately* underwhelming. This is why the dark night of Saint John of the Cross, named and celebrated at the onset of modernity, is actually the paradox of true divine presence and the dwindling to *nada* of false sacred power over us. Hence the silence of contemplation, also the nondramatic everydayness of eucharistic liturgy—bringing what Alison calls "the detox of our Nuremberg-ed imaginations"[47]—and the existential homelessness that contributes a characteristic cast to authentic spirituality in secular modernity. All because Christian baptism gathers us into *a rootlessness that trumps belonging,* in a world where unity and togetherness regularly conceal the corpses of victims. This is, as Alison names it, a "faith that is the gateway to a relatively benign secularity," a "strangely unreligious gift," leading us beyond the aforementioned "cheap togetherness and junk goodness."[48]

Of course, Christ and his saints are still to be imitated. Paul commends himself as a model—"be imitators of me as I am of Christ" (1 Cor 11:1)—though not in the rivalrous sense whereby some were setting him against Apollos, or indeed against Christ himself (1 Cor 3:4).[49] Paul underlines the point by his consistently ironic self-presentation, as Robert Hamerton-Kelly observes,[50] "boasting in his weakness" (2 Cor 11:30, 12:9), so it is clear that Christ is his model in eschewing the mimeticism of worldly success.

The withdrawal of Christ and the absence of God, where we find our new model of desire, entails a refusal to participate in world making, empire building, grand ideological scheming, and the egotistical self-assertion that masks the hollow ring of mimeticism. Instead of "being somebody" in "the real world"—the violently structured, hypermimetic world, that is—we become who we are truly meant to be in a "more real world" opened up by the true Word of God. What Girard calls the logos of Heraclitus, the violent principle of this world, always expels the Logos of John, as the prologue of John's Gospel testifies (Jn 1:1–18). There is no cultural place for the gospel, since by giving it an earthly home we betray it. That is, we assimilate it to the false sacred. Our alternative, though it leaves us with what feels like spiritual homelessness, is "the replacement [of] the God that inflicts violence with the God that only suffers violence, the Logos that is expelled."[51]

At the 2010 conference of the Colloquium on Violence and Religion, held at the University of Notre Dame, Anthony Bartlett suggested that Girard's downbeat ending in *Battling to the End* was unnecessarily minimal. It left only this hint of salutary withdrawal, from the likes of Hölderlin, as a sign that things could be different in an otherwise doomed world. Bartlett referred to a book by the Australian Catholic theologian Anthony J. Kelly, *The Resurrection Effect,* making a case that greater assurance is available within Christian faith. Kelly argues that the resurrection is a genuine force in history bearing an eschatological guarantee that the new creation will prevail.

Whatever assurance Girard might possibly offer, however, it will not be of the Hegelian sort, promising positive resolution in history. Girard's great achievement in *Battling to the End,* according to Alison, was to offer "the first genuinely post-Hegelian account of Christian eschatology and apocalyptic."[52] Yes, there is an unstoppability of the resurrection, and the Logos of John once spoken will not return void. But this truth is spoken, as it were, *under erasure.* Girard himself names the paradox, of an unrelenting historical advance of the gospel's impact matched by its apparent decline under secular modernity. Yet this power which undid the archaic sacred remains. Indeed, Girard mentions one further sign, in the way it besieged Nietzsche before his final collapse.[53] However, it cannot be triumphalized or institutionalized. Rather, its presence is *sacramental,* retaining the form of a sign, a cipher, an invitation to mystery that is real but not provable to the satisfaction of—that is, on the terms of—worldly mimetic fascination.

A Community of Witnesses

I have taken note that Girard does not wish to be a Christian apologist in ways that risk his world historical vision being discounted. While he wishes to proclaim Christ, he does not wish to do so to the detriment of Christ's own continuing work in the world. Perhaps this is why Girard writes little or nothing about the church. The Girardian theologian Jósef Niewiadomski once corrected me on this, in mock exasperation, complaining that Girard has no ecclesiology. Alison provides one, however, provisionally and in snippets, demonstrating how to cope graciously with a flawed ecclesial institution, as well as how to loyally inhabit the Roman Catholic Church without falling into a posture of mimetic opposition to its resurgent conservatism.[54] Raymund Schwager rightly insisted, however, that an ecclesiology must emerge from Girard's view of revelation and salvation rightly understood: "By gathering together into a peaceful community those human beings who, through the desire of their own hearts, constantly tend towards deceit and violence," Schwager argues, "God reveals himself as God. *The process of revelation is thus technically identical with the overcoming of violence among men and women.*"[55] So, to develop an earlier image based on Alison's "other other" and Girard's warning about inappropriate imitation of Christ, it seems that the nonmodel model calls into being a nontribal tribe—a new sort of human community existing not for its own satisfaction but for knowing and celebrating the truth, for the life of the world.

Giuseppe Fornari describes this community of Christian believers as the last *katéchon* in its actions throughout the world. "The hypothesis holds good and functions magnificently once we understand by community of believers not the church triumphant but a 'remnant' that bears witness and fights," he argues. "That is what happened under Nazism and Stalinism and again since then under the various regimes that have tried and are still trying, with varying degrees of success, to repeat the horrific deeds of those two ominous models."[56] The way this plays out, according to Hamerton-Kelly, is by symbolic refusal to endorse the false sacred lie in its various reappearances through history. "Since sacred power depends on the conspiracy of all to maintain it," he writes, "those who withhold consent from the conspiracy are dangerous and their gracious irony threatens the foundations. They are the 'nothings' that God uses to bring the 'somethings' to nothing (1 Cor 1:28)."[57]

Indeed, in *Battling to the End*, Girard goes so far as to name the Roman papacy as a new force for healing among the nations; it signifies peaceful mimesis since it has lost so much of its geopolitical power and because it stands above the sterile mimetic rivalry of conservatives and progressives in the church.[58] A small hint of ecclesial enthusiasm thus emerges, in a brief but highly suggestive endorsement of his own church's mission under John Paul II and Benedict XVI. "Catholicism has grown out of its childhood," Girard declares, "and become the last *Internationale*."[59]

Gardner, reflecting on *Battling to the End*, is concerned that "Girard risks contributing to the apocalypse he predicts by proposing Christian withdrawal from the fray."[60] Girard's emphasis on the papacy, however, especially Pope Benedict's insistence on the necessity of faith for preserving and revitalizing the modern order, suggests an alternative possibility. The withdrawal Girard insists on is chiefly from the encumbrance of mimetic rivalry and not as obviously from wider engagement or influence *tout court*. After all Pope Benedict, whom Girard endorses, is hardly a shrinking violet. I suggest that all nonmimetically entrapped figures can have a powerful impact on the hearts and minds of others thanks to good mimesis, influencing real-world outcomes in unexpected ways. Consequently, active engagement for the life of the world remains in keeping with Girard's program, following our conversion from rivalrous mimetic dynamics and their illusory promise of enhanced personal "being." This is what we find in the perennial witness of Christ's saints. But it also typifies a figure like Nelson Mandela who embraced public life having plainly renounced metaphysical desire, mimetic rivalry, and violent dreams of payback, hence coming to exercise significant global influence.

* * *

So we are left with faith, hope, and love, these three, as the only possible hedge against despair. Girard's confidence is not in a Hegelian resolution in history, as we have seen, though he has not entirely given up on history either. Thus I want to end on a note of mystery, and obligation, with no option apart from offering our violent, mimetic selves to God, who alone can make something different of us.

Some readers, searching in vain for a practical Girardian plan to counter the threat of our times, will feel that Girard leaves us with little concrete hope. But surely the answer is not some rational program of managed reform, some technique that glosses over the depth and the extent of humanity's violent mimetic disorder. This is a clear lesson from Girard's apocalyptic historiography in *Battling to the End*. Resurrection faith and confidence in the Holy Spirit—that repentance and conversion are forces in the real world that *are* bearing fruit—provide the only alternatives ultimately on offer. For Girard the Christian witness, God has broken through the false sacred in the person of Jesus Christ and now enlists us in resisting its return. This may not seem like much to some, but Saint Paul—the great convert from mimetic fascination and religious violence—was able to boast in the face of such weakness, knowing the paradox of Christ's power dwelling within him precisely when he was most powerless (2 Cor 12:9–10). The last word goes to Girard:

> This God cannot act with a strong hand in a way that men would consider divine. . . . God does not reign but he will reign. He reigns already for those who have accepted him. Through the intermediary of those who imitate [Jesus] and imitate the Father, the Kingdom is already among us. It is a seed that comes from Jesus and that the world cannot expel, even if it does all it can.[61]

NOTES

INTRODUCTION

1. Serres, "Receiving René Girard into the Académie Française," 5.
2. Girard, *Things Hidden Since the Foundation of the World*, 40.
3. Girard offers biographical reflections here and there throughout his published work and numerous interviews. Some more revealing personal ones have appeared recently in the *cahier* celebrating his election to the Académie française: see, e.g., Girard, "Souvenirs d'un jeune Français aux États-Unis"; see also Dupuy, "René en Amerique." A helpful biographical sketch is offered by James G. Williams in *The Girard Reader*. I will be saying more about Girard's Christian conversion in the conclusion to this volume.
4. A good sense of the personal, spiritual, and intellectual impact Girard has had on students, colleagues, and friends is evident in tribute after tribute reproduced in Goodhart et al., eds., *For René Girard* (2009).
5. See Eisenstedt, "Multiple Modernities."
6. See Wittrock, "Modernity: One, None, or Many?"
7. See Eisenstedt and Schluchter, "Paths to Early Modernities: A Comparative View"; also Wittrock, "Early Modernities: Varieties and Transitions."
8. Latour, *We Have Never Been Modern*.
9. See, e.g., Ward and Hoelzl, eds., *The New Visibility of Religion*.
10. See, e.g., Göle, "Snapshots of Islamic Modernities"; Eickelman, "Islam and the Languages of Modernity"; Euben, *The Enemy in the Mirror*.
11. See Dawkins, *The God Delusion*.
12. See Berger, ed., *The Desecularization of the World*.
13. I have written at greater length on this in chapter 2 of my *Abiding Faith*. See also Gillespie, *The Theological Origins of Modernity*.
14. See Durkheim, *The Elementary Forms of the Religious Life*.
15. Weber, *The Protestant Ethic and the Spirit of Capitalism*.
16. See Miller, *Consuming Religion;* also Carrette and King, *Selling Spirituality*.
17. See Berger, Davie, and Fokas, *Religious America, Secular Europe?*, chap. 3.

18. Ibid.

19. See Bruce, *God Is Dead.*

20. Girard, *Sacrifice,* 81.

21. Palaver, " . . . Essay on Islam and the Return of the Archaic," 9.

22. I am deeply indebted for my understanding of secular modernity to the "reform master narrative" as described by Charles Taylor in *A Secular Age,* in which the "porous" self is disembedded from holistic belonging in the "paleo-Durkheimian" world of the "ancien régime" and cast as a "buffered" self into the "nova world," "the immanent frame"—apart from my one concern that the "buffered" self is significantly unbuffered in mimetic terms. Taylor cites Girard sympathetically here and there throughout his massive volume, and seems to suggest that Girardian insight on these matters is significant; see, e.g., 821n64. I think Girard also lays bare some roots that Taylor has not uncovered. See also Wolfgang Palaver, "Religion und Gewalt: René Girards und Charles Taylors komplementäre Beiträge zu einer zeitgemäßen Theorie," in *Kommunitarismus und Religion,* ed. M. Kühnlein (Berlin: Akademie Verlag, 2010), 319–28.

23. Taylor, *Sources of the Self,* 405.

24. Blumenberg, *The Legitimacy of the Modern Age,* II.3.

25. See Taylor, *A Secular Age,* 773–76; Gillespie, *The Theological Origins of Modernity.*

26. Weber, *The Protestant Ethic and the Spirit of Capitalism.*

27. See Gauchet, *The Disenchantment of the World;* also Cloots, "Modernity and Christianity: Marcel Gauchet and the Christian Roots of the Modern Ways of Thinking."

28. See Gardner, "René Girard's Apocalyptic Critique of Historical Reason," 15.

29. Girard, *Quand ces choses commenceront,* 78.

Chapter One. **MIMESIS, MODERNITY, AND MADNESS**

1. From Greek words meaning "to imitate," *mimesis* is widely used in aesthetics and literary criticism, referring to representation. The nature of representation has always been contested, from Plato to postmodernity. Mimesis was decried by Plato as a suspect impoverishment of reality, while to the contrary Aristotle endorsed it as a (constitutively human) means of getting closer to the real. From the Enlightenment emerged a new emphasis on mimesis as representational creativity. Contemporary thinkers point to its key role in human adaptation. See, e.g., Erich Auerbach, *Mimesis: The Representation of Reality in Western Literature* (Princeton, NJ: Princeton University Press, 1953); Mihai Spariosu, ed., *Mimesis in Contemporary Theory*

(Philadelphia: John Benjamins, 1984); Michael Taussig, *Mimesis and Alterity* (New York: Routledge, 1993).

2. Girard, *Things Hidden Since the Foundation of the World*, 35; original emphasis.

3. Girard, *Deceit, Desire, and the Novel*, 161. I can think of no better current example than the novels of Michel Houllebecq.

4. Girard, *To Double Business Bound*, 94.

5. Girard, *Things Hidden*, 284.

6. Girard (with Marcus Müller), "Interview with René Girard," 12.

7. Girard, *A Theater of Envy*, 29–79, 234–42; the phrase is Hermia's, in her conversation with Lysander, concluding that it is a hellish thing: see *A Midsummer Night's Dream*, I.i.140.

8. Girard, *Deceit, Desire, and the Novel*, 45–52; Girard, *Resurrection from the Underground*, 47–50.

9. Girard, *A Theater of Envy*, 133.

10. Girard, "Violence, Scapegoating, and the Cross," 335. See also his "Conversation" (with Phil Rose), 25. Girard admits that the love of parents for their children need not be interpreted mimetically, nor sexual desire—in those rare cases "lorsque l'ombre des rivaux a déserté la couche des amoreux" (when the rivals' shadow deserted the lovers' couch); Girard, *Quand ces choses commenceront*, 30.

11. Girard, *Things Hidden*, 343.

12. Girard, *Deceit, Desire, and the Novel*, 10.

13. Girard, *A Theater of Envy*, 73.

14. Girard, *To Double Business Bound*, 2.

15. Girard, *Deceit, Desire, and the Novel*, 5.

16. Ibid., 1–2.

17. Livingston, *Models of Desire*, 64, 165. Girard does make sparing reference: see note 90, below.

18. Girard, *Things Hidden*, 417.

19. Ibid., 9. For a guide to office politics, negotiation, and business ethics from the perspective of Girard's mimetic theory, see Grote and McGeeney, *Clever as Serpents*.

20. Girard, "Love and Hate in Chrétien de Troyes *Yvain*," in *Mimesis and Theory*, 214–29.

21. See Fanon, *The Wretched of the Earth;* also a Girardian reflection on "colonial psychology" in chapter 3 of my *Abiding Faith*. This connection, which Michael Kirwan describes as "tantalizing," is mentioned in his *Girard and Theology*, 106–9.

22. Girard, *Deceit, Desire, and the Novel*, 9.

23. Girard, *Job*, 51.

24. Girard, *Evolution and Conversion*, 61.

25. Girard, *Deceit, Desire, and the Novel,* 104.

26. Girard, *Battling to the End,* 22.

27. Girard, *Oedipus Unbound,* 29. Girard's collaborator Jean-Michel Oughourlian points out that forbidden fruit in the Garden of Eden became desirable to Eve only because of her rivalry toward God; see Oughourlian, *The Genesis of Desire,* 96.

28. Girard, "Satan," in *The Girard Reader,* 194–210, on 198.

29. Elsewhere Girard identifies "scandal" with the aforementioned aura surrounding any mimetically illuminated object; see Girard, *Oedipus Unbound,* 68.

30. Girard, "The Question of Anti-Semitism in the Gospels," in *The Girard Reader,* 211–21, on 215.

31. Girard, *Things Hidden,* 426–27.

32. Ibid., 299.

33. Ibid., 297.

34. Ibid.

35. Girard, *To Double Business Bound,* vii.

36. Girard, *Things Hidden,* 26.

37. Girard, *Deceit, Desire, and the Novel,* 9.

38. Ibid., 117–18.

39. Ibid., 119; original emphasis.

40. Hobbes, *Leviathan,* 63; Kirwan, *Discovering Girard,* 29–30.

41. Hobbes, *Leviathan,* 64.

42. Girard, "Stendhal and Tocqueville," in *Mimesis and Theory,* 42–49.

43. Girard, *Deceit, Desire, and the Novel,* 138.

44. Ibid.

45. Girard, *Things Hidden,* 359.

46. Oughourlian, *The Puppet of Desire,* 151–52; see also Webb, *The Self Between,* 145–48.

47. Oughourlian, *The Puppet of Desire,* 152, 77–78.

48. Ibid., 170–71.

49. Girard, *Things Hidden,* 320.

50. Oughourlian, *The Puppet of Desire,* 113, 224.

51. Girard, "Hamlet's Dull Revenge: Vengeance in *Hamlet,*" in *A Theater of Envy,* 271–89, on 279–80.

52. Oughourlian, *The Puppet of Desire,* 168; Oughourlian, *The Genesis of Desire,* 102.

53. Oughourlian, *The Puppet of Desire,* 222–24.

54. Ibid., 132–44.

55. Ibid., 142; see also a fuller, Girard-influenced discussion of this episode in my *Abiding Faith,* 84–85.

56. Girard, "Postface: Mimetic Desire in the Underground," in the 1997 edition of his *Resurrection from the Underground,* 143–65, on 158.

57. Oughourlian, *The Puppet of Desire,* 144–72.

58. Ibid., 228.

59. Oughourlian, *The Genesis of Desire,* 102.

60. Girard, *Things Hidden,* 348.

61. Oughourlian, *The Genesis of Desire,* 102.

62. Girard, *Things Hidden,* 403.

63. Ibid., 303.

64. Girard, *To Double Business Bound,* 96.

65. Oughourlian, *The Genesis of Desire,* 105.

66. Girard, *Violence and the Sacred,* 169, 170–71, 250–51; see also Fleming, *René Girard,* 32–33.

67. Mack, "Introduction: Religion and Ritual," 14.

68. Girard (with Wolfgang Palaver), "René Girard im Gespräch I," in *Gewalt und Religion,* 33–65, on 52, using Palaver's unpublished English transcript of the interview, which was later translated into German for publication (my thanks to Professor Palaver for a copy of the original English text).

69. Fleming, *René Girard,* 36; original emphasis.

70. Ibid., 38–39.

71. Doran, "Introduction," in Girard, *Mimesis and Theory,* xvii–xviii.

72. Oughourlian, in conversation with Girard; see Girard, *Things Hidden,* 391.

73. Girard, *Things Hidden,* 350.

74. Ibid., 355.

75. Ibid., 361.

76. Girard, *To Double Business Bound,* 43.

77. Girard, *Violence and the Sacred,* 241.

78. Girard, *Things Hidden,* 356, 411.

79. See Golsan, *René Girard and Myth,* 24.

80. Fleming, *René Girard,* 33–34.

81. Golsan, *René Girard and Myth,* 21–22.

82. Fleming, *René Girard,* 34–35.

83. Girard, *To Double Business Bound,* 106.

84. Girard, *Things Hidden,* 353.

85. Ibid.

86. Girard, *To Double Business Bound,* 56, 68.

87. Girard, *Things Hidden,* 360.

88. Girard, "To You Your Father Should Be as a God: The Crisis of Degree in *A Midsummer Night's Dream,*" in *A Theater of Envy,* 167–73, on 168.

89. Girard, *Things Hidden,* 359.

90. For a rare acknowledgment of this influence, pointing to the family of origin along with the school and professional training as necessary

contexts, "assurent notre insertion dans la vie sociale," see Girard, "Les Appartenances," 22.

91. Girard, *Resurrection from the Underground,* 139.

92. Girard, *Things Hidden,* 417.

93. Livingston, *Models of Desire,* 171.

94. Morrison, *The Culture of Shame,* 60, 74–79, 195.

95. Girard, *The Scapegoat,* 155.

96. Morrison, *The Culture of Shame,* 76–77.

97. For a helpful exploration of such relationships (which, though non-Girardian, is readily amenable to a mimetic reading), see Solomon, "Attachment Repair in Couples Therapy." It is a pity that the more than capable Oughourlian does not explore this range of fertile Girardian resonances in his otherwise fascinating account, in *The Genesis of Desire,* of mimetic problems in intimate relationships.

98. Girard, *Things Hidden,* 354.

99. Ibid., 368.

100. Ibid., 370, 378. Very clear on this whole issue is Wilson, "What Do We Want and Why Do We Want It?"

101. Girard, *Things Hidden,* 377.

102. Ibid., 370.

103. Ibid., 369.

104. Girard, *Quand ces choses commenceront,* 31.

105. Atlan and Dupuy, "Mimesis and Social Morphogenesis," 1264.

106. Girard, *Deceit, Desire, and the Novel,* 162–64; see also Kaye, "Twenty-First-Century Victorian Dandy," for an account of this phenomenon in its current metrosexual form.

107. Alison, *Broken Hearts and New Creations,* 61.

108. Girard, *Things Hidden,* 371.

109. Girard, "Narcissism: The Freudian Myth Demythified by Proust," in *Mimesis and Theory,* 175–93, on 187.

110. Ibid., 180–82.

111. A nice image from Mack, "Introduction: Religion and Ritual," 48.

112. Girard, *Things Hidden,* 370; original emphasis. On 371, Girard describes Célimène's salon of admirers as "a real Versailles of coquetry!"

113. Girard, *Quand ces choses commenceront,* xx.

114. Girard, "Intellectuals as Castrators of Meaning" (interview by Giulio Meotti), 2. If Girard offers some acknowledgment of a *natural* homosexual inclination apart from mimesis, the gay Girardian theologian James Alison acknowledges *distorted* versions of homosexual behavior—in prison, in wartime—based mimetically on power, unequal advantage, and abuse. Alison argues consistently that homosexual inclination is the real but entirely natural and noncontroversial shape of human sexuality for about 3 percent

of the population. See Alison, *Broken Hearts and New Creations*, 11. The 3 percent point was made by Father Alison in conversation.

115. Girard, "René Girard im Gespräch I" (interview with Wolfgang Palaver), in *Gewalt und Religion*, 48. In this published version of the text, which appears in German translation, the quotation is, "Ich sage nicht, dass Homosexualität schlecht ist, sondern dass eine bestimmte Homosexualität von Shakespeare so interpretiert wird."

116. Girard, "Pride and Passion in the Contemporary Novel," in *Mimesis and Theory*, 33–41, on 37–38.

117. Ibid., 362–65.

118. Ibid., 335, 337, 343, 346, 347.

119. Alison, *Broken Hearts and New Creations*, 276.

120. Girard, *Deceit, Desire, and the Novel*, 188, 192.

121. Ibid., 184–85.

122. Ibid., 178.

123. Webb, *The Self Between*, 107.

124. Girard, *Deceit, Desire, and the Novel*, 177–78.

125. Girard, *A Theater of Envy*, 47.

126. Girard, "The Passionate Oxymoron in Shakespeare's *Romeo and Juliet*," in *Mimesis and Theory*, 274–89, on 282.

127. Girard, *Deceit, Desire, and the Novel*, 176, in a chapter titled "Masochism and Sadism"; original emphasis.

128. Ibid., 166, in a chapter titled "The Hero's Ascesis."

129. Girard, *Oedipus Unbound*, 1.

130. Girard, *A Theater of Envy*, 35.

131. Girard, *Things Hidden*, 415.

132. Girard, *Deceit, Desire, and the Novel*, 181.

133. Ibid., 70.

134. Girard, "Innovation and Repetition," in *Mimesis and Theory*, 230–45, on 240. In Shakespeare's character Bottom, Girard observes that "the need to contradict is just as mimetic in him as the need to copy." See "More than Fancy's Images: The Craftsmen in *A Midsummer Night's Dream*," in *A Theater of Envy*, 57–65, on 61.

135. Girard, "Bastards and the Antihero in Sartre," in *Mimesis and Theory*, 134–59; see 158, 155.

136. Girard, *Things Hidden*, 378.

137. Girard, *Deceit, Desire, and the Novel*, 261; original emphasis.

138. Girard, *Things Hidden*, 426.

139. Girard, *Deceit, Desire, and the Novel*, 254.

140. McKenna, "Scandal, Resentment, Idolatry," 24–25.

141. Ibid., 19.

142. Girard, *Deceit, Desire, and the Novel*, 184.

143. Ibid., 185.

144. Ibid., 184.

145. To my knowledge, Girard never refers to clergy sexual abuse. However, his discussion of how "Salome" is corrupted by the mimetic desire of Herod/Herodias, which is fixated on John the Baptist, might suggest an aspect of how Girard would respond; see Girard, *The Scapegoat*, 132–33. The systemic nature of this whole problem is not admitted by churches, with today's new pitch of clergy discipline (as necessary as it may be) representing the effective denial of any wider, institutional/cultural culpability; see my article, "An Abusive Church Culture? Clergy Sexual Abuse and Systemic Dysfunction in Ecclesial Faith and Life," *St Mark's Review* 205 (August 2008): 31–49.

146. Girard, *A Theater of Envy*, 4.

147. Girard, *Deceit, Desire, and the Novel*, 56.

148. Girard, *To Double Business Bound*, 96.

149. I sought to trace this process as a single arc in chapter 2 of my *Abiding Faith*, from medieval nominalism to nineteenth-century Russian nihilism, though without at that stage fully integrating the discussion with Girard's program.

150. Girard, *Deceit, Desire, and the Novel*, 270.

151. Girard, *Resurrection from the Underground*, 93.

152. Ibid., 95.

153. Girard, *Things Hidden*, 392.

154. Girard, *Deceit, Desire, and the Novel*, 265, in a chapter titled "The Dostoyevskian Apocalypse."

155. James G. Williams, "Foreword," in Girard, *Resurrection from the Underground*, 11.

156. Girard, *Resurrection from the Underground*, 62.

157. Ibid., 55.

158. Ibid., 76.

159. Ibid., 141.

160. Ibid., 88.

161. Girard, *Deceit, Desire and the Novel*, 253. Dostoyevsky's novel (titled *Besy* in the Russian original) is also known in English as *The Demons* or *Devils*.

162. Ibid., 254–55.

163. Girard, *Resurrection from the Underground*, 79.

164. Ibid., 23.

165. Girard, *To Double Business Bound*, 75.

166. Ibid., 61–62, in a chapter titled, "Strategies of Madness—Nietzsche, Wagner, and Dostoevski."

167. Girard, *Things Hidden*, 310.

168. Girard, *To Double Business Bound*, 74; original emphasis.

169. Ibid., 92 (see also 93, for more on the masochistic dimension of this self-immolation upon the obstacle).

170. Ibid., 75.

171. Girard, *Things Hidden*, 311. The Girardian psychotherapist Henri Grivois writes more clinically on these phenomena with particular reference to the vulnerability of teenagers in their uniquely ill-defined, in-between state: "Adolescents are mimetic torches waiting to be lit." His account of psychotic undifferentiation in mimetic terms fits with that of Oughourlian and Girard on madness as the hypermimetic confusion of subject and model, concluding helpfully that—rather than a private, intrapsychic phenomenon—"emergent madness is a collective event lived in solitude." See Grivois, "Adolescence, Indifferentiation, and the Onset of Psychosis," 116, 120.

172. Girard, *Things Hidden*, 421; see also "Monsters and Demigods in Hugo," in *Mimesis and Theory*, 125–33, on 129.

173. Girard, *Deceit, Desire, and the Novel*, 282.

174. See Girard, *Things Hidden*, 151.

175. Girard, *Resurrection from the Underground*, 89.

176. Girard, *Deceit, Desire, and the Novel*, 287.

177. See Girard, *A Theater of Envy*, 295.

178. Girard, *Deceit, Desire, and the Novel*, 282.

179. Girard, "L'Opposition au darwinisme s'est évaporée" (conversation with Hervé Morin).

180. See Hatfield, Cacioppo, and Rapson, *Emotional Contagion*, 2, 76 ff.

181. Selma Fraiberg, "Blind Infants and Their Mothers: An Examination of the Sign System," in *The Effect of the Infant on its Caregiver*, ed. M. Lewes and L. A. Rosenblum (New York: Wiley, 1974), 217; cited in Hatfield, Cacioppo, and Rapson, *Emotional Contagion*, 88.

182. Jean Piaget, *Play, Dreams and Imitation in Childhood* (New York: Norton, 1962).

183. A. N. Meltzoff and M. K. Moore, "Newborn Infants Imitate Adult Facial Gestures," *Child Development* 54 (1983): 702–9, cited in Meltzoff and Gopnik, "The Role of Imitation in Understanding and Developing a Theory of Mind," 342.

184. Meltzoff and Gopnik, "The Role of Imitation," 341.

185. Ibid., 342.

186. Meltzoff and Moore, "Infant Intersubjectivity," 50–53.

187. Meltzoff and Gopnik, "The Role of Imitation," 343.

188. Meltzoff and Moore, "Persons in Representation," 20–26.

189. Meltzoff and Gopnik, "The Role of Imitation," 350–54.

190. Oughourlian, *The Genesis of Desire*, 89.

191. Iacoboni, *Mirroring People*, 24–25.

192. Ibid., 34–38.

193. Ibid., 28–30.

194. Ibid., 30–34.

195. Ibid., 38–42; see also Gallese, "The Two Sides of Mimesis," 28.

196. Rizzolatti and Sinigaglia, *Mirrors in the Brain*, xi, 114, 125.

197. Gallese, "The Two Sides of Mimesis," 32, 33, 34.

198. Iacoboni, *Mirroring People*, 11–12.

199. Rizzolatti and Sinigaglia, *Mirrors in the Brain*, 153–59; Iacoboni, *Mirroring People*, 36–37.

200. Iacoboni, *Mirroring People*, 74–78; Rizzolatti and Sinigaglia, *Mirrors in the Brain*, 124–31 (photograph on 126).

201. Iacoboni, *Mirroring People*, 77–78; Rizzolatti and Sinigaglia, *Mirrors in the Brain*, 168–69.

202. Iacoboni, *Mirroring People*, 200–203.

203. Ap Dijksterhuis, "Why We Are Social Animals: The High Road to Imitation as Social Glue," in *Perspectives on Imitation*, vol. 2, ed. Susan Hurley and Nick Chater (Cambridge, MA: MIT Press, 2005), 207–20; cited in Iacoboni, *Mirroring People*, 201.

204. Rizzolatti and Sinigaglia, *Mirrors in the Brain*, 151.

205. Iacoboni, *Mirroring People*, 116–20.

206. Ibid., 124.

207. Ibid., 168–74.

208. Ibid., chaps. 8–10.

209. Oughourlian, *The Genesis of Desire*, 95. Girard welcomes the discovery of mirror neurons in "A Conversation" (with Phil Rose), 30.

210. Garrels, "Imitation, Mirror Neurons, and Mimetic Desire," 78–79. Professor Gallese informed me in a private communication, in response to my suggestions along this line (having read his paper cited above), that measuring the MNS for subjects' "empathy" toward others unlike themselves (either racially different, for instance, or disfigured) is under way. These experiments might provide insight into how Girardian scapegoats are "chosen"—how they attract preconscious attention so that a crowd's wrath "naturally" falls on them. This phenomenon begins my discussion in the next chapter.

Chapter Two. **VIOLENCE, THE SACRED CANOPY**

1. Girard, *Violence and the Sacred*, chap. 3.

2. Girard, *Evolution and Conversion*, 137.

3. Ibid., 66.

4. Girard, *Job*, 27.

5. See Otto's classic rejoinder to Kant's too rational account of religion, *Das Heilige* (1917)—a title rather self-defeatingly rendered into English as *The Idea of the Holy* (Oxford: Oxford University Press, 1923).

6. Schwager, *Must There Be Scapegoats?*, 20.

7. Girard, "The Question of Anti-Semitism in the Gospels," in *The Girard Reader*, 219.

8. Girard, *Sacrifice*, 44.

9. Ibid., 23.

10. Girard, *Things Hidden*, 13, 32; see also Girard, "Violence and Religion: Cause or Effect?," 2; and "The Bloody Skin of the Victim" (interview with Wolfgang Palaver), 60. I wrote about religion and spirituality under the sway of commodification in chapter 1 of my *Abiding Faith*.

11. A term I use in chapter 1 of my *Abiding Faith*.

12. Girard, *Sacrifice*, 48–49.

13. Girard, *Things Hidden*, 96.

14. Bertonneau, "The Gist of René Girard" (no pagination in online version).

15. Girard, *Evolution and Conversion*, 96.

16. Ibid., 99.

17. Ibid., 112.

18. Girard (with Markus Müller), "Interview with René Girard," 3.

19. Girard, "Interview René Girard" (the *Diacritics* interview, later reproduced in *To Double Business Bound*), 32 (in the *Diacritics* version).

20. Girard, *Violence and the Sacred*, 221; Girard, *Things Hidden*, 91; Girard, "Violence, Scapegoating, and the Cross," 335.

21. Girard, *Things Hidden*, 97.

22. Ibid., 98.

23. Girard, *Evolution and Conversion*, 101.

24. Girard, *Things Hidden*, 98; Girard, *Evolution and Conversion*, 105.

25. Girard, *Things Hidden*, 98.

26. Ibid., 94.

27. Ibid., 87.

28. Girard, *Evolution and Conversion*, 105.

29. Ibid., 106.

30. Ibid., 108–9.

31. Ibid., 110.

32. Girard, *Things Hidden*, 99, 81.

33. Girard, *Evolution and Conversion*, 107, 110.

34. Ibid., 109–10.

35. Girard, *Things Hidden*, 102.

36. Ibid., 96.

37. Ibid., 100; also *Evolution and Conversion*, 105.

196 | Notes to Pages 63–65

38. Girard, "Generative Scapegoating," 248–49. The Girardian scholar James G. Williams, translator of Girard's book *I See Satan Fall Like Lightning,* notes there that Girard confines himself to a single victim for the sake of simplicity, but a class of victims can also be referred to, such as foreigners: see 35n2.

39. Girard, in conversation with Renato Rosaldo in a "Discussion" at the end of Hamerton-Kelly, ed., *Violent Origins,* 248 (emphasis mine).

40. Girard, *Battling to the End,* ix.

41. Girard, *Things Hidden,* 103.

42. Girard proposes that burial customs, like all rituals, recall the founding murder, so that, for example, burial mounds imitate the heap of stones over a victim's body that remains after a stoning; see *Things Hidden,* 91.

43. Girard, *Things Hidden,* 68–73; Girard, *Evolution and Conversion,* 116–19.

44. Girard, *Evolution and Conversion,* 116, referring to Carrasco, *City of Sacrifice.*

45. Girard, *Evolution and Conversion,* 120–21.

46. Ibid., 121.

47. Girard (with Markus Müller), "Interview," 11; see also Girard, *Violence and the Sacred,* 262.

48. Girard, *Evolution and Conversion,* 103–4.

49. Ibid., 113.

50. Girard's significant attention to the very earliest possible human existence as nevertheless demanding the taboos and rituals that he grounds in the surrogate victim mechanism seems to trump the critique of the Irish spiritual writer Diarmuid O'Murchu in a book on the rehabilitation of desire, that is, that Girard's theory is only essentially relevant from well into the Neolithic, before which a less hierarchical and more free range version of human life was supposedly in place. See O'Murchu, *The Transformation of Desire,* 36. Here the shade of Rousseau's noble savage seems to be present.

51. Mack, "Introduction: Religion and Ritual," 22–32; Palaver, "Violence and Religion," 125.

52. Girard, *Things Hidden,* 73; see also Girard, "Disorder and Order in Mythology," 93. Nor am I persuaded. With this proposition in mind—about the hunt founding human culture—I recently watched a television documentary on contemporary African hunter-gatherers. This small group spent an exhausting day pursuing a spiny anteater, matter-of-factly and unceremoniously skewering the poor thrashing thing in its burrow—which they had spent hours laboriously digging out under a hot sun—then cooking its fatty skin to sustain them in the field before taking the choice portions back to their village. The sense I had was of a routinized, skilled, workmanlike yet convivial undertaking, evincing a well-established set of practices. To me this

hunt looked more like the fruit of a human social order than the means of its founding.

53. Girard, "Disorder and Order in Mythology," 96.

54. Girard, *Things Hidden*, 84–85; see also Girard (with Markus Müller), "Interview," 11.

55. Girard, *Evolution and Conversion*, 125.

56. Gans, "Introductory Remarks," in the special 1996 edition of *Anthropoetics*, "Generative Anthropology," 1.

57. Eric Gans, *Originary Thinking: Elements of Generative Anthropology* (Stanford: Stanford University Press, 1993), 8–9; cited in Girard, *Evolution and Conversion*, 123.

58. Bartlett, "From First Hesitation to Scenic Imagination: Originary Thinking with Eric Gans," 93, 104. This long article provides an overview of Gans's theoretical program.

59. Ibid., 91.

60. Ibid., 141.

61. Gans, "René et moi," 19–25, on 24 (I refer elsewhere to another article by Gans with the same title, from *Anthropoetics*).

62. Gans, "The Origin of Language: Violence Deferred or Violence Denied?," 15.

63. Ibid., 5–7.

64. Girard (with Markus Müller), "Interview," 10.

65. Gans, "The Origin of Language," 9.

66. Girard, *Evolution and Conversion*, 123. Having said that, Girard refuses to adjudicate between three major theories about when human language actually began, claiming insufficient expertise; see Girard, "A Conversation" (with Phil Rose), 29.

67. Girard, *Evolution and Conversion*, 127–28; also Girard, *Job*, 76.

68. Bertonneau, "The Gist of René Girard."

69. Girard, *Things Hidden*, 32.

70. Ibid., 42.

71. Girard, "Generative Scapegoating," 93 (original emphasis).

72. Girard, "Violence, Scapegoating, and the Cross," 336.

73. Girard, *I See Satan Fall Like Lightning*, 90–91.

74. Girard, *Things Hidden*, 12.

75. Girard, *I See Satan Fall Like Lightning*, 88.

76. Girard, *Dieu, une invention?*, 56; see also Girard in conversation, "Scapegoats and Saviours," 8.

77. Girard, *Things Hidden*, 82.

78. Girard, *I See Satan Fall Like Lightning*, 100.

79. Girard, "The Bloody Skin of the Victim" (interview with Wolfgang Palaver), 60 (emphasis mine).

80. Girard, *Violence and the Sacred*, 18.
81. Ibid., 134.
82. Ibid., 20.
83. Ibid., 33.
84. Ibid., 33–34, 108; see also Girard, *Things Hidden*, 75 ff.
85. Girard, *Violence and the Sacred*, 57.
86. Girard, "Violence, Scapegoating, and the Cross," 338.
87. Girard, "Hamlet's Dull Revenge: Vengeance in *Hamlet*," in *A Theater of Envy*, 271–89; see 274.
88. Girard, "Violence Renounced," 315.
89. Girard, *Violence and the Sacred*, chap. 3; see also Girard, *Oedipus Unbound*.
90. Alain de Botton, *Status Anxiety* (New York: Pantheon, 2004), 147.
91. Girard, *Battling to the End*, 19. A fine cinematic example is provided by an allegorical 2009 sci-fi film, *District 9,* in which the scapegoated Wikus is accused of having sex with the despised, insectlike aliens that are rounded up and confined in South Africa.
92. Girard, *Violence and the Sacred*, 92.
93. Ibid., 269. Likewise, Girard sees intertribal rivalry as internal rivalry exported; see 279.
94. Ibid., 95; see also Girard, *Things Hidden*, 156.
95. Girard, *Violence and the Sacred*, 96.
96. See Latour, *We Have Never Been Modern*.
97. Girard, *Things Hidden*, 13, 91.
98. Girard, "Violence, Scapegoating, and the Cross," 337; also a range of examples in chapter 7 of Girard, *Job*, titled, "Jezebel Trampled to Death under the Horses' Hooves." This is also a common theme in the Psalms, as discussed by Girard in "Violence in Biblical Narrative," 389.
99. Girard, *Battling to the End*, 22.
100. Girard, "The Anthropology of the Cross," in *The Girard Reader*, 270–71.
101. Girard, *Things Hidden*, 52.
102. Girard, *Violence and the Sacred*, 107.
103. Ibid., 304.
104. Girard, *Things Hidden*, 72; see also Girard, "The Anthropology of the Cross," in *The Girard Reader*, 270–71.
105 Girard, *Violence and the Sacred*, 120–26.
106. Ibid., 125.
107. Girard, *Job*, 41. We enjoy a similar catharsis today thanks to the brutality of thrillers, which Girard says are the closest we get to the lynch mob; see his *Oedipus Unbound*, 101.
108. Girard, *Violence and the Sacred*, 136.

109. Girard, "The Bloody Skin of the Victim" (interview with Wolfgang Palaver), 62; also Girard, *I See Satan Fall Like Lightning*, 116–17.

110. Girard, *Violence and the Sacred*, 141–42. The shocking extent of sacrificial violence against women in the charnel house of Tenochtitlan is cataloged by Carrasco in *City of Sacrifice*.

111. Girard, *Job*, 78.

112. Girard, *Violence and the Sacred*, 150.

113. Ibid., 150–62.

114. Ibid., 237.

115. Girard, "From Ritual to Science," 20. See also a related discussion of technology as the offspring of ritual in Girard, *Quand ces choses commenceront*, 84, 90–95.

116. Girard, "From Ritual to Science," 15.

117. Ibid., 17. So that line from Monty Python's comic film *The Life of Brian*, involving the mishearing of Jesus' Sermon on the Mount, turns out to be most apt: "blessed are the cheese makers."

118. Girard, *Violence and the Sacred*, 316.

119. Girard, *The Scapegoat*, 1–2, 12; see also chapter 5, "Texts of Persecution," in Girard, *Things Hidden;* and chapter 6, "Sacrifice," in Girard, *I See Satan Fall Like Lightning*.

120. Girard, *The Scapegoat*, 9–10. Girard suggests that such confession represents the only self-empowerment left open to powerless victims, providing them at least with an illusion of self-determination in front of their persecutors. Influenced by his tormentors, Job in like manner came to doubt his own innocence before God (Job 9:27–29); see Girard, *Job*, 128–29.

121. Girard, *The Scapegoat*, 8.

122. Ibid., 12–14.

123. Ibid., 15.

124. Girard, "Violence and Representation in the Mythical Text," in *To Double Business Bound*, 195.

125. Girard, *The Scapegoat*, 18.

126. Girard, "Violence and Religion," 3.

127. Girard, *The Scapegoat*, 18–19.

128. Ibid., 81 (original emphasis).

129. Ibid., 20.

130. Ibid., 21.

131. Ibid., 22.

132. Ibid., 22.

133. Ibid., 23.

134. See also chapter 4, "Myth: The Invisibility of the Founding Murder," in Girard, *Things Hidden*.

135. Girard, *The Scapegoat*, 24.

136. Ibid., 25. Girard offers a close reading of the Oedipus myth in chapter 2 of *Oedipus Unbound*.

137. Girard, *The Scapegoat*, 25–26.

138. Ibid., 27, 29.

139. Girard, "The Anthropology of the Cross," in *The Girard Reader*, 267.

140. Girard in discussion, in Hamerton-Kelly, ed., *Violent Origins*, 227; see also a related discussion of myth by Girard, "Python and His Two Wives: An Exemplary Scapegoat Myth," in *The Girard Reader*, 119, 131.

141. Girard, *The Scapegoat*, 38.

142. Ibid., 38. Girard's discussion of the Native American Dogrib myth—of a woman guilty of bestiality (whose puppies were also children), who was banished (the primal murder) but ended up watching over the tribe—offers another classic example of this twofold transference in myth (see 49–50).

143. Ibid., 41, 45–46, 51.

144. Girard, "Generative Scapegoating," 103.

145. Girard, *The Scapegoat*, 57–63.

146. Ibid., 74; the Baldr-Curetes-Titans discussion occurs in chapter 6.

147. Ibid., 80, 83.

148. Ibid., 83.

149. Ibid., 84–85; see also 85–87 for Girard's discussion of a single myth combining all these strategies to water down the blame: that of Cadmus, founder of Thebes.

150. Ibid., 88–94.

151. Girard, "Violence, Scapegoating, and the Cross," 339.

152. Girard, "Interview René Girard," 41.

153. Girard in discussion, in Hamerton-Kelly, ed., *Violent Origins*, 227. "Hurrah for the Anglicans," one might add, though it would be better if we Anglicans had not recommended witch-hunting in our own church around issues of sexual orientation.

154. See, e.g., Girard, "Generative Scapegoating," 79, 94.

155. Girard, *The Scapegoat*, 41 (emphasis mine).

156. See Girard, *Evolution and Conversion*, 86, where he defends this usage against the English alternative "unconscious," which he rejects for its Freudian connotations (see chap. 1, above).

157. Girard, *Things Hidden*, 126.

158. Girard, *Sacrifice*, chap. 2, "The Founding Myths of Vedic Sacrifice," 30–61.

159. Ibid., 65

160. Ibid., 88–93.

161. Ibid., 95.

Chapter Three. **SCRIPTURE AND SECULARIZATION**

1. Williams, "Steadfast Love and Not Sacrifice," 77–78; see also chap. 9.

2. Girard, *Things Hidden*, 142; Girard (with Markus Müller), "Interview with René Girard," 4; see also Grote, "The Imitation of Christ as Double-Bind," 494.

3. I also note Jacob's final leave-taking from his duplicitous father-in-law, Laban, with whom he has been locked in mimetic tit-for-tat for decades, when a heap of stones is set up as a witness between them—perhaps a sign of the immolation that has been avoided, cementing a pact of strategic mutual avoidance and hence a real if imperfect resolution of crisis (Gn 31:46–54). Such reserve also marks Jacob's handling of Esau postreconciliation, wisely ensuring some physical separation between the two of them (Gn 33:12–17).

4. Girard, *Things Hidden*, 143, 148.

5. Ibid., 143. From elsewhere in the Hebrew Bible Baillie adds the figures of Micaiah, who escaped the collective violence of four hundred false prophets by his countertranscendent vision of the real God and his court, and Susanna, in whose story we see the birth of judicial due process as the guilty are condemned in place of the innocent (Baillie, *Violence Unveiled*, 173–77, 189–93).

6. Girard, *Things Hidden*, 143.

7. Ibid.

8. Ibid., 240. Baillie adds an observation on the importance of ritual at the tent of meeting in the Exodus account of Israel's desert sojourn, representing the typical care characteristic of tribal societies in which properly performed ritual is essential for containing the threat of violence. He notes that Hebrew priests at the tent of meeting vest with all the care we would expect today from the bomb squad—and for good reason, with a holocaust for the sons of Aaron reflecting the consequence of their ritual failure (Ex 28; Lv 10:1–3) (see Baillie, *Violence Unveiled*, 150, 152). Williams understands such punishing wrath from God in these narratives as a metaphor for collective violence, so that fire from God is really a reference to mob action (see Williams, *The Bible, Violence, and the Sacred*, 124). He is convinced of this because Exodus and its God seem so far from the normal run of mythical violence. While Egyptian literature blamed the Israelites for Egypt's plagues (as we would expect from myths and persecution texts) and while Israel—oppressed and subject to the murder of its firstborn—provided Egypt with a ready supply of scapegoats, nevertheless a different national identity emerged under Moses, beyond his early dabbling in mimetic rivalry and murder. Israel rejected the victim identity and departed on its own course. Egypt then collapsed into a mimetic crisis of self-destructive violence thanks to the absence

of its accustomed scapegoats, which is how Williams reads Exodus imagery of the Red Sea rolling back on Israel's pursuers (Ex 10) (see Williams, *The Bible, Violence, and the Sacred,* 77–81, 89). None of this makes sense with a violent mythological god. Rather, for Williams, as he reads Exodus, "Israel's religious revolution shines through the text: although many features of the ancient sacred order and sacrificial violence remain in the narrative, the narrator's sympathy lies not with the dominant social order, that of the Egyptians, but with those who are expelled. Whatever the problems of mimetic desire, rivalry, and sacrificial violence that remain in the book of Exodus, as in the Bible as a whole, a breakthrough has occurred here" (89).

9. Girard, *Things Hidden,* 148.

10. Ibid., 149.

11. Ibid.

12. Ibid., 151–52.

13. Williams, *The Bible, Violence, and the Sacred,* 60. Williams refers to versions ascribed to Pompeius Trogus and Chaeremon, respectively.

14. Girard, *Things Hidden,* 152.

15. Girard, "Violence Renounced," 318.

16. Girard, *Quand ces choses commenceront,* 57 (translation mine).

17. Girard, *Things Hidden,* 152. I note that even while imprisoned Joseph is immediately recognized as a worthwhile person and put in charge of the prison, as he had been put in charge of Potiphar's household, and would likewise be elevated by Pharaoh.

18. Ibid., 152; see also Girard, "Mimesis and Violence," in *The Girard Reader,* 17–18.

19. Claus Westermann, *Genesis 37-50: A Commentary* (Minneapolis: Augsburg; London: SPCK, 1986), 28.

20. See "The Story of Two Brothers," in *Ancient Near-Eastern Texts Relating to the Old Testament,* 3rd ed. with Supplement, ed. James B. Pritchard (Princeton: Princeton University Press, 1969), 23–25. The story is also available on the Internet by searching under its title.

21. Lefebure, *Revelation, the Religions, and Violence,* 31.

22. Bata appears to be the victim of collective murder three times on his way to becoming Pharaoh, apart from which the sacrifice of his penis, rated highly symbolic of the self and its power in the ancient Near East (Girard viewing Jewish circumcision as replacing earlier human sacrifice), sounds significantly like a primal murder under erasure—not to mention the fish eating it, recalling all those other animal assailants surrounding the victim to which our attention has been drawn, who represent the primal lynch mob. As for nobody becoming divine in this story, we recall that Bata and Anubis were already gods in Egypt and that this story is their prequel, if you like. We note too that Bata ends up as Pharaoh, who is of course a divinity. As for Bata being declared innocent, this is only because everybody

already knows that he has become a god so he must have been innocent. This is how the surrogate victim mechanism works: first the universal imputation of guilt, then the collective murder, then retroactively the innocence once the reconciling mechanism of collective violence has worked its magic and the victim has been divinized. Genesis never divinized Joseph, however, and while Anubis is only reconciled once Bata's penis sacrifice has taken place, Joseph has champions from the start in the figures of Reuben/Judah.

23. Girard, *The Scapegoat*, 199. The Girardian literary scholar Giuseppe Fornari provides another example, from Euripides' last play, *Iphegenia at Aulis*. An old slave—a powerless, pitying onlooker who has refused the logic of violence—looks outward from the sacrificial labyrinth of Greek culture on behalf of the playwright, "awaiting the revelation of an infinite love to push back the frontiers of its sacrificial awareness." He likens this moment to the expectant ending of the Old Testament. See Fornari, "Labyrinthine Theories of Sacrifice," 187.

24. Girard, *Sacrifice*, chap. 2, 65, 87–92, 94–95.

25. Girard, *I See Satan Fall Like Lightning*, 9.

26. Ibid., 12.

27. Ibid., 9 (original emphasis).

28. Ibid., 12. Williams addresses the earlier commandments more fully than Girard, but in commenting on the Third Commandment, about God's name not being taken in vain, he confirms Girard's reading of the Commandments in terms of God's liberating purposes, because "the name, which the people know and have and may call upon, is the perpetual Word that separates order from disorder, life from death, peoplehood from slavery" (Williams, *The Bible, Violence, and the Sacred*, 110). Williams goes on to emphasize the ways in which undifferentiation and hence chaos are guarded against in the Decalogue: by maintaining proper social boundaries with regard to property, wives, authoritative customs, and religious traditions—with respect for parents reflecting a healthy awareness of a proper order of things, against the possibilities of mimetic desire giving rise to social chaos, as Girard also points out. (See Williams, *The Bible, Violence, and the Sacred*, 108–13; Girard, *I See Satan Fall Like Lightning*, 7–13; see also my little book, *The Ten Commandments and Ethics Today* [Melbourne: Acorn, 2008], a set of Girard-inspired retreat addresses on the Ten Commandments given at an Australian Benedictine monastery).

29. Girard, *Things Hidden*, 154. I discussed Douglas and Girard together in chapter 3 of my *Abiding Faith*.

30. Girard, *Things Hidden*, 157; also "Mimesis and Violence," in *The Girard Reader*, 18.

31. Girard, *I See Satan Fall Like Lightning*, 28–30.

32. Williams, "Steadfast Love and Not Sacrifice," 96.

33. Williams, *The Bible, Violence, and the Sacred*, 162.

34. Schwager, *Must There Be Scapegoats?*, 134.

35. Girard, *Things Hidden*, 157.

36. Williams, "'Steadfast Love and Not Sacrifice,'" 86.

37. Ibid., 89–91.

38. Baillie reads this passage more positively, with the fire from heaven as a metaphor for the violent crowd unleashed by Elijah as part of an anti-sacrificial turn against religions of human sacrifice (Baillie, *Violence Unveiled,* 169–73). I find Alison more persuasive.

39. Alison, "Theology Amidst the Stones and Dust," in *Faith beyond Resentment,* 30.

40. Williams makes a similar point about Jeremiah, who reluctantly accepts "that God's refusal directly to answer his questions and complaints means that God transcends the mimetic situation in which the prophet and his persecutors oppose one another" (Williams, *The Bible, Violence, and the Sacred,* 148).

41. Alison, "Spluttering up the Beach to Nineveh," in *Faith beyond Resentment.*

42. Alison, "The Exilic Transformation of Anger into Love," in *Faith beyond Resentment.*

43. Girard, *Things Hidden,* 447.

44. See Girard, "Violence in Biblical Narrative." He refers to C. S. Lewis, *Reflections on the Psalms* (New York: Harcourt, Brace, and World, 1958).

45. Girard, "The Bloody Skin of the Victim" (interview with Wolfgang Palaver), 61.

46. See Girard, "Violence in Biblical Narrative," 391; "The Bloody Skin of the Victim," 62; *I See Satan Fall Like Lightning,* 116.

47. Girard, "Violence in Biblical Narrative," 392.

48. Girard, *The Scapegoat,* 104.

49. Girard, "Violence in Biblical Narrative," 392.

50. Ibid.

51. Girard, *Job: The Victim of His People,* 27.

52. Ibid., 35, 111–16; see also *The Scapegoat,* 104.

53. Girard, *I See Satan Fall Like Lightning,* 117.

54. Girard, *Job,* 131.

55. See Bailie, *Violence Unveiled,* 136; Schwager, *Must There Be Scapegoats?,* 43,

56. Schwager, *Must There Be Scapegoats?,* 61–62.

57. Ibid., 131–32.

58. Williams, "'Steadfast Love and Not Sacrifice,'" 98.

59. Girard, "Generative Scapegoating," 141.

60. Girard, *Things Hidden,* 158.

61. Fraser, *Christianity and Violence*, 26. Zechariah appeared in 2 Chronicles and was hence the last of these in the Bible as Jesus knew it; see Mt 23:34–36; Lk 11:50–51.

62. Girard, *Things Hidden*, 158–60; see also Girard, "The Question of Antisemitism in the Gospels," in *The Girard Reader*, 220–21.

63. Girard, *Things Hidden*, 162.

64. Ibid., 165.

65. Girard, "The Evangelical Subversion of Myth," 39.

66. Girard, *Things Hidden*, 178.

67. Ibid., 167–74.

68. Baillie, *Violence Unveiled*, 166.

69. Schwager, *Jesus in the Drama of Salvation*, 130.

70. Girard, *Things Hidden*, 178–79.

71. Girard, "Violence Renounced," 319.

72. Girard, *Things Hidden*, 180–82. There is quite a body of Girardian literature on the nonviolent atonement.

73. Ibid., 192–93.

74. Ibid., 187 (original emphasis).

75. Ibid., 195.

76. Ibid., 203.

77. Ibid., 213–19; see also Girard, "Foreword," in Williams, *The Bible, Violence, and the Sacred*, viii; also "Are the Gospels Mythical?," 7; and "An Interview with René Girard," in Golsan, *René Girard and Myth*, 130–31.

78. Ibid., 193.

79. Ibid., 223.

80. Girard, *The Scapegoat*, 101; see also Girard, "Foreword," in Williams, *The Bible, Violence, and the Sacred*, ix.

81. Girard, *The Scapegoat*, 105–9.

82. Ibid., 110–11.

83. Ibid., 118–20.

84. Ibid., 127.

85. Ibid., 127–45.

86. Ibid., 146.

87. Ibid., 149–58. Girard also points to the thieves crucified with Jesus (Mk 15:27–32) as mimetic figures who "insult Jesus in imitation of the crowd, in a last desperate effort to rejoin the crowd, to deny their crucifixion" (Girard, "Violence and Religion," 6). More recently Girard has added the revealing of mimetic rivalries to Jesus' other major revelation, the scapegoat mechanism. "Christ exasperated mimetic rivalries," he argues. "He agreed to be their victim in order to reveal mimetic rivalries to the eyes of all. He caused them to appear everywhere: in the society, in families." See Girard, *Battling to the End*, 103.

I note, too, how Peter's threefold rehabilitation by Jesus (Jn 21:15–22), expunging his threefold denial, provides Peter with a means to demonstrate the disavowal of his former mimeticism. When Jesus asks, "Simon son of John, do you love me more than these?," Peter's nonmimetically competitive reply makes no reference to these others, as once it might: "Yes, Lord; you know that I love you." Jesus is ensuring that he can commit the care of his sheep and lambs to Peter, which would not be possible if he remained in thrall to mimetic envy and rivalry—though a lapse follows immediately, in the infamous exchange over the beloved disciple, where Peter asks, "What about him?" The same care taken by Jesus should also be applied by those who choose today's bishops and popes.

88. Girard, *The Scapegoat*, 165–82.

89. Ibid., 182–83.

90. Girard, *I See Satan Fall Like Lightning*, 123; see also Girard, *Sacrifice*, 95.

91. Girard, *I See Satan Fall Like Lightning*, 132–35.

92. Girard, "Are the Gospels Mythical?," 7.

93. Girard, *I See Satan Fall Like Lightning*, 125.

94. Ibid., 131.

95. Ibid., 139, 142.

96. Ibid., 142, 182; see also Girard, *Evolution and Conversion*, 224.

97. Ibid., 149–50.

98. Ibid., 150.

99. Girard, "Satan," in *The Girard Reader*, 209.

100. Girard, "Ratzinger Is Right" (interview with Nathan Gardels), 4.

101. Girard, *I See Satan Fall Like Lightning*, 192.

102. Girard, "The Evangelical Subversion of Myth," 35.

103. Girard, *Evolution and Conversion*, 210.

104. Girard, "Violence Renounced," 313.

105. Ibid., 315.

106. Girard, *Things Hidden*, 235.

107. Ibid., 231.

108. Girard, "Generative Scapegoating," 117.

109. See Alison, *Raising Abel*.

110. See Serres, "Ego Credo."

111. Alison, "Sacrifice, Law, and the Catholic Faith: Is Secularity Really the Enemy?," in *Broken Hearts and New Creations*, 89.

112. Girard, "Violence, Difference, Sacrifice" (interview with Rebecca Adams), 33.

113. Alison, *Raising Abel*, 108.

114. Girard, "Mimesis and Violence," in *The Girard Reader*, 18–19; see also, *Things Hidden*, 249–54.

115. Bandera, *The Sacred Game,* 234.

116. Girard, *Things Hidden,* 225. At one time Girard was particularly dismissive of Hebrews, due to its liberal use of sacrificial concepts (*Things Hidden,* 224). He has since disavowed this position, recognizing Hebrews' deconstructive use of sacrificial language in order to *undermine* sacrificial religion, also newly appreciating self-sacrifice once freed from the sacrificial mechanism. Schwager encouraged this reappraisal, in *Jesus in the Drama of Salvation,* 183. As Hardin points out, "Hebrews discerns a crisis in the old sacrificial system" but, "while using the language of sacrifice, rejects all connections between violence and the sacred. Instead, Hebrews offers a new paradigm of what real self-giving (human and divine) is really about" (see Hardin, "Sacrificial Language in Hebrews," 113, 116). But Girard had already recanted, telling Rebecca Adams that he had been completely wrong not to appreciate the evolution of sacrifice beyond its violent, primal religious sense, and its function in modern celebrations of victimhood. He confessed, "I scapegoated Hebrews and I scapegoated sacrifice"—missing, for instance, the positive version of sacrifice in Solomon's judgment between two women (1 Kgs 3:16–28), where the real mother offered to sacrifice her rightful claim if it secured her child's safety (see Girard, "Violence, Difference, Sacrifice," 29; see also *Evolution and Conversion,* 215–17). Girard later describes his early antipathy to the possibility of a valid Christian self-sacrifice as the last gasp of his antichurch avant-gardism; see his "Apocalyptic Thinking after 9/11" (with Robert Doran), 29–30. Sarah Coakley criticizes the "Girard bandwagon" for tying sacrifice to violence (see her "Sacrifice Regained"), but I fear she is flogging a dead horse. For a fine Girardian theological reflection on how sacrifice can be read positively, especially as regards the Eucharist, see Robert J. Daly, *Sacrifice Unveiled.*

117. Hamerton-Kelly, *Sacred Violence,* 188.

118. See Girard, *I See Satan Fall Like Lightning,* chap. 4, "The Horrible Miracle of Apollonius of Tyana."

119. Ibid., 167.

120. Ibid., 165–66.

121. Ibid., 168.

122. Girard, *Evolution and Conversion,* 239.

123. McMahon, "Violence-Religion-Law," 200.

124. Helpful here is a short history of Christian complicity in the violent sacred, as well as many countervailing examples demonstrating true fidelity to the gospel, provided as part of the 2000 Boston conference of the Colloquium on Violence and Religion, which addressed violence as it appears under the auspices of the various world religions: see Daly, "Violence and Institution in Christianity."

125. Girard, "Generative Scapegoating," 140.

126. Baillie, *Violence Unveiled*, 67–71.

127. Girard, "Great Rome Shall Suck Reviving Blood: The Founding Murder in *Julius Caesar*," in *A Theater of Envy*, 200–209.

128. Girard, "Let's Be Sacrificers but Not Butchers, Caius: Sacrifice in *Julius Caesar*," in *A Theater of Envy*, 210–19, on 217–18.

129. Baillie, *Violence Unveiled*, 86. "A London Fête" can be viewed online, e.g., at http://oldpoetry.com/opoem/101691-Coventry-Patmore-A -London-F-te.

130. Baillie, *Violence Unveiled*, 98.

131. Bandera, *The Sacred Game*, 12.

132. Ibid., 23.

133. Ibid., 28–29.

134. Ibid., 186.

135. Ibid., 29, 36.

136. Ibid., 196.

137. Ibid., 186.

138. Ibid., 36–37.

139. Ibid., 31.

140. Ibid., 31–32.

141. Girard, "Generative Scapegoating," 118.

142. Girard, *I See Satan Fall Like Lightning*, 179.

143. Girard, *Sacrifice*, 66. I note in this connection Girard's dismissal of Joseph Campbell, author of *The Hero with a Thousand Faces* (Bollingen Series 17 [New York: Pantheon, 1949]), who assimilates biblical narrative to pagan myth to confect a popular nondogmatic, nonexclusive spiritual wisdom. Girard identifies this positivist mainstay of contemporary "spirituality" rhetoric with the first literary attack on Christianity that we know about—by the aforementioned second-century philosopher Celsus—with its claim that Christianity is no different from paganism (see also Girard, "Violence, Scapegoating, and the Cross," 347; and *The Scapegoat*, 100–101). This charge, echoed in the romantic escapism of Campbell's Jungian-inspired project, misses the violence and the *dogmatic noninclusivity* of myth, along with biblical distinctiveness. "Instead of being marvellously imaginative maps of 'the unconscious,'" as Baillie counters, "myths are the narrative remnants of the source of human unconsciousness" (*Violence Unveiled*, 130). We know from Girard that this unconscious lies in the unacknowledged mimetic nexus of our lives, rather than in any Freudian depth of the mind, and that the founding murder is also cloaked in unconsciousness.

144. Girard, "Generative Scapegoating," 116–17.

145. Girard, "Nietzsche versus the Crucified," in *The Girard Reader*, 246–53.

146. Girard, "The Founding Murder in the Philosophy of Nietzsche," 231.

147. Ibid., 256; see also *Evolution and Conversion*, 220–21. The Nietzsche reference to Aphorism #125, "The Madman," is in *The Gay Science: With a Prelude in Rhymes and an Appendix in Songs* (1887), trans. Walter Kaufmann (New York: Random House, 1974), 181.

148. Girard, "The Founding Murder in the Philosophy of Nietzsche," 246; see also *Evolution and Conversion*, 220.

149. Girard, "Generative Scapegoating," 117.

150. Girard, "Interview," in Golsan, *René Girard and Myth*, 133.

151. Girard, "The Twofold Nietzschian Heritage," in *I See Satan Fall Like Lightning*, 173.

152. Ibid., 173; see also Girard, "Violence and Religion," 6.

153. Girard, "The Twofold Nietzschian Heritage," in *I See Satan Fall Like Lightning*, 175; see also 171.

154. Bandera, *The Sacred Game*, 258, 270.

155. Ibid., 173.

156. Ibid., 295.

157. Girard, "An Interview with René Girard," in *To Double Business Bound*, 227.

158. Girard, *Things Hidden*, 184; see also Girard's interview with Wolfgang Palaver, "René Girard im Gespräch I," 60, in *Gewalt und Religion;* and McKenna, *Violence and Difference*, 138–39.

159. Girard, *I See Satan Fall Like Lightning*, 181.

160. Gardner, "René Girard's Apocalyptic Critique of Historical Reason," 6.

161. See Bandera, *The Sacred Game*, 254.

162. Milbank, *Theology and Social Theory*, 280.

163. Girard, *Battling to the End*, xi.

164. Girard, "The Founding Murder in the Philosophy of Nietzsche," 142–43; see also Girard, *Quand ces choses commenceront*, 169.

Chapter Four. **MODERN INSTITUTIONS AND VIOLENCE**

1. Girard, *Battling to the End*, 18.

2. Girard, *Things Hidden*, 28.

3. Thiel, "The Straussian Moment," 193.

4. Girard, *Evolution and Conversion*, 262.

5. I thank my New Testament colleague John Painter for helping me clarify this double usage, which might suggest that Paul is personalizing what is essentially a process—something Girard also does in his discussions

of Satan. My opting for the first of these two Greek spellings when trans-literating the word reflects the most common usage in Girardian literature and is not intended to indicate any preference between them or to make a point.

6. Hamerton-Kelly likens this function to that of Old Testament law, according to Paul (Gal 3:23–24), as a custodian until Christ's coming, "hold-ing bad violence in check by good violence, holding society together until the truth could be made known" (Hamerton-Kelly, *Sacred Violence*, 76).

7. Girard, *I See Satan Fall Like Lightning*, 186. Paul emphasizes our real but circumscribed obligation to obey these authorities, as Girard dis-cusses on 98.

8. Girard, *Evolution and Conversion*, 13, 244. Details here are limited. Indeed, both for this chapter and the next the amount of Girardian writing on matters under consideration varies from a lot to very little—though, as mentioned in the introduction, there is no fault in Girard having focused on the literary and historical past rather than on these contemporary issues. Nevertheless, on this or that topic where Girard's own engagement is limited it is possible to fill gaps with insights from the secondary Girardian literature and from my own informed reflection.

9. Francis Fukuyama, *Trust: The Social Virtues and the Creation of Pros-perity* (New York: Free Press, 1995).

10. Dupuy, "Panic and the Paradoxes of the Social Order," 221–23.

11. See Palaver, "Hobbes and the KATÉCHON," 61–68 passim.

12. Girard, *Celui par qui le scandale arrive*, 149 (translation mine). Note here one of Girard's rare signals that he is not a pacifist. This is an issue I say more about in the conclusion of this study.

13. Dietrich Bonhoeffer, *Ethics* (1949), ed. Eberhard Bethge, trans. Neville Horton Smith (London: Collins, 1964), 108.

14. Lawrence, "Philosophy, History, and Apocalypse in Voegelin, Strauss, and Girard," 126.

15. Palaver, "Hobbes and the KATÉCHON," 70.

16. Bossy, "Elementary Forms of Durkheim," 15–16.

17. For this helpful distinction I am indebted to Emilio Gentile, *Politics as Religion.*

18. Bellah, "Civil Religion in America," 18.

19. Gentile, *Politics as Religion,* 136.

20. Pascal, *Pensées* (1670), ed. Dominique Descotes, Brunschvicg ver-sion (Paris: Flammarion, 1976), #102 (Lafuma edition, #118) (translation mine).

21. Bernard Mandeville, *The Fable of Bees: Or, Private Vices, Public Bene-fits* (1714) (Indianapolis: Liberty Fund, 1998); see Girard, *Evolution and Conversion*, 244.

22. Adam Smith, *An Inquiry into the Nature and Causes of the Wealth of Nations* (1776), ed. Edwin Cannan (Chicago: University of Chicago Press, 1976), IV.2. para. 9.

23. Friedrich Hayek, *The Constitution of Liberty* (1960) (London: Routledge, 2008), chap. 3, "The Common Sense of Progress," 36–48.

24. Sung, *Desire, Market and Religion*, 36, 43.

25. Kitzmüller, "Economy as a Victimizing Mechanism," 22, 26, 36.

26. As argued, e.g., by Tom Friedman in his apologia for globalization, *The Lexus and the Olive Tree* (New York: Farrar, Straus & Giroux, 1999).

27. Beaudin and Gauthier, "The Uncontrolled Return of the Passions in the Economic and Political Sacrificial 'Soteriology' of Our Times," 185.

28. Anspach, "Global Markets, Anonymous Victims."

29. Dumouchel, "Indifference and Envy," 150–53.

30. Ibid., 154.

31. Anspach, "Global Markets, Anonymous Victims."

32. Girard, *Evolution and Conversion*, 248.

33. In *L'Enfer des choses;* see Palaver, "Envy or Emulation," 140.

34. Dumouchel, "Indifference and Envy," 155–57; Steinmair-Pösel, "Economy and Mimetic Theory," 78–79.

35. Kitzmüller, "Economy as a Victimizing Mechanism," 33, 35.

36. Vaughan, "The Punitive Consequences of Consumer Culture," 205.

37. On this whole phenomenon, see, e.g., Akerlof and Schiller, *Animal Spirits*, though they do not mention the mimetic theory.

38. Gächter and Thöni, "Envy, Status and Economy," 59.

39. Steinmair-Pösel, "Economy and Mimetic Theory," 77.

40. Gans, "The Market and Resentment," 96, 102.

41. Baudrillard, *Consumer Society*, 139, 141, 143.

42. Ibid., 92–93. I have written at greater length on consumer culture in *Abiding Faith*, 22–46.

43. Baudrillard, *Consumer Society*, 166.

44. Ibid., 196.

45. Ibid., 184.

46. Frank, *Falling Behind*, 57–58.

47. Rousseau feared that this "tendency of democratic politics to collapse the various hierarchical differentiations into the one fundamental differentiation of rich and poor must be a strong encouragement to the growth of envy." See Ward, "Transforming Passion into Compassion," 258.

48. Wilkinson and Pickett, *The Spirit Level*, 261.

49. Girard, "'What Is Occurring Today Is Mimetic Rivalry on a Planetary Scale'" (interview with Henri Tincq). The online version is unpaginated.

50. See Saunders, *Arrival City*.

51. Girard, *Evolution and Conversion*, 248. See also Orléan, "The Origin of Money"; Goux, "Primitive Money, Modern Money."

52. Weber, *The Protestant Ethic and the Spirit of Capitalism*.

53. Walter Benjamin, *Selected Writings*, Vol. 1: 1913–1926, ed. M. Bullock and M. W. Jennings (Cambridge, MA: Belknap Press, 1996), 288–91; cited in Palaver, "Envy or Emulation," 154n12.

54. Girard, "Interview" (with Markus Müller), 6–7. See also the larger treatment of this question by Wolfgang Palaver, "Challenging Capitalism as Religion: Hans G. Ulrich's Theological and Ethical Reflections on the Economy," *Studies in Christian Ethics* 20, no. 2 (2007): 215–30.

55. Elsewhere, Girard ascribes this idea to his long-standing conversation partners Jean-Pierre Depuy and Paul Dumouchel (see *Evolution and Conversion*, 79).

56. Girard, *Evolution and Conversion*, 79; also Girard, *Battling to the End*, 216.

57. Girard, *Evolution and Conversion*, 7.

58. Ibid., 242–43; see also Kitzmüller, "Economy as a Victimizing Mechanism," 31. Girard also acknowledges the way American capitalist culture avoids internal mediation by the division of labor, along with social and geographic mobility—presumably for escaping whichever hothouse of mimetic rivalry, either by moving up or by moving out.

59. Girard, *Evolution and Conversion*, 245.

60. Girard, "The Innocent Victim Has a Defender" (interview with Attilio Scarpellini), 3.

61. Girard, *Evolution and Conversion*, 247. Indeed, he thinks that an interdisciplinary team would be necessary to work out how mimesis and surviving aspects of the old false sacred play out in such an immensely complicated system (see 245).

62. Dupuy, "Detour and Sacrifice," 73.

63. Girard, *Evolution and Conversion*, 244, 264n18.

64. Kitzmüller, "Economy as a Victimizing Mechanism," 36.

65. See chapter 3 of my *Abiding Faith*, "Modernity and Its Victims." I remain especially pleased with my Girardian reading of George Orwell's essay, "Shooting an Elephant," in that chapter.

66. Girard, *Evolution and Conversion*, 246–47.

67. Anspach, "Desired Possessions," 187.

68. Thiel, "The Straussian Moment," 212.

69. Ibid.

70. Gardner, "Democracy and Desire in *The Great Gatsby*," 273.

71. Girard, "Eating Disorders and Mimetic Desire," 6.

72. Ibid., 8–9.

73. Ibid., 12.

74. Ibid., 17–19.

75. Girard, "Une conversation avec René Girard" (with Mark Anspach and Laurence Tacou), in Girard, *Anorexie et désir mimétique*, 89–123; see 100, 123 (translation mine). This little volume contains a French translation from the English of Girard's essay "Eating Disorders and Mimetic Desire," an interpretive essay by Jean-Michel Oughourlian, and this transcribed conversation between Girard, Anspach, and Tacou.

76. Ibid., 114 (translation mine).

77. Girard, "Eating Disorders and Mimetic Desire," 17.

78. Ibid., 14.

79. Levy-Navarro, "Lean and Mean: Shakespeare's Criticism of Thin Privilege," in *The Culture of Obesity in Early and Late Modernity*, 67–109; see 86.

80. Ibid., 68, 109.

81. Levy-Navarro, "Towards a Constructionist Fat History," in *The Culture of Obesity in Early and Late Modernity*, 1–33, on 12.

82. The shame theorists are probably right that overweight people today are "filling up" against emptiness and despair in an uncaring environment, but then the result of such self-medication against shame can be more shame (see, e.g., Morrison, *The Culture of Shame*, 88–89). The lack of "being," inspiring both the eating and shame over the result, is more accurately understood mimetically. It can entail a mimetic rejection of thinness as a playing field on which competition is feared, e.g., withdrawing from the mimetically charged realms of sexual rivalry or high-level employment.

83. Ward, "Abortion as a Sacrament," 26–27. Girard reads the American abortion debate in terms of competitive victimage; see Girard, *Quand ces choses commenceront*, 71.

84. Ward, "Abortion as a Sacrament," 26.

85. Ibid., 30.

86. The American focus of these examples reflects the Girardian literature, as an earlier chapter recalled European instances of anti-Semitism and crusading violence. My own country has an unenviable record of injustice toward Aboriginals, including sacrificial violence. Europe struggles with immigrants, while even enviably multicultural Australia is now politically bipartisan in harshly treating asylum seekers. So I am not attacking America. We Australians have every reason to respect America and her *katéchon* function for decisive help in fighting off Japanese aggression during World War II. Of course, questions remain about American compromises with foreign dictators and excesses of mimetic violence such as Abu Ghraib.

87. McKenna, "The Law's Delay," 209–10.

88. McKenna, *Violence and Difference*, 198.

89. See Kratter, "Twilight of the Vampires."

90. See Palaver, "On Violence."

91. Oughourlian, *The Genesis of Desire*, 115.

92. See Pahl, *Empire of Sacrifice.*

93. Frederick Douglass, *Narrative of the Life of Frederick Douglass, an American Slave* (1845) (New York: Barnes and Noble Classics, 2003), 72–75, 100–106.

94. Smith, "Black-on-Black Violence," 42.

95. Arens, "Dead Man Walking," 25.

96. Girard, *Evolution and Conversion*, 73.

97. The U.S. Supreme Court judgement in the matter of *Herrera v. Collins* is available at http://caselaw.lp.findlaw.com/scripts/getcase.pl?court=us &vol=506&invol=390 (last accessed May 2011).

98. McBride, "Capital Punishment as the Unconstitutional Establishment of Religion," final paragraph (my online version is unpaginated).

99. Gardner, "Democracy and Desire in *The Great Gatsby*," 291–92.

Chapter Five. **WAR, TERROR, APOCALYPSE**

1. Fornari, "Figures of Antichrist," 16.

2. See Palaver, "Carl Schmitt's 'Apocalyptic' Resistance against Global Civil War," 70.

3. See Huntington, "The Clash of Civilizations," 40–41.

4. Palaver, "Carl Schmitt's 'Apocalyptic' Resistance against Global Civil War," 71.

5. Gardner, "René Girard's Apocalyptic Critique of Historical Reason," 17 (original emphasis).

6. Fornari, "Figures of Antichrist," 30.

7. Enzensberger, *Civil Wars*, 23.

8. Ibid., 47.

9. Morrow, "Violence and the Sacred in Northern Ireland," 156.

10. See Schmitt, *The Concept of the Political.*

11. Palaver, "Carl Schmitt's 'Apocalyptic' Resistance against Global Civil War," 76.

12. Cavanaugh, *The Myth of Religious Violence*, 41.

13. Ibid., 77.

14. Ibid., 176.

15. Ibid., 162, 226.

16. Ibid., 194.

17. Ibid., 201–2.

18. Ibid., 211.

19. Ibid., 230.

20. See Richardson, *What Terrorists Want*, 61.

21. See, e.g., Girard, *Resurrection from the Underground*, 109.

22. Dupuy, "Anatomy of 9/11," 40 (original emphasis). See also André Glucksmann, *Dostoevski à Manhattan* (Paris: Laffont, 2002).

23. Girard and Anspach, "A Response: Reflections from the Perspective of Mimetic Theory," 143–44.

24. Ibid., 145. In a Girard-influenced French article, Pierrette Poncella argues that the modern state provides the terrorist's model-obstacle, while there are three categories of sacrifice: terrorists who sacrifice themselves to unify their community and, on the side of the state, both the terrorists who are sacrificed to help unify the state (here I think of public U.S. rejoicing on the killing of Bin Laden) and the hostages allowed to die so that worse destruction is averted; see Poncella, "Terrorisme et sacre," 187–89. I question any implication of a "clash of civilizations," however.

25. Girard, "René Girard im Gespräch I" (interview with Wolfgang Palaver), in *Gewalt und Religion*, 31–65, on 65. In this example of young suicide bombers being glorified we find a rare instance of Girard allowing the sacrificial mechanism (at least some of) its archaic divinizing outcome with a modern victim.

26. Girard, *Celui par qui le scandale arrive*, 23–24 (original emphasis) (translation by Dupuy, in "Anatomy of 9/11," 41).

27. Girard, *Battling to the End*, 215. Stephen Gardner overstates Girard's critique of Islam, in an essay devoted in part to establishing Girard's political conservatism; see Gardner, "René Girard's Apocalyptic Critique of Historical Reason," 15.

28. Girard, "'What Is Occurring Today Is Mimetic Rivalry on a Planetary Scale'" (interview with Henri Tincq). My online version of this brief article does not have standard pagination, so subsequent references to it are not given page numbers. It is a short document, however, and the references are easy to find.

29. Dupuy echoes this point, in "Anatomy of 9/11," 44. Palaver notes that this global cry for redress in the rhetoric of Bin Laden is widespread— from continuing Shiite anger over the death of Husain to the grievances claimed by Aum Shinrikyo to justify its gas attacks on the Tokyo subway— and takes up Vamik Volkan on the "egoism of victimization" to conclude that "terrorism is closely connected to a vengeful instrumentalization of victimhood." See Palaver, "The Ambiguous Cachet of Victimhood," 79, 76.

30. Girard, "'What Is Occurring Today Is Mimetic Rivalry on a Planetary Scale'" (interview with Henri Tincq).

31. Ibid.

32. Girard, *Violence and the Sacred*, 4–5.

33. See Girard, *Battling to the End*, 211–17. A 2009 compilation of this material with other parts of *Battling to the End* provides an overview of the

whole book: see Girard, "Of War and Apocalypse" (though there is more terrorism material in the original).

34. Dupuy would concur, grounding 9/11 "in a logic of identity, similarity, imitation, and fascination" (Dupuy, "Anatomy of 9/11," 40). Palaver, too, who concludes, "Fundamentalist terrorism is not primarily rooted in cultural differences or in poverty and economic underdevelopment but, to the contrary, in a world in which people paradoxically become more resentful as they move closer to those who are better off." See Palaver, "Carl Schmitt's 'Apocalyptic' Resistance against Global Civil War," 72.

35. Girard, *Battling to the End*, 211.

36. Ibid.

37. Ibid., 212. The more general impotence of shame and humiliation is set at the heart of terrorist psychology by James W. Jones, in an explicitly Girardian discussion, with young men denied proper developmental opportunities seeking out charismatic models. These offer a sense of belonging, with little tolerance for anything vague, unclear, unstructured, and insufficiently authoritarian (see Jones, *Blood That Cries Out from the Earth*, 121, 134, 146). In other contexts, Girard acknowledges such hypermimetic proneness.

38. Ibid., 212.

39. Raban, "My Holy War" (my online version is not properly paginated).

40. Girard, *Battling to the End*, 213.

41. Ibid., 214, 215.

42. Ibid., 215.

43. Ibid., 216.

44. Girard, "The Bloody Skin of the Victim" (interview with Wolfgang Palaver), 65.

45. Girard, "Intellectuals as Castrators of Meaning" (interview with Guilio Meotti), 4.

46. Girard, *Battling to the End*, 213.

47. Ibid., 214.

48. Ibid., 215.

49. Interpreting Islamic violence has proved elusive for Girardians. At the 2000 Conference of the Colloquium on Violence and Religion, in Boston, an Islamic scholar declared Islam's de jure peacefulness and was challenged by Robert Hamerton-Kelly over much de facto violence. Response from the floor suggested that Islam itself should not be scapegoated. See Qamar-ul Huda, "The Problems of Violence and Conflict in Islam"; Hamerton-Kelly, "Response to Qamar-ul Huda"; and "Discussion Summary"; found together in *Contagion* 9 (September 2002): 80–108.

50. Girard, *Battling to the End*, 216.

51. Girard, "A Conversation" (with Phil Rose), 34.

52. Girard, "Apocalyptic Thinking after 9/11" (interview with Robert Doran), 25, 28.

53. Ibid., 23. Peter Thiel would agree, suggesting that this religiously badged clash with Western nonseriousness reflects Schmitt's point about the need for a defining struggle to create unity within a constituency; see Thiel, "The Straussian Moment," 191.

54. Ibid., 31. Girard of course admits outright false sacred regressions within Christianity, such as the lynching of blacks in the U.S. South but also less straightforward examples such as the sacrificial rhetoric of World War I retaining some elements of truth in the midst of immense falsehood (see 32). Dupuy offers what appears to be a clarification, pointing to the archaic sacred remaining in the essentially mechanical rather than consciously religious violence of crowds—hence the frenzied tearing limb from limb of two Israeli soldiers by a Ramallah crowd in 2000, for instance, has more to do with Dionysus than the Islam that provided the interpretive, symbolizing, ritualizing, embedding context of the atrocity; see Dupuy, "Anatomy of 9/11," 48–49.

55. Depuy, "Anatomy of 9/11," 42.

56. Palaver, "Islam and the Return of the Archaic," 9. As mentioned in the introduction, however, Taylor's account of this process of disembedding must be held together with an awareness that secular modern individuals remain profoundly entwined in mimeticism.

57. See Göle, "Snapshots of Islamic Modernities."

58. Eickelman, "Islam and the Languages of Modernity," 131.

59. Euben, *Enemy in the Mirror*, 166–67.

60. See Calvert, "'The World Is an Undutiful Boy!': Sayyid Qutb's American Experience," 101.

61. Excellent here is Gafaiti, "'Hyperculturalization' after September 11."

62. Murawiek, *The Mind of Jihad*, 105. I have written more on this in *Abiding Faith*, 71–74.

63. Murawiek, *The Mind of Jihad*, 161.

64. Ibid., 227, 251–52, 310, 313.

65. Cavanaugh, *The Myth of Religious Violence*, 228–29.

66. Murawiek, *The Mind of Jihad*, 161.

67. Ibid., 267.

68. Girard, *Battling to the End*, 67.

69. Asad, *Suicide Bombing*, 63.

70. Ibid., 66.

71. Juergensmeyer, *Terror in the Mind of God*, 15, 188.

72. Ibid., 210.

73. Richardson, *What Terrorists Want*, 56.

74. Ibid., 87.
75. Ibid., 57–69.
76. McKenna, "Scandal, Resentment, Idolatry," 7.
77. Ibid., 13.
78. Ibid., 3.
79. Raban, "My Holy War" (my online version not properly paginated).
80. Ibid.
81. Ibid. See also Calvert, "'The World Is an Undutiful Boy!': Sayyid Qutb's American Experience."
82. Raban, "My Holy War."
83. Ibid.
84. Husain, *The Islamist.*
85. Palaver, "Islam and the Return of the Archaic," 9.
86. Girard, *Things Hidden,* 440.
87. Girard, "The Dostoyevskian Apocalypse," in *Deceit, Desire, and the Novel,* 281.
88. Girard, "Satan," in *The Girard Reader,* 209.
89. See, e.g., Girard, "An Interview with René Girard," in *To Double Business Bound,* 227; Girard, *Things Hidden,* 136–37, 186–87.
90. Girard, *Battling to the End,* xvi, x, xi, 105.
91. Ibid., x.
92. Ibid., xi.
93. Haven, "René Girard: Stanford's Provocative *Immortel,*" 4.
94. Girard, *Battling to the End,* xi, 5.
95. I thank my colleague in the Canberra Girard Reading Group, Peter Stork, for bringing this important distinction to my attention.
96. Clausewitz, *On War,* 1.vi.
97. Ibid., 1.iii.
98. Ibid., 1.iv.
99. Ibid., 1.v.
100. Girard, *Battling to the End,* 9; cf. 14, 19.
101. Clausewitz, *On War,* 1.xxv.
102. Girard, *Battling to the End,* 17; see also 13–14.
103. Clausewitz, *On War,* 1.xxiv.
104. Girard, *Battling to the End,* 1. Michel Serres, on formally welcoming Girard into L'Académie française, said that we cannot interpret the inexplicable mass violence of the twentieth century without Girard's mimetic theory. See Serres, "Receiving René Girard into the Académie Française," 8.
105. Girard also identifies mimetic forces powerfully at work in Clausewitz's assessment of Napoleon. "Clausewitz's view of Napoleon is extremely vast," Girard remarks. "But he's totally mimetic. Napoleon he hates so cordially that he loves him." See Girard, "A Conversation" (with Phil Rose), 35.

106. Girard, *Battling to the End*, 14.

107. Ibid., 18.

108. Ibid., 4, 6, 19.

109. Ibid., xii (original emphasis).

110. Ibid., 66.

111. Ibid., 10.

112. Ibid., xii.

113. Ibid., 15–17.

114. Ibid., 15.

115. Ibid., 16–17.

116. Ibid.; see chap. 7.

117. Ibid., 21.

118. Ibid., 173.

119. Ibid., 21. See also Girard, "Intellectuals as Castrators of Meaning" (interview with Guilio Meotti), 4.

120. Girard, *Battling to the End*, 17.

121. Ibid., 20.

122. Ibid., 67.

123. Ibid.

124. Ibid., 21.

125. Ibid., 42.

126. Ibid., 18.

127. Ibid., 19.

128. Ibid., 20. Paul Dumouchel describes genocide as a sacrificial ritual—no more, no less—requiring only a sacrificial population without defenders, a violent past providing models for the action, a sense of loss to be made up by those held responsible, and a mimetic peer group to help get things going; see Dumouchel, "Mimetismes et génocides," 251.

129. Girard, *Battling to the End*, 216. Girard has confined his reflections to apocalyptic passages in the Gospels (see, e.g., 110). Concerning the Book of Revelation, the Girardian New Testament scholar Stephen Finamore (in *God, Order, and Chaos*, 177–78) concludes that

> the whole book [i.e., Revelation] could be read as a representation of the transfer of sovereignty over the earth to God and God's agents from God's adversaries. The transfer is brought about in a process generated by God's revelation of truth achieved in Jesus and in which those who follow Jesus participate. The existing patterns of human social life slowly disintegrate in the light of their exposure to the truth of their own nature. The exposure of truth makes it impossible for traditional forms of human social order to re-establish themselves and no new form of order can be achieved without the 'destruction' of the forces

of mimetic rivalry. Only when this is achieved can a form of order not based on existing systems of differentiation become possible. The process by which this occurs is represented in terms drawn from the Holy War traditions of Israel and is the wrath of God. It is God's because God has acted to reveal the truth and so generate the process. The violence itself is human. However, since the existing forms of differentiation are undermined, the social chaos of the crisis is experienced by the participants as having a cosmic dimension. That, it is suggested, is the pattern and framework of the narrative of Revelation.

130. Girard, *Battling to the End,* 21.
131. Ibid., xvii.
132. Ibid. I think that Girard offers a slightly fuller picture of this task on 13.

CONCLUSION

1. For now, I refer to the discussion of these critiques in Kirwan, *Discovering Girard;* see chapter 4, "Method and Objections," 87–111.
2. Girard, "Apocalyptic Thinking since 9/11" (interview with Robert Doran), 26–27 (original emphasis).
3. Girard, *Battling to the End,* xvii.
4. See Haven, "René Girard: Stanford's Provocative *Immortel,*" 5.
5. Girard, "Conversion in Literature and Christianity" (1999), in *Mimesis and Theory,* 269.
6. Girard, "Marcel Proust" (1962), in *Mimesis and Theory,* 69.
7. Girard, *Resurrection from the Underground,* 105.
8. Ibid., 140. See also Graham, "St. Augustine's Novelistic Conversion."
9. See Hampton, "Beyond Reciprocal Violence—René Girard and Siegfried Sassoon." In a nice coincidence, the mimetically tortured Sassoon was received into the Roman Catholic Church at the age of seventy after instruction by Dom Sebastian Moore, OSB, a subsequent Girard aficionado and mentor to James Alison, and still going strong in his nineties. See also Max Egremont, *Siegfried Sassoon: A Life* (New York: Farrar, Straus & Giroux, 2005).
10. Girard, "Does Not the Stone Rebuke Me for Being More Stone than It?": *The Winter's Tale* (Act 5, Scene 3)," in *A Theater of Envy,* 334–42, on 342 (original emphasis).
11. See, e.g., Alison, "On Learning to Say 'Jesus Is Lord': A 'Girardian' Confession," in *Faith beyond Resentment,* 147–69; Alison, "Confessions of a Former Marginaholic" and "The Strangeness of This Passivity," in *On Being Liked,* 65–77 and 131–46.

12. Williams, "*Magister Lucis:* In the Light of René Girard," 166.

13. Girard, "Entretien" (with Mark R. Anspach).

14. Girard, "Intellectuals as Castrators of Meaning" (interview with Guilio Meotti), 2.

15. Girard, "Souvenirs d'un jeune Français aux États-Unis" (Memories of a Young Frenchman in the United States), 30. See also Girard, "Violence, Difference, Sacrifice" (interview with Rebecca Adams), 11–16. Jean-Pierre Dupuy, marking Girard's reception into l'Académie française, suggests that Girard could only have discovered mimeticism in the mimetic laboratory that is the United States, and only in his own personal recovery from its worst excesses; see Dupuy, "René en Amerique," 51.

16. Girard, "A Conversation with René Girard," in *The Girard Reader*, 285.

17. For the fullest account of his conversion, see Girard, *Quand ces choses commenceront*, 217–23. The train journey details are on 219.

18. Girard, "Epilogue: The Anthropology of the Cross" (interview with James G. Williams), in *The Girard Reader*, 285–86.

19. Ibid., 288.

20. See, e.g., Girard, "The Goodness of Mimetic Desire," in *The Girard Reader*, 63–64; also "Violence, Difference, Sacrifice" (interview with Rebecca Adams), 24.

21. Girard, *I See Satan Fall Like Lightning*, 15.

22. Girard, *Battling to the End*, 35. He says he had thought this at the time of *Things Hidden*.

23. Ibid., x.

24. Ibid., 101.

25. Girard, *Things Hidden*, 430–31.

26. Girard, *I See Satan Fall Like Lightning*, 13–14.

27. Alison, *Broken Hearts and New Creations*, x.

28. Girard, *I See Satan Fall Like Lightning*, 17; see also Baillie, "Sacrificial Violence in Homer's *Iliad*."

29. Grote, "The Imitation of Christ as Double Bind: Toward a Girardian Spirituality," 496.

30. See Girard's comments on this culture in "Intellectuals as Castrators of Meaning" (interview with Guilio Meotti), 2.

31. Girard, "An Interview with René Girard," in Golsan, *René Girard and Myth*, 146.

32. Grote, "The Imitation of Christ as Double Bind," 493.

33. Marr, *Tools for Peace;* see also his "Stewardship of Goods in the Rule of Benedict."

34. Girard, "Epilogue: The Anthropology of the Cross" (interview with James M. Williams), in *The Girard Reader*, 278–79.

35. Girard, "Hamlet's Dull Revenge: Vengeance in Hamlet," in *A Theater of Envy*, 271–89, on 282.

36. Girard, *Battling to the End*, 24, 217.

37. Ibid., xiii.

38. Ibid., 63.

39. Ibid., 182.

40. Girard, "A Conversation" (with Phil Rose), 34.

41. Girard, *Battling to the End*, 183.

42. See Palaver, "The Ambiguous Cachet of Victimhood," 73. For a fine, albeit imagined, speech by President George W. Bush in this spirit—a speech that I wish could have been given in the aftermath of 9/11, though of course nothing remotely like it was possible—see Bellinger, *The Trinitarian Self*, 130–38.

Could it be that Girard's recipe for containing the violence of war in its mimetically volatile modern form is to take firm but restrained steps to head off conflict (e.g., France invading the Rhineland to prevent German rearmament) combined with an approach to defense involving nonviolent resistance—given his Clausewitzian insight that defense ensures the escalation of violence? Firm action to prevent war from getting started coupled with serious but nonviolent resistance in the face of aggression might then constitute the sort of strategy Girard would commend for restraining the escalation to extremes. We remember of course that nonviolent resistance is not the same as pacifism.

43. Gardner, "René Girard's Apocalyptic Critique of Historical Reason," 15.

44. See Wink, *Engaging the Powers*; see also Roedel, "Sacrificial and Nonsacrificial Mass Nonviolence."

45. Girard, *Battling to the End*, 125.

46. Ibid., 122 (original emphasis).

47. Alison, "Worship in a Violent World," in *Undergoing God*, 38.

48. Alison, "Sacrifice, Law, and the Catholic Faith: Is Secularity Really the Enemy?," in *Broken Hearts and New Creations*, 87, 90–91, 89, respectively.

49. See, e.g., Swartley, "Discipleship and Imitation of Jesus/Suffering Servant: The Mimesis of New Creation," 218–45. I also wrote on this theme of imitating Paul in chapter 4 of my *Abiding Faith*.

50. Hamerton-Kelly, *Sacred Violence*, 174–75.

51. Girard, *Things Hidden*, 275.

52. Alison, "Postface to the 2010 Edition of *Raising Abel*," 203.

53. Girard, *I See Satan Fall Like Lightning*, 174.

54. See especially Alison's new postface to the 2010 edition of *Raising Abel*, 206–8, where he admits having occasionally forgotten this as a Roman Catholic.

55. Schwager, *Must There Be Scapegoats?*, 119 (original emphasis).

56. Fornari, "Figures of Antichrist," 36. Thomas Merton, overwhelmed on first seeing the Trappist Abbey of Gethsemani in Kentucky, declared it the place that held America together. Reflecting on this, the American spiritual writer Kathleen Norris declares the monastery, like the church at large, to be a city planted among the nations for their healing; see Norris, *The Cloister Walk* (New York: Riverhead, 1996), 378.

57. Hamerton-Kelly, *Sacred Violence*, 84–85. See also Oberprantacher, "Beyond Rivalry? Rethinking Community in View of Apocalyptic Violence."

58. Girard, *Battling to the End*, 177.

59. Ibid., 199. The same point is made by a German Catholic priest and New Testament scholar who resigned his Tübingen chair to join an alternative community of Christian witness: see Gerhard Lohfink, *Does God Need the Church? Toward a Theology of the People of God* (1998), trans. Linda M. Maloney (Collegeville, MN: Michael Glazier, 1999), 288.

60. Gardner, "René Girard's Apocalyptic Critique of Historical Reason," 14–15.

61. Girard, *Job*, 157–58.

BIBLIOGRAPHY

Akerlof, George A., and Robert J. Shiller. *Animal Spirits: How Human Psychology Drives the Economy, and Why It Matters for Global Capitalism.* Princeton: Princeton University Press, 2009.

Alison, James. *Broken Hearts and New Creations: Intimations of a Great Reversal.* London: Continuum, 2010.

———. *Faith beyond Resentment: Fragments Catholic and Gay.* London: Darton, Longman and Todd, 2001.

———. *The Joy of Being Wrong: Original Sin through Easter Eyes.* New York: Herder and Herder, 1998.

———. *Knowing Jesus* (1993). 2d ed. London: SPCK, 1998.

———. *On Being Liked.* London: Darton, Longman and Todd, 2003.

———. "Postface for the 2010 Edition of *Raising Abel*," In *Raising Abel: The Recovery of the Eschatological Imagination,* 199–209. London: SPCK, 2010.

———. *Raising Abel: The Recovery of the Eschatological Imagination.* New York: Crossroad Herder, 2003.

———. *Undergoing God: Dispatches from the Scene of a Break-In.* London: Darton, Longman and Todd, 2006.

Anspach, Mark R. "Desired Possessions: Karl Polanyi, René Girard, and the Critique of the Market Economy." *Contagion* 11 (2004): 181–88.

———. "Global Markets, Anonymous Victims." *Unesco Courier* (May 2001). Available at www.mimetictheory.org/bios/articles/Anspach_UNESCO.pdf (last accessed May 2011).

———. "Introduction: l'anorexie et l'esprit du temps." In René Girard (with Jean-Michel Oughourlian, Mark R. Anspach, and Laurence Tacou), *Anorexie et désir mimétique,* 14–36. Paris: Éditions de L'Herne, 2008.

———. "Violence against Violence: Islam in Comparative Context." In *Violence and the Sacred in the Modern World,* edited by Mark Juergensmeyer, 9–29. London: Frank Cass, 1991.

———, ed. *René Girard.* Cahiers de L'Herne. Paris: Éditions de L'Herne, 2008.

Appleby, R. Scott. "Fire and Sword: Does Religion Promote Violence?" *Commonweal* (9 April 2010): 12–17.

Arbuckle, Gerald A. *Violence, Society and the Church: A Cultural Approach.* Collegeville, MN: Liturgical Press, 2004.

Arens, Edmund. *"Dead Man Walking:* On the Cinematic Treatment of Licensed Public Killing." *Contagion* 5 (1998): 14–29.

Asad, Talal. *On Suicide Bombing.* Welleck Library Lectures. New York: Columbia University Press, 2007.

Atlan, Henri, and Jean-Pierre Dupuy. "Mimesis and Social Morphogenesis: Violence and the Sacred from a Systems Analysis Viewpoint." In *Applied Systems and Cybernetics,* vol. 3, *Human Systems, Sociocybernetics, Management and Organizations,* edited by G. E. Lasker, 1263–67. New York: Pergamon Press, 1981.

Baillie, Gil. "Sacrificial Violence in Homer's *Iliad.*" In *Curing Violence,* edited by Mark I. Wallace and Theophus H. Smith, 45–70. Sonoma, CA: Polebridge Press, 1994.

———. *Violence Unveiled: Humanity at the Crossroads.* New York: Crossroad, 1995.

Bandera, Cesáreo. *The Sacred Game: The Role of the Sacred in the Genesis of Modern Literary Fiction.* University Park: Pennsylvania State University Press, 1994.

Bartlett, Andrew. "Review Essay: From First Hesitation to Scenic Imagination: Originary Thinking with Eric Gans." *Contagion* 15–16 (2008–9): 89–172.

Baudrillard, Jean. *The Consumer Society: Myths and Structures* (1970). Translated by Chris Turner, with an Introduction by George Ritzer. London: Sage, 1998.

Beaudin, Michael, and Jean-Marc Gauthier. "The Uncontrolled Return of the Passions in the Economical and Political Sacrificial 'Soteriology' of Our Times: Theological Perspectives." In *Passions in Economy, Politics and the Media: In Discussion with Christian Theology,* edited by Wolfgang Palaver and Petra Steinmair-Pösel, 175–95. Beiträge zur mimetischen Theorie 17. Wien: Lit Verlag, 2005.

Bellah, Robert N. "Civil Religion in America." *Daedalus* 96, no. 1 (Winter 1967): 1–21.

Bellinger, Charles K. "The Joker Is Satan, and So Are We: Girard and *The Dark Knight.*" *Journal of Religion and Film* 13, no. 1 (April 2009). Available at www.unomaha.edu/jrf/vol13.no1/JokerSatan.htm (last accessed May 2011).

———. *The Trinitarian Self: The Key to the Puzzle of Violence.* Princeton Theological Monograph Series. Eugene, OR: Pickwick, 2008.

Berger, Peter, ed. *The Desecularization of the World: Resurgent Religion and World Politics.* Washington, DC: Ethics and Public Policy Center; Grand Rapids, MI: Eerdmans, 1999.

Berger, Peter, Grace Davie, and Effie Fokas. *Religious America, Secular Europe? A Theme and Variations.* Aldershot: Ashgate, 2008.

Bertonneau, Thomas F. "The Gist of René Girard: Truth Versus the Crowd in His Two Most Recent Books." *First Principles* (8 October 2008). Available at www.firstprinciplesjournal.com/articles.aspx?article=1104 &theme=hiedu&page=4&loc=b&type=ctbf (last accessed May 2011).

Blumenberg, Hans. *The Legitimacy of the Modern Age.* Translated by Robert M. Wallace. Cambridge, MA: MIT Press, 1983.

Bossy, John. "Some Elementary Forms of Durkheim." *Past and Present* 95 (May 1982): 3–18.

Bruce, Steve. *God Is Dead: Secularization in the West.* Oxford: Blackwell, 2002.

Calvert, John. "'The World Is an Undutiful Boy!': Sayyid Qutb's American Experience." *Islam and Muslim-Christian Relations* 11, no. 1 (2000): 87–103.

Campbell, Colin. *The Romantic Ethic and the Spirit of Modern Consumerism* (1987). York: Alcuin Academics, 2005.

Carrasco, David. *City of Sacrifice: The Aztec Empire and the Role of Violence in Civilization.* Boston: Beacon, 1999.

Carrette, Jeremy, and Richard King. *Selling Spirituality: The Silent Takeover of Religion.* London: Routledge, 2005.

Casanova, José. "Secularization, Enlightenment, and Modern Religion." In *Public Religions in the Modern World,* 11–39, 235–47. Chicago: University of Chicago Press, 1994.

Cavanaugh, William T. *The Myth of Religious Violence: Secular Ideology and the Roots of Modern Conflict.* Oxford: Oxford University Press, 2009.

Clausewitz, Carl von. *On War* (1832). Translated by Michael Howard and Peter Paret. Abridged with an Introduction and Notes by Beatrice Heuser. Oxford: Oxford World Classics, 2007.

Cloots, André. "Modernity and Christianity: Marcel Gauchet on the Christian Roots of Modern Ways of Thinking." *Milltown Studies* 61 (2008): 1–30.

Coakley, Sarah. "Sacrifice Regained: The Rationality of Christian Belief." Inaugural Lecture as Norris-Hulse Professor of Divinity, University of Cambridge, 13 October 2009. Available at http://www.abdn.ac.uk /gifford/documents/Norris-Hulse_Professor_of_Divinity_-_Inaugu ral_lecture.pdf (last accessed April 2013).

Cowdell, Scott. *Abiding Faith: Christianity Beyond Certainty, Anxiety, and Violence.* Eugene, OR: Cascade, 2009.

Daly, Robert J. *Sacrifice Unveiled: The True Meaning of Christian Sacrifice.* London: T&T Clark, 2009.

———. "Violence and Institution in Christianity." *Contagion* 9 (2002): 4–33.

Dawkins, Richard. *The God Delusion*. Boston: Houghton Mifflin, 2006.

Doran, Robert. "Editor's Introduction: Literature as Theory." In *Mimesis and Theory*, by René Girard and edited by Robert Doran, xi–xxvi. Cultural Memory in the Present. Stanford: Stanford University Press, 2008.

Dumouchel, Paul. "Hobbes and Secularization: Christianity and the Political Problem of Religion." *Contagion* 2 (1995): 39–56.

———. "Indifference and Envy: The Anthropological Analysis of Modern Economy." *Contagion* 10 (2003): 149–60.

———. "Inside Out: Political Violence in the Age of Globalization." *Contagion* 15–16 (2008–9): 173–84.

———. "Miméticismes et génocides." In *René Girard*, edited by Mark R. Anspach, 247–54. Cahiers de L'Herne. Paris: Éditions de L'Herne, 2008.

———, ed. *Violence and Truth: On the Work of René Girard* (1985). London: Athlone, 1988.

Dupuy, Jean-Pierre. "Anatomy of 9/11: Evil, Rationalism, and the Sacred." *SubStance* 37, no. 1 (2008): 33–51.

———. "Detour and Sacrifice: Illich and Girard." In *For René Girard: Essays in Friendship and in Truth*, edited by Sandor Goodhart, Jørgen Jørgensen, Tom Ryba, and James G. Williams, 57–77. Studies in Violence, Mimesis, and Culture. East Lansing: Michigan State University Press, 2009.

———. "Panic and the Paradoxes of the Social Order." In *Passions in Economy, Politics and the Media: In Discussion with Christian Theology*, edited by Wolfgang Palaver and Petra Steinmair-Pösel, 215–33. Beiträge zur mimetischen Theorie 17. Wien: Lit Verlag, 2005.

———. "René en Amérique." In *René Girard*, edited by Mark R. Anspach, 51–54. Cahiers de L'Herne. Paris: Éditions de L'Herne, 2008.

Durkheim, Emile. *The Elementary Forms of the Religious Life: A Study in Religious Sociology*. Translated by Joseph Ward Swain. New York: Macmillan, 1915.

Eickelman, Dale F. "Islam and the Languages of Modernity." *Daedalus* 129, no. 1 (Winter 2000): 119–35.

Eisenstadt, S. N. "Multiple Modernities." *Daedalus* 129, no. 1 (Winter 2000): 1–30.

Eisenstadt, S. N., and Wolfgang Schluchter. "Introduction: Paths to Early Modernities—A Comparative View." *Daedalus* 127, no. 3 (Summer 1998). 1–18.

Enzensberger, Hans Magnus. *Civil Wars: From L.A. to Bosnia*. Translated by Piers Spence and Martin Chalmers. New York: New Press, 1994.

Euben, Roxanne L. *The Enemy in the Mirror: Islamic Fundamentalism and the Limits of Modern Rationalism*. Princeton: Princeton University Press, 1999.

Fanon, Frantz. *The Wretched of the Earth.* Translated by Constance Farrington. New York: Grove Press, 1963.

Finamore, Stephen. *God, Order, and Chaos: René Girard and the Apocalypse.* Paternoster Biblical Monographs. Eugene, OR: Wipf and Stock, 2009.

Fleming, Chris. *René Girard: Violence and Mimesis.* Cambridge: Polity, 2004.

Fornari, Giuseppe. "Figures of Antichrist: The Apocalypse and Its Restraints in Contemporary Political Thought." *Innsbrucker Discussionspapiere zu Weltordnung, Religion und Gewalt* 31 (2009): 1–39. Reprinted in *Contagion* 17 (2010): 53–85.

———. "Labyrinthine Theories of Sacrifice: The *Cretans* by Euripides." *Contagion* 4 (1997): 163–88.

Frank, Robert H. *Falling Behind: How Rising Inequality Harms the Middle Class.* Berkeley: University of California Press, 2007.

Fraser, Giles. *Christianity and Violence: Girard, Nietzsche, Anselm and Tutu.* Affirming Catholicism. London: Darton, Longman and Todd, 2001.

Gächter, Simon, and Christian Thöni. "Envy, Status, and Economy: An Empirical Approach." In *Passions in Economy, Politics and the Media: In Discussion with Christian Theology,* edited by Wolfgang Palaver and Petra Steinmair-Pösel, 37–65. Beiträge zur mimetischen Theorie 17. Wien: Lit Verlag, 2005.

Gafaïti, Hafid. "'Hyperculturization' after September 11: The Arab-Muslim World and the West." *SubStance* 37, no. 1 (2008): 98–117.

Gallese, Vittorio. "The Two Sides of Mimesis: Girard's Mimetic Theory, Embodied Simulation and Social Identification." *Journal of Consciousness Studies* 16, no. 4 (2009): 21–44.

Gans, Eric. "The Market and Resentment." In *Passions in Economy, Politics and the Media: In Discussion with Christian Theology,* edited by Wolfgang Palaver and Petra Steinmair-Pösel, 85–102. Beiträge zur mimetischen Theorie 17. Wien: Lit Verlag, 2005.

———. "The Origin of Language: Violence Deferred or Violence Denied?" *Contagion* 7 (2000): 1–17.

———. "René et moi" (Chronicles of Love and Resentment). *Anthropoetics* 307 (25 September 2004). Available at www.anthropoetics.ucla.edu /views/vw307.htm (last accessed May 2011).

———. "René et moi." In *For René Girard: Essays in Friendship and in Truth,* edited by Sandor Goodhart, Jørgen Jørgensen, Tom Ryba, and James G. Williams, 19–25. Studies in Violence, Mimesis, and Culture. East Lansing: Michigan State University Press, 2009.

Gardner, Stephen L. "Democracy and Desire in *The Great Gatsby.*" In *Passions in Economy, Politics and the Media: In Discussion with Christian Theology,* edited by Wolfgang Palaver and Petra Steinmair-Pösel, 273–94. Beiträge zur mimetischen Theorie 17. Wien: Lit Verlag, 2005.

————. "René Girard's Apocalyptic Critique of Historical Reason: Limiting Politics to Make Way for Faith." *Contagion* 18 (2011): 1–22.

Garrels, Scott R. "Imitation, Mirror Neurons, and Mimetic Desire: Convergence between the Mimetic Theory of René Girard and Empirical Research on Imitation." *Contagion* 12–13 (2006): 47–86.

Gauchet, Marcel. *The Disenchantment of the World: A Political History of Religion* (1985). Translated by Oscar Burge, with a Foreword by Charles Taylor. New French Thought. Princeton: Princeton University Press, 1997.

Gentile, Emilio. *Politics as Religion* (2001). Translated by George Staunton. Princeton: Princeton University Press, 2006.

Gillespie, Michael Allen. *The Theological Origins of Modernity.* Chicago: University of Chicago Press, 2008.

Girard, René (with Jean-Michel Oughourlian, Mark R. Anspach, and Laurence Tacou). *Anorexie et désir mimétique.* Paris: Éditions de L'Herne, 2008.

————. "Apocalyptic Thinking after 9/11: An Interview with René Girard" (interview with Robert Doran). *SubStance* 37, no. 1 (2008): 20–32.

————. "Les Appartenances." In *Politiques de Caïn: Dialogues avec René Girard,* edited by Domenica Mazzù, 19–33. Paris: Desclée de Brouwer, 2004.

————. "Are the Gospels Mythical?" *First Things,* April 1996. Available at www.firstthings.com/article/2007/10/002-are-the-gospels-mythical-11 (last accessed May 2011).

————. *Battling to the End: Conversations with Benoît Chantre* (2007). Translated by Mary Baker. Studies in Violence, Mimesis, and Culture. East Lansing: Michigan State University Press, 2010.

————. "The Bloody Skin of the Victim" (interview with Wolfgang Palaver). In *The New Visibility of Religion: Studies in Religion and Cultural Hermeneutics,* edited by Graham Ward and Michael Hoelzl, 59–67. Continuum Resources in Religion and Political Culture. London: Continuum, 2008.

————. *Celui par qui le scandale arrive: Entretiens avec Maria Stella Barberi.* Paris: Hachette Littératures, 2008.

————. "A Conversation with René Girard (August 2006/May 2007)" (with Phil Rose). *Contagion* 18 (2011): 23–38.

————. *Deceit, Desire, and the Novel: Self and Other in Literary Structure* (1961). Translated by Yvonne Freccero. Baltimore: Johns Hopkins University Press, 1965

————. "Discussion" (with Renato Rosaldo, Walter Burkert, Burton Mack, Jonathan Z. Smith et al.). In *Violent Origins: Walter Burkert, René Girard, and Jonathan Z. Smith on Ritual Killing and Cultural Formation,* edited by Robert Hammerton-Kelly, 177–88, 206–35, 245–56. Stanford: Stanford University Press, 1987.

————. "Disorder and Order in Mythology." In *Disorder and Order: Proceedings of the Stanford International Symposium (Sept. 14–16, 1981),* edited by

Paisley Livingston, 80–97. Stanford Literature Studies. Saratoga, CA: Anma Libri, 1984.

———. "Eating Disorders and Mimetic Desire." *Contagion* 3 (1996): 1–20.

———. "Entretien" (with Mark R. Anspach). In *René Girard,* edited by Mark R. Anspach, 22–28. Cahiers de L'Herne. Paris: Éditions de L'Herne, 2008.

———. "The Evangelical Subversion of Myth." In *Politics and Apocalypse,* edited by Robert Hamerton-Kelly, 29–49. Studies in Violence, Mimesis, and Culture. East Lansing: Michigan State University Press, 2007.

——— (with Pierpaolo Antonello and João Cezar de Castro Rocha). *Evolution and Conversion: Dialogues on the Origins of Culture.* London: Continuum, 2007.

———. "Foreword by René Girard." In *The Bible, Violence, and the Sacred: Liberation from the Myth of Sanctioned Violence,* by James G. Williams, vii–x. San Francisco: HarperSanFrancisco, 1991.

———. "The Founding Murder in the Philosophy of Nietzsche." In *Violence and Truth: On the Work of René Girard* (1985), edited by Paul Dumouchel, 227–46. London: Athlone, 1988.

———. "From Ritual to Science." In *Mapping Michael Serres,* edited by Niran Abbas, 10–23. Studies in Literature and Science. Ann Arbor: University of Michigan Press, 2008.

———. "Generative Scapegoating" (followed by "Discussion"). In *Violent Origins: Walter Burkert, René Girard, and Jonathan Z. Smith on Ritual Killing and Cultural Formation,* edited by Robert Hamerton-Kelly, 73–105; 106–45. Stanford: Stanford University Press, 1987.

——— (with Wolfgang Palaver). *Gewalt und Religion: Ursache oder Wirkung? Herausgegeben, mit zwei Gesprächen und einem Nachwort von Wolfgang Palaver.* Berlin: Matthes & Seitz, 2010.

———. *The Girard Reader.* Edited by James G. Williams. New York: Crossroad, 1996.

———. "The Innocent Victim Has a Defender. And He Is in Jerusalem" (interview with Attilio Scarpellini). *L'Espresso* 25 (12 June 2003). Original title "The God of the Apocalypse." Available at http://chiesa .espresso.repubblica.it/articolo/6956?eng=y (last accessed May 2011).

———. "Intellectuals as Castrators of Meaning: An Interview with René Girard" (interview by Guillio Meotti). *Il Foglio* (20 March 2007). Translated by Paul N. Faraone and Christopher S. Morrissey. *First Principles* (28 August 2008). Available at www.firstprinciplesjournal.com/articles .aspx?article=1086&theme=home&loc=b (last accessed May 2011).

———. "Interview" (with Richard J. Golsan). In *René Girard and Myth: An Introduction,* by Richard J. Golsan, 129–49. Theorists of Myth. London: Routledge, 2002.

———. "Interview René Girard." *Diacritics* 8, no. 1 (Spring 1978): 31–54. Reprinted as "An Interview with René Girard," in René Girard, *To*

Double Business Bound: Essays on Literature, Mimesis, and Anthropology (1978) (London: Athlone, 1988), 199–229.

———. "Interview with Réne Girard" (interview with Marcus Müller). *Anthropoetics* 2, no. 1 (June 1996): 1–13.

———. *I See Satan Fall Like Lightning* (1999). Translated by James G. Williams. Maryknoll, NY: Orbis; Ottawa: Novalis; Leominster: Gracewing, 2001.

———. *Job: The Victim of His People* (1985). Translated by Yvonne Freccero. Stanford: Stanford University Press, 1987.

———. *Mimesis and Theory: Essays on Literature and Criticism, 1953–2005.* Edited with an Introduction by Robert Doran. Cultural Memory in the Present. Stanford: Stanford University Press, 2008.

———. *Oedipus Unbound: Selected Writings on Rivalry and Desire.* Edited with an Introduction by Mark R. Anspach. Stanford: Stanford University Press, 2004.

———. "On War and Apocalypse." *First Things* 195 (August–September 2009): 17–22. Adapted from *Battling to the End.*

———. "L'Opposition au darwinisme s'est évaporée" (conversation with Hervé Morin). *Le Monde* (2 October 2009): *Les Livres,* 10.

———. "Origins: A View from the Literature." In *Understanding Origins: Contemporary Views on the Origin of Life, Mind and Society,* edited by Francisco J. Varela and Jean-Pierre Dupuy, 27–42. Dordrecht: Kluwer, 1992.

———. *Quand ces choses commenceront: Entretiens avec Michel Tregeur.* Paris: Arléa, 1994.

———. "Ratzinger Is Right" (interview with Nathan Gardels). *New Perspectives Quarterly* 22, no. 3 (Summer 2005). Available at www.dig italnpq.org/archive/2005_summer/10_girard.html (last accessed May 2011).

———. *Resurrection from the Underground: Feodor Dostoyevsky* (1963, 1976). Edited and translated with a Foreword by James G. Williams. New York: Crossroad, 1997.

———. *Sacrifice* (2003). Translated by Matthew Pattillo and David Dawson. Breakthroughs in Mimetic Theory. East Lansing: Michigan State University Press, 2011.

———. *The Scapegoat* (1982). Translated by Yvonne Freccero. Baltimore: Johns Hopkins University Press, 1986.

———. "Scapegoats and Saviours: In Conversation" (with Austen Ivereigh, James Alison, and Michael Kirwan). *The Tablet* (16 October 2004). 8–9.

———. "Souvenirs d'un jeune Français aux États-Unis." In *René Girard,* edited by Mark R. Anspach, 29–34. Cahiers de L'Herne. Paris: Éditions de L'Herne, 2008.

————. *A Theater of Envy: William Shakespeare* (1991). South Bend, IN: St. Augustine's Press, 2004.

———— (with Jean-Michel Oughourlian and Guy Lefort). *Things Hidden since the Foundation of the World* (1978). Translated by Stephen Bann and Michael Metteer. London: Continuum, 2003.

————. *To Double Business Bound: Essays on Literature, Mimesis, and Anthropology* (1978). London: Athlone, 1988.

————. "Violence and Religion: Cause or Effect?" *Hedgehog Review* 6, no. 1 (22 March 2004): 8–13.

————. *Violence and the Sacred* (1972). Translated by Patrick Gregory. Baltimore: Johns Hopkins University Press, 1977.

————. "Violence, Difference, Sacrifice: A Conversation with René Girard" (interview with Rebecca Adams). *Religion and Literature* 25, no. 2 (Summer 1993): 11–33.

————. "Violence in Biblical Narrative." *Philosophy and Literature* 23, no. 2 (1999): 387–92.

————. "Violence Renounced: Response by René Girard." In *Violence Renounced: René Girard, Biblical Studies, and Peacemaking*, edited by Willard M. Swartley, 308–20. Institute of Mennonite Studies; Studies in Peace and Scripture 4. Telford, PA: Pandora Press; Scottdale, PA: Herald Press, 2000.

————. "Violence, Scapegoating, and the Cross." In *The Evolution of Evil*, edited by Gayman Bennett, Martinez J. Hewlett, Ted Peters, and Robert John Russell, 334–48. Religion, Theology, and the Natural Sciences. Göttingen: Vandenhoeck & Ruprecht, 2008.

————. "'What Is Occurring Today Is Mimetic Rivalry on a Planetary Scale': René Girard on September 11" (interview with Henri Tincq). *Le Monde* (6 November 2011). Translated by Colloquium on Violence and Religion. Available at www.morphizm.com/politix/girard911.html (last accessed May 2011).

Girard, René, and Mark R. Anspach. "A Response: Reflections from the Perspective of Mimetic Theory." In *Violence and the Sacred in the Modern World*, edited by Mark Juergensmeyer, 141–48. London: Frank Cass, 1991.

Girard, René, Mark R. Anspach, and Laurence Tacou. "Une conversation avec René Girard." In René Girard (with Jean-Michel Oughourlian, Mark R. Anspach, and Laurence Tacou), *Anorexie et désir mimétique*, 89–123. Paris: Éditions de L'Herne, 2008.

Girard, René, André Gounelle, and Alain Houziauz. "Débat." In René Girard, André Gounelle, and Alain Houziauz, *Dieu, une invention?*, 105–19. Questions de la vie. Ivry-sur-Seine: Les Editions de l'Atelier, 2007.

————. *Dieu, une invention?* Questions de la vie. Ivry-sur-Seine: Les Editions de l'Atelier, 2007.

Göle, Nilüfer. "Snapshots of Islamic Modernities." *Daedalus* 129, no. 1 (Winter 2000): 91–117.

Golsan, Richard J. *René Girard and Myth: An Introduction.* Theorists of Myth. London: Routledge, 2002.

Goodhart, Sandor, Jørgen Jørgensen, Tom Ryba, and James G. Williams, eds. *For René Girard: Essays in Friendship and in Truth.* Studies in Violence, Mimesis, and Culture. East Lansing: Michigan State University Press, 2009.

Goux, Jean-Joseph. "Primitive Money, Modern Money." In *Understanding Origins: Contemporary Views on the Origin of Life, Mind and Society,* edited by Francisco J. Varela and Jean-Pierre Dupuy, 145–49. Dordrecht: Kluwer, 1992.

Graham, Tyler. "St. Augustine's Novelistic Conversion." *Contagion* 5 (1998): 135–54.

Grande, Per Bjørnar. *Mimesis and Desire: An Analysis of the Religious Nature of Mimesis and Desire in the Work of René Girard.* Köln: Lap Lambert Academic Publishing, 2009.

Grivois, Henri. "Adolescence, Indifferentiation, and the Onset of Psychosis." *Contagion* 6 (1999): 104–20.

Grote, Jim. "The Imitation of Christ as Double-Bind: Toward a Girardian Spirituality." *Cistercian Studies* 29, no. 4 (1994): 485–98.

Grote, Jim, and John McGeeney. *Clever as Serpents: Business Ethics and Office Politics.* Collegeville, MN: Liturgical Press, 1997.

Guggenberger, William. "*Homo Oeconomicus* and the Mimetic Man: Vanity and Pride in the Ethics of Adam Smith." In *Passions in Economy, Politics and the Media: In Discussion with Christian Theology,* edited by Wolfgang Palaver and Petra Steinmair-Pösel, 123–38. Beiträge zur mimetischen Theorie 17. Wien: Lit Verlag, 2005.

Hammerton-Kelly, Robert G. "Response to Qamar-Ul Huda." *Contagion* 9 (2002): 99–104.

———. *Sacred Violence: Paul's Hermeneutic of the Cross.* Minneapolis: Fortress, 1992.

———. "A Tribute to René Girard on His 70th Birthday." *Contagion* 1 (1994): ix–xii.

———, ed. *Politics and Apocalypse.* Studies in Violence, Mimesis, and Culture. East Lansing: Michigan State University Press, 2007.

———. *Violent Origins: Walter Burkert, René Girard, and Jonathan Z. Smith on Ritual Killing and Cultural Formation.* Stanford: Stanford University Press, 1987.

Hampton, Charles. "Beyond Reciprocal Violence—René Girard and Siegfried Sassoon." *Practical Theology* 1, no. 1 (2008): 65–83.

Hardin, Michael. "Sacrificial Language in Hebrews: Reappraising René Girard." In *Violence Renounced: René Girard, Biblical Studies, and Peacemaking,* edited by Willard M. Swartley, 103–19. Institute of Mennonite Studies; Studies in Peace and Scripture 4. Telford, PA: Pandora Press; Scottdale, PA: Herald Press, 2000.

Hatfield, Elaine, John T. Caccioppo, and Richard L. Rapson. *Emotional Contagion.* Studies in Emotion and Social Interaction. Cambridge: Cambridge University Press; Paris: Éditions de la Maison des Sciences de l'Homme, 1994.

Haven, Cynthia. "History Is a Test and Mankind Is Failing It: René Girard Scrutinizes the Human Condition from Creation to Apocalypse." *Stanford Magazine* (July–August 2009). Photography by Michael Sugrue. Available at www.stanfordalumni.org/news/magazine/2009/julaug /features/girard.html (last accessed May 2011).

———. "René Girard: Stanford's Provocative *Immortel* Is a One-Man Institution." *Stanford University News* (11 June 2008). Available at http:// news.stanford.edu/news/2008/june11/girard-061108.html (last accessed May 2011).

Hénaf, Marcel. "Global Terror, Global Vengeance?" *SubStance* 37, no. 1 (2008): 72–97.

Hobbes, Thomas. *Leviathan: or, The Matter, Forme and Power of a Commonwealth Ecclesiasticall and Civil* (1651). Oxford: Basil Blackwell, 1946.

Huda, Qamar-ul. "The Problems of Violence and Conflict in Islam." *Contagion* 9 (2002): 80–98.

Huntington, Samuel P. "The Clash of Civilizations?" *Foreign Affairs* 72, no. 3 (Summer 1993): 22–49.

Hurlbut, William B. "Mimesis and Empathy in Human Biology." *Contagion* 4 (1997): 14–25.

Husain, Ed. *The Islamist: Why I Became an Islamic Fundamentalist, What I Saw Inside, and Why I Left.* London: Penguin, 2007.

Iacoboni, Marco. *Mirroring People: The New Science of How We Connect with Others.* New York: Farrar, Straus & Giroux, 2008.

Jones, James W. *Blood That Cries Out from the Earth: The Psychology of Religious Terrorism.* New York: Oxford University Press, 2008.

Juergensmeyer, Mark. "Sacrifice and Cosmic War." In *Violence and the Sacred in the Modern World,* edited by Mark Juergensmeyer, 101–17. London: Frank Cass, 1991.

———. *Terror in the Mind of God: The Global Rise of Religious Violence.* 3rd ed. Berkeley: University of California Press, 2003.

———, ed. *Violence and the Sacred in the Modern World.* London: Frank Cass, 1991.

Kaye, Jeremy. "Twenty-First-Century Victorian Dandy: What Metrosexuality and the Heterosexual Matrix Reveal about Victorian Men." *Journal of Popular Culture* 42, no. 1 (2009): 103–22.

Kelly, Anthony J. *The Resurrection Effect: Transforming Christian Life and Thought.* Maryknoll, NY: Orbis, 2008.

Kerr, Fergus. "Revealing the Scapegoat Mechanism: Christianity after Girard." In *Philosophy, Religion and the Spiritual Life,* edited by Michael McGhee, 161–75. Royal Institute of Philosophy Supplement 32. Cambridge: Cambridge University Press, 1992.

Kirwan, Michael. *Discovering Girard.* Cambridge, MA: Cowley, 2005.

———. *Girard and Theology.* London: T&T Clark, 2009.

Kitzmüller, Erich. "Economy as a Victimising Mechanism." *Contagion* 2 (1995): 17–38.

Kratter, Matthew. "Twilight of the Vampires: History and the Myth of the Undead." *Contagion* 5 (1998): 30–45.

Latour, Bruno. *We Have Never Been Modern* (1991). Translated by Catherine Porter. Cambridge, MA: Harvard University Press, 1993.

Lawrence, Fred. "Philosophy, History, and Apocalypse in Voegelin, Strauss, and Girard." In *Politics and Apocalypse,* edited by Robert Hamerton-Kelly, 95–137. Studies in Violence, Mimesis, and Culture. East Lansing: Michigan State University Press, 2007.

Lefebure, Leo D. *Revelation, the Religions, and Violence.* Maryknoll, NY: Orbis, 2000.

Levy-Navarro, Elena. *The Culture of Obesity in Early and Late Modernity: Body Image in Shakespeare, Jonson, Middleton, and Skelton.* Basingstoke: Palgrave Macmillan, 2008.

Lewis, Michael. *Shame: The Exposed Self.* New York: Free Press, 1992.

Livingston, Paisley. *Models of Desire: René Girard and the Psychology of Mimesis.* Baltimore: Johns Hopkins University Press, 1992.

Loughlin, Gerard. "René Girard (b. 1923): Introduction." In *The Postmodern God: A Theological Reader,* edited by Graham Ward, 96–104. Oxford: Blackwell, 1997.

Loy, David R. "The Religion of the Market." *Journal of the American Academy of Religion* 65, no. 2 (Summer 1997): 275–90.

Lynd, Helen Merrell. *On Shame and the Search for Identity.* New York: Harvest, 1958.

Mack, Burton. "Introduction. Religion and Ritual." In *Violent Origins: Walter Burkert, René Girard, and Jonathan Z. Smith on Ritual Killing and Cultural Formation,* edited by Robert Hamerton-Kelly, 1–70. Stanford: Stanford University Press, 1987.

Marr, Andrew. "Stewardship of Material Goods in the Rule of Benedict." In *Passions in Economy, Politics, and the Media: In Discussion with Christian*

Theology, edited by Wolfgang Palaver and Petra Steinmair-Pösel, 163–73. Beiträge zur mimetischen Theorie 17. Wien: Lit Verlag, 2005.

———. *Tools for Peace: The Spiritual Craft of St. Benedict and René Girard.* Lincoln, NE: iUniverse, 2007.

Martin, David. *On Secularization: Towards a Revised General Theory.* Aldershot: Ashgate, 2005.

Marvin, Carolyn, and David W. Ingle. "Blood Sacrifice and the Nation: Revisiting Civil Religion." *Journal of the American Academy of Religion* 64, no. 4 (Winter 1996): 767–80.

McBride, James. "Capital Punishment as the Unconstitutional Establishment of Religion: A Girardian Reading of the Death Penalty." *Journal of Church and State* 37, no. 2 (Spring 1995): 263–88.

McKenna, Andrew J. "The Law's Delay: Cinema and Sacrifice." *Legal Studies Forum* 15, no. 3 (1991): 199–211.

———. "Scandal, Resentment, Idolatry: The Underground Psychology of Terrorism." *Anthropoetics* 8, no. 1 (Spring–Summer 2002). Available at www.anthropoetics.ucla.edu/ap0801/resent.htm (last accessed May 2011).

———. *Violence and Difference: Girard, Derrida, and Deconstruction.* Urbana: University of Illinois Press, 1992.

McMahon, Edward. "Violence-Religion-Law: A Girardian Analysis." In *Curing Violence,* edited by Mark I. Wallace and Theophus H. Smith, 182–203. Sonoma, CA: Polebridge Press, 1994.

Meltzoff, Andrew N., and Alison Gopnik. "The Role of Imitation in Understanding Persons and Developing a Theory of Mind." In *Understanding Other Minds: Perspectives from Autism,* edited by Simon Baron-Cohen, Helen Tager-Flusberg, and Donald J. Cohen, 335–66. Oxford: Oxford University Press, 1993.

Meltzoff, Andrew N., and M. Keith Moore. "Infant Intersubjectivity: Broadening the Dialogue to Include Imitation, Identity and Intention." In *Intersubjective Communication and Emotion in Early Ontogeny,* edited by Stein Bråten, 47–62. Cambridge: Cambridge University Press; Paris: Éditions de la Maison des Sciences de l'Homme, 1998.

———. "Persons in Representation: Why Infant Imitation Is Important for Theories of Human Development." In *Imitation in Infancy,* edited by Jacqueline Nadel and George Butterworth, 9–35. Cambridge: Cambridge University Press, 1999.

Milbank, John. *Theology and Social Theory: Beyond Secular Reason.* Oxford: Blackwell, 1990.

Miller, Vincent J. *Consuming Religion: Christian Faith and Practice in a Consumer Culture.* New York: Continuum, 2005.

Moore, Sebastian. *The Contagion of Jesus: Doing Theology as If It Mattered.* Edited by Stephen McCarthy. Maryknoll, NY: Orbis, 2007.

Morrison, Andrew P. *The Culture of Shame.* New York: Ballantine Books, 1996.

Morrow, Duncan. "Violence and the Sacred in Northern Ireland." *Contagion* 2 (1995): 145–64.

Murawiec, Laurent. *The Mind of Jihad.* Cambridge: Cambridge University Press, 2008.

Nathanson, Donald L., ed. *The Many Faces of Shame.* New York: Guildford Press, 1987.

Oberprantacher, Andreas. "Beyond Rivalry: Rethinking Community in View of Apocalyptic Violence." *Contagion* 17 (2010): 175–87.

O'Murchu, Diarmid. *The Transformation of Desire: How Desire Became Corrupted—and How We Can Reclaim It.* London: Darton, Longman and Todd, 2007.

Orléan, André. "The Origin of Money." Translated by Paisley Livingston. In *Understanding Origins: Contemporary Views on the Origin of Life, Mind and Society,* edited by Francisco J. Varela and Jean-Pierre Dupuy, 113–43. Dordrecht: Kluwer, 1992.

Oughourlian, Jean-Michel. *The Genesis of Desire* (2007). Translated by Eugene Webb. Studies in Violence, Mimesis, and Culture. East Lansing: Michigan State University Press, 2010.

———. "Preface." In René Girard (with Jean-Michel Oughourlian, Mark R. Anspach, and Laurence Tacou), *Anorexie et désir mimétique,* 7–13. Paris: Éditions de L'Herne, 2008.

———. *The Puppet of Desire: The Psychology of Hysteria, Possession, and Hypnosis.* Translated by Eugene Webb. Stanford: Stanford University Press, 1991.

Pahl, Jon. *Empire of Sacrifice: The Religious Origins of American Violence.* New York: New York University Press, 2010.

Palaver, Wolfgang. "The Ambiguous Cachet of Victimhood: On Violence and Monotheism." In *The New Visibility of Religion: Studies in Religion and Cultural Hermeneutics,* edited by Graham Ward and Michael Hoelzl, 68–87. Continuum Resources in Religion and Political Culture. London: Continuum, 2008.

———. "Carl Schmitt's 'Apocalyptic' Resistance against Global Civil War." In *Politics and Apocalypse,* edited by Robert Hamerton-Kelly, 69–94. Studies in Violence, Mimesis, and Culture. East Lansing: Michigan State University Press, 2007.

———. "Envy or Emulation: A Christian Understanding of Economic Passions." In *Passions in Economy, Politics, and the Media: In Discussion with Christian Theology,* edited by Wolfgang Palaver and Petra Steinmair-Pösel, 139–62. Beiträge zur mimetischen Theorie 17. Wien: Lit Verlag, 2005.

———. " . . . Essay on Islam and the Return of the Archaic." *Bulletin of the Colloquium on Violence and Religion* 37 (October 2010): 6–10.

———. "A Girardian Reading of Schmitt's *Political Theology.*" *Telos* 93 (Fall 1992): 43–68.

———. "Hobbes and the KATÉCHON: The Secularization of Sacrificial Christianity." *Contagion* 2 (1995): 57–74.

———. "On Violence: A Mimetic Perspective." *Innsbrucker Theologische Leseraum* (23 February 2002). Available at www.uibk.ac.at/theol/lese raum/texte/137.html (last accessed May 2011).

———. "Schmitt's Critique of Liberalism." *Telos* 102 (Winter 1995): 43–71.

———. "Violence and Religion: Walter Burkert and René Girard in Comparison." *Contagion* 17 (2010): 121–37.

Palaver, Wolfgang, and Petra Steinmair-Pösel, eds. *Passions in Economy, Politics and the Media: In Discussion with Christian Theology.* Beiträge zur mimetischen Theorie 17. Wien: Lit Verlag, 2005.

Poncela, Pierrette. "Terrorisme et sacre: Une interpretation sacrificielle du terrorisme." In *Terrorisme et culture: Pour une anthroplogie stratégique,* édited by Jean-Paul Charnay, 183–89. Travaux du Centre d'études et des recherches sur les stratégies et les conflits. Paris: Université de Paris-Sorbonne, 1981.

Raban, Jonathan. "My Holy War: What Do a Vicar's Son and a Suicide Bomber Have in Common?" *New Yorker* (4 February 2002): 28–37.

Renfrew, Colin. *Prehistory: The Making of the Human Mind* (2007). London: Phoenix, 2008.

Richardson, Louise. *What Terrorists Want: Understanding the Enemy, Containing the Threat* (2006). New York: Random House, 2007.

Rizzolatti, Giacomo, and Corrado Sinigaglia. *Mirrors in the Brain: How Our Minds Share Actions, Emotions, and Experience* (2006). Translated by Frances Anderson. Oxford: Oxford University Press, 2008.

Roedel, John. "Sacrificial and NonSacrificial Mass Nonviolence." *Contagion* 15–16 (2008–9): 221–36.

Saunders, Doug. *Arrival City: The Final Migration and Our Next World.* Sydney: Allen & Unwin, 2010.

Scheler, Max. *Ressentiment* (1912). Translated by Lewis B. Coser and William W. Holdheim. Marquette Studies in Philosophy. Milwaukee, WI: Marquette University Press, 2003.

Schmitt, Carl. *The Concept of the Political* (1932). Expanded ed. Translated with an Introduction by George Schwab et al. Chicago: University of Chicago Press, 2007.

Schwager, Raymund. *Banished from Eden: Original Sin and Evolutionary Theory in the Drama of Salvation* (1997). Translated by James Williams.

Inigo Text 9. Leominster: Gracewing; New Malden: Inigo Enterprises, 2006.

———. *Jesus in the Drama of Salvation: Toward a Biblical Doctrine of Redemption*. Translated by James G. Williams and Paul Haddon. New York: Crossroad, 1999.

———. *Jesus of Nazareth: How He Understood His Life* (1991). Translated by James G. Williams. New York: Crossroad, 1998.

———. *Must There Be Scapegoats? Violence and Redemption in the Bible* (1978, 1987). 2nd ed. Translated by Maria L. Assad. Leominster: Gracewing; New York: Crossroad, 2000.

Scott, Kyle. "A Girardian Critique of the Liberal Democratic Peace Theory." *Contagion* 15–16 (2008–9): 45–62.

Serres, Michel. "Ego Credo." *Contagion* 12–13 (2006): 1–11.

———. "Receiving René Girard into the Académie Française." In *For René Girard: Essays in Friendship and in Truth*, edited by Sandor Goodhart, Jørgen Jørgensen, Tom Ryba, and James G. Williams, 1–17. Studies in Violence, Mimesis, and Culture. East Lansing: Michigan State University Press, 2009.

Smith, Fred. "Black-on-Black Violence: The Intramediation of Desire and the Search for a Scapegoat." *Contagion* 6 (1999): 32–44.

Solomon, Marion F. "Attachment Repair in Couples Therapy: A Prototype for Treatment of Intimate Relationships." *Clinical Social Work Journal* 37 (2009): 214–23.

Steinmair-Pösel, Petra. "Economy and Mimetic Theory." In *Passions in Economy, Politics, and the Media: In Discussion with Christian Theology*, edited by Wolfgang Palaver and Petra Steinmair-Pösel, 67–84. Beiträge zur mimetischen Theorie 17. Wien: Lit Verlag, 2005.

Sung, Jung Mo. *Desire, Market and Religion*. Reclaiming Liberation Theology. London: SCM Press, 2007.

Swartley, Willard M. "Discipleship and Imitation of Jesus/Suffering Servant: The Mimesis of New Creation." In *Violence Renounced: René Girard, Biblical Studies, and Peacemaking*, edited by Willard M. Swartley, 218–45. Institute of Mennonite Studies; Studies in Peace and Scripture 4. Telford, PA: Pandora Press; Scottdale, PA: Herald Press, 2000.

———, ed. *Violence Renounced: René Girard, Biblical Studies, and Peacemaking*. Institute of Mennonite Studies; Studies in Peace and Scripture 4. Telford, PA: Pandora Press; Scottdale, PA: Herald Press, 2000.

Taylor, Charles. *A Secular Age*. Cambridge, MA: Belknap Press, 2007.

———. *Sources of the Self: The Making of the Modern Identity*. Cambridge, MA: Harvard University Press, 1989.

Thiel, Peter. "The Straussian Moment." In *Politics and Apocalypse*, edited by Robert Hamerton-Kelly, 189–218. Studies in Violence, Mimesis, and Culture. East Lansing: Michigan State University Press, 2007.

Vanheeswijck, Guy. "The Place of René Girard in Contemporary Philosophy." *Contagion* 10 (2003): 95–110.

Varela, Francisco J., and Jean-Pierre Dupuy, eds. *Understanding Origins: Contemporary Views on the Origin of Life, Mind and Society.* Dordrecht: Kluwer, 1992.

Vattimo, Gianni, and René Girard. *Christianity, Truth, and Weakening Faith: A Dialogue* (2006). Edited by Pierpaolo Antonello and translated by William McCuaig. New York: Columbia University Press, 2010.

Vaughn, Barry. "The Punitive Consequences of Consumer Culture." *Punishment and Society* 4, no. 2 (2002): 195–211.

Wallace, Mark I., and Theophus H. Smith, eds. *Curing Violence.* Sonoma, CA: Polebridge Press, 1994.

Ward, Bernadette Waterman. "Abortion as a Sacrament: Mimetic Desire and Sacrifice in Sexual Politics." *Contagion* 7 (2000): 18–35.

Ward, Bruce. "Transforming Passion into Compassion: Rousseau and the Problem of Envy in Modern Democracy." In *Passions in Economy, Politics, and the Media: In Discussion with Christian Theology,* edited by Wolfgang Palaver and Petra Steinmair-Pösel, 253–72. Beiträge zur mimetischen Theorie 17. Wien: Lit Verlag, 2005.

Ward, Graham, and Michael Hoelzl, eds. *The New Visibility of Religion: Studies in Religion and Cultural Hermeneutics.* Continuum Resources in Religion and Political Culture. London: Continuum, 2008.

Webb, Eugene. *The Self Between: From Freud to the New Social Psychology of France.* Seattle: University of Washington Press, 1993.

Weber, Max. *The Protestant Ethic and the Spirit of Capitalism* (1904–5). Translated (1958) by Talcott Parsons. Mineola, NY: Dover, 2003.

Wilkinson, Richard, and Kate Pickett. *The Spirit Level: Why More Equal Societies Almost Always Do Better.* London: Allen Lane, 2009.

Williams, James G. *The Bible, Violence, and the Sacred: Liberation from the Myth of Sanctioned Violence.* With a Foreword by René Girard. San Francisco: HarperSanFrancisco, 1991.

———. "Foreword: René Girard." In *Resurrection from the Underground,* by René Girard, edited by James G. Williams, 7–14.

———. "*Magister Lucis:* In the Light of René Girard." In *For René Girard: Essays in Friendship and in Truth,* edited by Sandor Goodhart, Jørgen Jørgensen, Tom Ryba, and James G. Williams, 159–67. Studies in Violence, Mimesis, and Culture. East Lansing: Michigan State University Press, 2009.

———. "René Girard: A Biographical Sketch." In René Girard, *The Girard Reader,* edited by James G. Williams, 1–6. New York: Crossroad, 1996.

———. "René Girard without the Cross? Religion and the Mimetic Theory." *Anthropoetics* 2, no. 1 (June 1996). Available at www.anthropoetics .ucla.edu/ap0201/girardw.htm (last accessed May 2011).

———. "'Steadfast Love and Not Sacrifice': A Nonsacrificial Reading of the Hebrew Scriptures." In *Curing Violence,* edited by Mark I. Wallace and Theophus H. Smith, 71–99. Sonoma, CA: Polebridge Press, 1994.

Wilson, Bruce W. "What Do We Want and Why Do We Want It? Chasing after the Wind: Coquetry, Metaphysical Desire and God." *St. Mark's Review* 202 (2007): 3–9.

Wink, Walter. *Engaging the Powers: Discernment and Resistance in a World of Domination.* Minneapolis: Fortress Press, 1992.

Wittrock, Björn. "Early Modernities: Varieties and Transitions." *Daedalus* 127, no. 3 (1998): 19–40.

———. "Modernity: One, None, or Many? European Origins and Modernity as a Global Condition." *Daedalus* 129, no. 1 (Winter 2000): 31–60.

INDEX

Terms following *and* in parentheses after a main entry are related terms covered in the pages indexed.

SCOTT COWDELL

is associate professor and research fellow in public and contextual theology at Charles Sturt University, Canberra, Australia, and canon theologian of the Canberra-Goulburn Anglican Diocese. He is author and editor of a number of books, including *Violence, Desire, and the Sacred: Girard's Mimetic Theory Across the Disciplines* (edited with Chris Fleming and Joel Hodge).